Bauwelt Fundamente 174

Edited by

Elisabeth Blum
Jesko Fezer
Günther Fischer
Angelika Schnell

Florian Strob (Ed.)

Architect of Letters
Reading Hilberseimer

Bauverlag

Birkhäuser

Gütersloh · Berlin

Basel

The Bauwelt Fundamente series was founded in 1963
by Ulrich Conrads; it was edited from the early 1980s to
2015 jointly with Peter Neitzke.
Supervising editor of this volume: Günther Fischer

Design of the series since 2017 by Matthias Görlich using
the design by Helmuth Lortz, 1963

Front cover: Detroit area, planning diagram, c. 1945,
published in: Hilberseimer, Ludwig. 1949. *The New Regional Pattern: Industries and Gardens, Workshops and
Farms*. Chicago: Theobald, p. 173 (image detail)

Back cover: Ludwig Hilberseimer, Weißenhof Settlement
Single-family residence, 1927, © Ludwig Karl Hilbers-
eimer Papers, Ryerson and Burnham Art and Architecture
Archives, Art Institute of Chicago

Library of Congress Control Number: 2022942365

Bibliographic information published by the German
National Library
The German National Library lists this publication in the
Deutsche Nationalbibliografie; detailed bibliographic
data are available on the Internet at http://dnb.dnb.de.

This publication is also available as an e-book
(ISBN PDF 978-3-0356-2486-1)

Distribution via bookstores is exclusively through
Birkhäuser Verlag.
© 2022 Birkhäuser Verlag GmbH, Basel
P.O. Box 44, 4009 Basel, Switzerland
Part of Walter de Gruyter GmbH, Berlin/Boston
and Bauverlag BV GmbH, Gütersloh, Berlin

bau ‖ ‖ verlag

Printed in Germany

ISBN 978-3-0356-2485-4

9 8 7 6 5 4 3 2 1
www.birkhauser.com

Edition Bauhaus 59

Edited for the Bauhaus Dessau Foundation
by Florian Strob

Bauhaus Dessau Foundation
Director and CEO: Barbara Steiner
Gropiusallee 38
06846 Dessau-Roßlau, Germany

The Bauhaus Dessau Foundation is a non-profit foundation under public law. It is institutionally supported by
the Federal Government Commissioner for Culture and
the Media, the State of Saxony-Anhalt and the City of
Dessau-Roßlau.

The publication *Architect of Letters: Reading Hilbers-
eimer* is part of the research project *Bauhaus im Text /
Bauhaus Written Heritage* (2020-2022), funded by the
Ministry of Science, Energy, Climate Protection and
Environment of the State of Saxony-Anhalt.

SACHSEN-ANHALT
Ministerium für
Wissenschaft, Energie,
Klimaschutz und Umwelt

MIX
Papier aus verantwor-
tungsvollen Quellen
FSC® C089473

Contents

Introduction

Architect of Letters: Reading Hilberseimer

Florian Strob

Introduction

In his years as professor of urban and regional planning at the Illinois Institute of Technology (IIT) in Chicago, Ludwig Hilberseimer walked three
times a week from his apartment at 1510 North Dearborn Street to the IIT at
3360 South State Street. That makes 8.5 kilometers, six times per week and
12 hours of walking. He crossed Chicago from north to south and back again
(see González Martínez 2015, 52–53).

When we inquired about two photographs by Pius Pahl of Hilberseimer on the
day of the closing of the Bauhaus in 1933, his son, Peter Jan Pahl, himself a renowned civil engineer, told my colleague that our inquiry brought back memories of a long walk with Hilberseimer through a cold Chicago winter.

The photograph by Pahl shows a smoking Hilberseimer next to Lilly Reich and
surrounded by Bauhaus students (fig. 1). 1933, the year of the closing of the
Bauhaus, marks a veritable turning point in Hilberseimer's life. Born in 1885
in Karlsruhe, he studied architecture at the local technical university (Technische Hochschule Karlsruhe) between 1906 and 1910, but left without a formal
degree, and went—via a short stint in an architectural office in Bremen—to Berlin, where he would live until he left Germany for the United States in 1938.

After working for the architect Heinrich Lassen, he led a planning office for
the construction of Zeppelin airship halls during the years of World War I.
The 1920s and 1930s were dominated by his networks in avant-garde circles;
he was active in numerous groups, such as the Arbeitsrat für Kunst, Novembergruppe, Werkbund, Der Ring, and the German section of CIAM. He wrote
articles, essays, and books on contemporary art, architecture, and eventually, city planning.

His built projects were few; he seemed to have realized buildings under his
own name only in the decade between 1926 and 1936. His impressive network

Figure 1: "Consultation on the doorstep" on the day of the closure of the Bauhaus in Berlin (Ludwig Hilberseimer and some Bauhaus students), 1933, photo: Pius E. Pahl

as well as his many publications secured him, however, a place among the leading architects of the time. His authority was one of erudition and discourse. He was hired by the second director of the Bauhaus, Hannes Meyer, to teach architecture theory *(Baulehre)*, and continued under the third and last director, Ludwig Mies van der Rohe, to teach urban planning and housing *(Stadtplanung und Siedlungswesen)*. He was a revered and influential teacher.

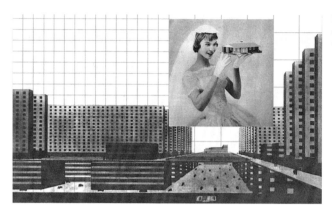

Figure 2: Mona Mahalls and Asli Serbests, *The House Alice Built*, 2018

In his time at the Bauhaus, he was involved in the urban planning of the extension for the Dessau-Törten Housing Estate. Together with several theoretical urban projects, the scientific analysis of sunlight, density, and other aspects, Dessau-Törten is part of a shift in Hilberseimer's urban thinking. His seminal *Großstadtarchitektur* of 1927 was an examination of the capitalist city of speculation, his urban proposal for a Hochhausstadt (1924) attempted a vertical solution of its defaults. Dessau-Törten, however, sought to find answers in what Hilberseimer called *Mischbebauung* (mixed-type development), the combination of apartment buildings for childless couples or singles and single-family homes with gardens. It is this concept of mixed-type development that he continued to advance in the following decades (see "Visuals", p. 290–291, fig. 28–32).

After the National Socialists closed the Bauhaus, and, in fact, would only allow it to reopen if Hilberseimer and Wassily Kandinsky would be dismissed, Hilberseimer was neither able to teach at public institutions nor publish anymore in Germany (with few exceptions). He worked as an architect, finishing two houses in Berlin, and otherwise occupied himself with theoretical or unbuilt projects. The main achievement of these years was, in retrospect, the writing process for what would later become his first major English-language publication, *The New City* (1944). 1933 marks the beginning of this long writing process, in which, based on his teaching at the Bauhaus, he distilled and

Figure 3: Adrian Phiffer,
Hero of Generic Architecture, 2019, video still

formulated his *Principles of Planning*, as the subtitle of *The New City* is called. The trained architect became a planner.

Hilberseimer the planner taught from 1938 until shortly before his death in 1967 as professor of city and regional planning at the IIT in Chicago. Like at the Bauhaus, the students in Chicago referred fondly to him as Hilbs. He followed *The New City* with *The New Regional Pattern* (1949) and *The Nature of Cities* (1955), both rewriting and extending *The New City* toward a more and more globalized view of what had started as the integration of city and landscape. Always having considered the history of urban planning and architecture, his last books turned to the history of modernity and his own past; a monograph on Mies van der Rohe in 1956 was followed by *Entfaltung einer Planungsidee* in 1963; *Contemporary Architecture: Its Roots and Trends* in 1964; and *Berliner Architektur der 20er Jahre* in 1967.

It would be all too easy to paint the picture of a stubborn, cold man dissecting the modern city. This is Hilberseimer reduced to one image, namely what he had called the schema of a high-rise city (Hochhausstadt, 1924, see "Visuals", p. 278, fig. 9–10). It might be his most efficacious image, causing an unrelenting production of images across different cultural spheres and political affiliations, two recent examples of which are shown here (figs. 2 and 3).

Returning to Hilberseimer on his walk through an icy Chicago, as told by Peter Jan Pahl, what came to my mind was a well-known photograph of one of

Hilberseimer's few built architectural projects, his contribution for the 1927 Weißenhof estate in Stuttgart (see "Visuals", p. 280, fig. 13). We see a man in a black suit and a briefcase in hand from behind, possibly walking home after work; we might think of Robert Musil's *Der Mann ohne Eigenschaften* (*The Man without Qualities*, 1930–43) or Neue Sachlichkeit. This image as much as Hilberseimer's architectural design is an emblem of its time. It could also be read as an attempt at expressing something universal or generic: We see in front of the house in Weißenhof an exemplary man, an exemplary lived existence in modernity, absorbing what is around him, with his back to the audience, focused on the task ahead.

Maybe we can read Hilberseimer as this single man walking then, not a man without qualities but someone unwilling to be in the limelight, to show his face to the world. The facade of his Weißenhof house seems to negate expression. Face and facade seem to fall together. Architecture, for Hilberseimer, was to do with construction, not composition; it was constructivist and attempted to "break with the illusionism of Renaissance art" (Anderson 2012, 47). First demanding an "objective-collective expression" in architecture and later promoting the "invisible city" that hid architecture beneath greenery (Kilian 2002, 67 and 104), Hilberseimer left the design of facades, like speaking at public events, mostly to others (Mies van der Rohe in the first, or Alfred Caldwell in the latter case).

In his writings, Hilberseimer put the human being at the center of his thoughts on urbanism and planning, yet without considering a specific person, but precisely someone, a man, a person walking the grid of a quintessentially modern city (Chicago), a placeholder in an experiment, if you will, a figure of thought in order to think the future, a type.

My suggestion is to think about Hilberseimer, the author of the works discussed in this volume, not in terms of biographical research or pulling someone out of someone else's shadow or creating the next hero of modernity. What Hilberseimer set out to do, he described himself in *Großstadtarchitektur*: "By thoroughly systematizing design, typifying building elements, and standardizing details, a set of models will result that can accommodate every variation and expression, just as the letters of the alphabet, words, and the principles of grammar, in spite of their apparent exhaustion, become something completely new in the hands of a creative person" (Hilberseimer 2012, 149–50). Typification is, one could argue, the underlying concept for his thinking. Accordingly, Hilberseimer called his drawings for urban projects "schemas": they were in most cases not to be considered architectural designs.

The title of this volume of essays, *Architect of Letters*, refers to the architect as writer, as well as to this particular understanding of Hilberseimer's work: he wrote a grammar for others to use. Reading Hilberseimer thus means at least a double task. Firstly, readers are best advised to move away from the obsession with certain powerful imagery and tend toward the author. And indeed, all essays collected here gain valuable new insights by looking at various of Hilberseimer's texts. Secondly, when analyzing or simply looking at his many unbuilt projects, it will be helpful to consider reading the underlying "grammar" of these visuals.

The volume in its breadth of approaches and thematic focuses attempts to correct the understanding of Hilberseimer's work as self-referential and his position as one of an outsider in the history of modern architecture and urban planning. While he was the rare case of a former art critic among urban planners, he was a well-connected man of stupendous knowledge and learning: the contributors of this volume trace an astonishing array of references in his works. Ludwig Hilberseimer, in his various roles as architect, art critic, urban planner, and teacher, was a veritable referencing phenomenon (without necessarily mentioning his sources or being mentioned by others himself). As an author, he was seldomly the first, but rather positioned himself at the center of a wide-flung net of references. He advocated certain ideas, good solutions for what he saw as pressing problems of his time. His writing did not, it seems, promote originality, but processing information, development and reduction to the essence.

Through the lens of his works, we see a man walking the grid of a quintessential modern city again. On his way from his apartment at 1510 North Dearborn Street to the IIT at 3360 South State Street, Hilberseimer experienced the density of the capitalist city, the cars rushing past him, down to the leafy streets of the IIT campus, and back again. Two realms that can be said to define the development of his thinking, two realms that appear to be continuous in Chicago's cityscape as well as in Hilberseimer's work. It is this modern city that we still live in today.

His close collaborator and friend, Ludwig Mies van der Rohe, once remarked on Hilberseimer's legacy: "But maybe the importance of his work will finally come out. The present concern about energy conservation, solar orientation, environmental controls, etc., were long-time common issues in Hilbs's work" (Danforth 1988, 13). Ecology and the dire need to change our modern cities in the fight against climate change make the case for looking at modernity through the Hilberseimer lens. One of his main "grammatical" inventions is the settlement unit, which proposes to combine "buildings for commerce and administration located within a green belt, and then houses of the residential area surrounded by a park containing schools, playgrounds, and community buildings. This park area would make the settlement part of the landscape and create an organic relation between city and country" (Hilberseimer 1944, 107).

Everyday life in such a settlement unit would be lived largely without cars: you would walk through the park to reach schools or community buildings or the playground. I think back to Hilberseimer on his two-hour-long walks through Chicago and see—and hear—and smell a lot of traffic. Quite the contrast to his imagined settlement unit.

The so-called fifteen-minute city, as promoted today by the city of Paris and many others, might come to mind. The aim of this initiative is to take the individual and their needs seriously and to locate the essentials of life within walking distance, thereby reducing car traffic significantly. Chrono-urbanism was advanced by urbanists and researchers from other fields, particularly in regards to challenges of digitization, climate change, and lately in response to pandemics (see Moreno et. al. 2021). The Hilberseimer from 1955 sounds—Mies van der Rohe would have not been surprised—rather contemporary in 2022:

> The unit we propose [...] contains within itself all the essentials of a small
> community. Its size would be determined by walking distances which

would nowhere exceed fifteen to twenty minutes. The number of people living within such a unit would be determined by the number of people working in offices and factories which are part of the unit. Density would vary accordingly. [...] As each unit would contain all the essentials of a community, its population should be large enough to meet the social and personal requirements of the individual, large enough to offer variety in work and in life, large enough to support necessary communal, cultural, and hygienic institutions. But it should also be small enough to preserve an organic community life, so that democracy might prevail and each individual participate in community activities (Hilberseimer 1955, 193).

Hilberseimer, as mentioned earlier, wrote a grammar for others to use. It seems timely to reconsider the architect of letters for our own age, we might discover potentials in the modern cities we live in that were previously overlooked.

This volume is not the first to draw attention to Hilberseimer's works and determine his legacy. Following early interest in Italy, particularly for the Berlin period, the architect Vittorio Gregotti edited in 1986 an issue of *Rassegna* that was dedicated to the work of Hilberseimer and presented, among other things, a list of works and projects from 1885 to 1938 by Christine Mengin. While this Italian publication—a somewhat European undertaking with authors from Germany, France and Italy—focused largely on Hilberseimer's Berlin years, the volume *In the Shadow of Mies: Ludwig Hilberseimer: Architect, Educator, and Urban Planner*, edited by Richard Pommer, David Spaeth, and Kevin Harrington in 1988, looked mostly at Hilberseimer's later years in Chicago after 1938.

In the Shadow of Mies was followed by K. Michael Hays with his seminal study *Modernism and the Posthumanist Subject: The Architecture of Hannes Meyer and Ludwig Hilberseimer* in 1992. Ten years later, Markus Kilian in his doctoral dissertation "Großstadtarchitektur und New City: Eine planungsmethodische Untersuchung der Stadtplanungsmodelle Ludwig Hilberseimers" reconsidered the urban planner for the German discourse and, to a certain extent, bridged the divide caused by exile. Something Richard Anderson, with his English-language edition of *Großstadtarchitektur, Metropolisarchitecture and Other Essays* (2012) did in the reverse direction, making some of the early Hilberseimer texts available for the American discourse. Three of the most recent voices turning our attention to the works of Hilberseimer are Charles Waldheim, Plácido González Martínez, and Philipp Oswalt. Waldheim introduced the notion of ecological urbanism into the discussion of Hilberseimer's work, a notion that links Hilberseimer to current concerns in architecture and urban planning (see above). In his study *In Light of Hilberseimer: The Genesis and Legacy of The New City,* González Martínez aims to make legible the interdependence of life and work and to show the continuities within Hilberseimer's theoretical work. Oswalt finally made a strong case for reevaluating Hilberseimer's achievements at the Bauhaus (see *Hannes Meyers neue Bauhauslehre,* Bauwelt Fundamente 164).

Architect of Letters: Reading Hilberseimer presents for the first time since 1988 an overview of current concerns with and research into Hilberseimer's legacy. It was my objective from the start to collect a broad variety of approaches, generations, and fields and to show the wealth of material when reading Hilberseimer. This was all in order to avoid the fractured reception of the past, as sketched above, and to provoke further investigation. The essays of this volume are organized into four chapters, delineating four major strands in Hilberseimer's output: the city, housing, the region, and media. A fifth chapter gives the reader and, particularly, the student of architecture and urban planning an overview of the built and unbuilt projects. Without aiming at presenting anything complete, this fifth chapter tells of Hilberseimer's intellectual development visually and thus complements the four previous chapters. Here, too, the reception of only a few images of the Berlin period is to be corrected.

The essays of this volume are based on talks given at the international conference *Ludwig Hilberseimer: Infrastructures of Modernity,* which took place at the Bauhaus Dessau Foundation in October 2021, and coincided with the opening of an exhibition at the Bauhaus Museum Dessau (October 2021–March 2022), *Ludwig Hilberseimer: Infrastructures of The New City.* The annual theme of the Bauhaus Dessau Foundation for 2021 was infrastructure.

The conference and exhibition as well as the critical edition of Hilberseimer's *The New City. Principles of Planning* and this volume of essays are part of the research project *Bauhaus Written Heritage* (2020–2022). I would like to thank Claudia Perren, former director of the Bauhaus Dessau Foundation, for her encouragement and support from my first ideas for this research project in 2018 onwards.

I would like to thank the Ministry of Science, Energy, Climate Protection and Environment of the State of Saxony-Anhalt for the generous funding of the research project, as well as the Fritz Thyssen Foundation for significant additional funding for the conference. The whole research project, including this publication, would not have been possible without the support of The Art Institute of Chicago. Alison Fisher, Harold and Margot Schiff Curator of Architecture and Design at the Art Institute of Chicago, and Zoë Ryan, former John H. Bryan Chair and Curator of Architecture and Design at the Art Institute of Chicago until November 2021, were very supportive from the start. I wish to thank Nathaniel Parks and J.T. de la Torre for their resourceful help with the work in the Ryerson and Burnham Art and Architecture Archives and our image requests.

I am particularly grateful to the scholars participating in the conference and contributing to this volume. The organization of the conference and exhibition were managed by Anne-Zora Westphal and the editing of this publication by Caroline Jansky. I would like to thank Anne-Zora and Caroline as well as the whole project team (Laura Gieser, Karoline Lemke, Annika Padoan, Andreas Schätzke, Clarissa Seidel, Ulrich and Wolfgang Thöner) for their great work.

It is worth mentioning that this volume of essays will be published in the Bauwelt Fundamente series, where Hilberseimer himself published *Entfaltung einer Planungsidee* – as number 6 of the series, in 1963 (see "Visuals", p. 314, fig. 67). Sixty years later, I am grateful to the series editors, in particular Günther Fischer, and Katharina Kulke from Birkhäuser for publishing *Architect of Letters: Reading Hilberseimer* as number 174 of Bauwelt Fundamente.

Dessau and Berlin, May 2022

City

Hilberseimer Reconsidered: Commitments and Continuities

Charles Waldheim

> "City planning is a social task."
> Ludwig Hilberseimer, *The New City*

For most audiences concerned with modern architecture and urbanism, Ludwig Hilberseimer remains among the most controversial and divisive architects of the twentieth century. The German urbanist's work has been variously characterized as "menacing," "alienating," "painful," and "devoid of human life." Numerous critics derided him as "hopelessly out of fashion" (see Fabricius 2013, 39, 49–50n1; Pommer 1988, 16–17; Rykwert 1984, 126; and Blundell Jones 1989, 75). To this day, the most dominant historical accounts describe Hilberseimer as a minor or marginal figure in twentieth-century architecture and urbanism, toiling in the shadows of his more influential and significant colleagues. Yet Hilberseimer has also been regularly rediscovered by generation after generation of architects, historians, and theorists. The authors assembled here quite rightly understand the significance of Hilberseimer's work for contemporary audiences. Over the past decades, Hilberseimer's life and work have been the subject of vigorous and ongoing research by historians, architects, and urbanists working on both sides of the Atlantic. That important work continues, and we are better informed today than perhaps at any other time in the recent past given the increasing communication between scholars and researchers as well as by important publications such as this and institutions such as the Bauhaus Dessau Foundation and the Art Institute of Chicago, among others.[1] Perhaps appropriately, much of that intellectual energy has rightly gone toward the close reading of specific episodes or encounters, publications, or projects. It is also true that many of the more influential accounts of Hilberseimer as a progressive figure focused on his earlier commitments to the historical avant-garde while in Berlin, and an approach to the city that Hilberseimer himself ultimately repudiated in the 1930s in favor of his more mature intellectual commitments.

This essay traces the outlines of what might be a complementary trajectory, something more longitudinal or transversal in support of the ongoing project of recuperating Hilberseimer for broader audiences in architecture and the urban arts. The scholarship on Hilberseimer, focused as it has been on individual cases produced on different continents and in different languages, has tended to reinforce an episodic reading of his work. Hilberseimer's unique biography, political exile, and loss of his native language all reinforce this tendency. Instead, however, this essay proposes a reading of Hilberseimer's primary intellectual and cultural contributions as constituting a single ongoing work committed to the city as a social project. Hilberseimer's commitment to socialism was based upon the evident failures of the capitalist city and an aspiration toward the equitable distribution of economic and environmental resources. He understood the design of the city as a cultural project manifesting a worldview through creative and open-minded inquiry in the service of social change.

The origins of this singular project might be seen to coincide with his appointment to the Bauhaus in 1928 and the economic and political shocks of 1929–30. It took various forms—teaching, publications, and projects both academic and professional—and was supported and enabled by different individuals and institutions. Collectively, those discrete episodes and encounters enabled Hilberseimer to accumulate a well-resolved set of positions on a range of topics central to the shape of the city.

Hilberseimer's project developed through three primary intellectual commitments, all of which share his conception of the city as a cultural project and his understanding of his work of city planning as a form of cultural production in service of new social conditions. Over time, these commitments iterated, combined, and evolved to approach something comprehensive and synthetic. First was a conception of urban order as shaped by and expressive of the dominant economic structures and political economies of the culture, while developing designs to spatially insulate citizens from the worst impacts of that political economy. Second was a commitment to the natural environment and a proto-ecological understanding of the relations between the shape of the city and its natural contexts, thus allowing for the ordering of the new city to preserve and equitably distribute natural resources. Third, and perhaps most significantly, was an ethic that situates points one and two in the context of a socialist notion of fairness, including the equitable distribution of economic and ecological resources toward cultural ends. These first two topics, the economic and ecological, have received significant attention in recent scholarship. Yet Hilberseimer's deeply held socialist commitment to fairness and equity, while comparatively understudied, is both timely and urgent given the challenges associated with the city today.[2] Hilberseimer was a contributor to the journal *Sozialistische Monatshefte* (Socialist Monthly Bulletins) edited by Joseph Bloch. The journal was among the revisionist voices within the trade union base of the Social Democratic Party and included a range of political opinions from Marxist through anarchist thought. While some have described Hilberseimer as a communist, the historical record of Hilberseimer's political commitments is more nuanced and mixed.[3] Moreover, Hilberseimer considered city planning a cultural form and professional vocation rather than a strictly political act, per se. While there is ample evidence of his deeply held commitment to socialist values of equitable distribution and access, there is little evidence of Hilberseimer's commitment to state communism. Rather, Hilberseimer is more often remembered as professing a position somewhere between ambivalence and passive resistance to the construct of the state itself, preferring the autonomy of the "Republic Hilberseimer."[4] Hilberseimer's studies of mixed housing developments in the late 1920s and early 1930s serve as a suitable entry point. His low-level aerial view of mixed-type housing (*Mischbebauung*) of 1930 offers an early glimpse of this longer-term project of a radically reconceived urban form (see "Visuals", p. 291, fig. 31). In this initial iteration of what would become a durable strategy over the coming decades, Hilberseimer punctuated a horizontal carpet of low-rise courtyard and L-shaped garden houses with mid-rise slab apartment buildings. This strategy allowed for all units to enjoy ample sun while maintaining a level of density and a variety of building types suitable for various generations and family structures. This urban structure was supported through the public ownership of the land itself as well as the design and maintenance of extensive public parks and private gardens. Hilberseimer continued to elaborate the historical, cultural, and intellectual aspects of this new city in a German-language manuscript on the elements of urban planning, which he completed in Berlin following the closure of the Bauhaus. Upon his exile to America in 1938, Hilberseimer began the arduous task of translating that manuscript into English. By 1943, the translation was complete. That same year, Mies secured Hilberseimer an invitation to curate an exhibition on planning for the postwar future at the Art Institute of Chicago. *The City: Organism & Artifact* opened in October 1944 and was accompanied by the publication of Hilberseimer's *The New City: Principles of Planning.*[5] The exhibition made frequent reference to the publication as further evidence in addition to the material on view, and both included extensive illustrations for a radically reimagined postwar Chicago. Notable among them is Hilberseimer's diagram of Chicago's proposed replanning from 1942 (see "Visuals", p. 301, fig. 49).

The exhibition and publication were both positively received, and Hilberseimer was subsequently invited to advise the newly formed South Side Planning Board as it considered the renewal of that portion of Chicago after the war. Hilberseimer assumed this advisory role as a middle-aged European intellectual with a mature vision for shaping the contemporary city based on a lifelong socialist commitment to equity. But there was little in his education or experience that prepared him for the politics of urban renewal and race in the United States. Despite his socialist convictions, Hilberseimer was seemingly incapable of seeing the injustice of the racist practices of slum clearance and urban renewal.[6] He left scant trace, in public or private, of any consideration of the disproportionate impact of his advocacy for radical urban change on the African American communities displaced through those practices. Equally, Hilberseimer was unable or unwilling to engage in the realpolitik of Chicago's development culture and resolute in his refusal to compromise. Mies famously remarked of his longtime colleague's strained relationship with Chicago planners and developers: "With Hilbs you take everything or nothing. And these people don't want that."[7]

In 1949 Hilberseimer published *The New Regional Pattern: Industries and Gardens, Workshops and Farms*, his second major English-language book on planning. It built upon *The New City* and restated his principles of planning while republishing several key diagrams and drawings. In contrast to his prior work, *The New Regional Pattern* was explicitly regional and national in scope, focusing on the infrastructural networks, geological determinates, and ecological potentials of Hilberseimer's decentralized urban order. In the text, Hilberseimer cited Henry Ford's assertion from the 1920s that industry would decentralize the American city: "Industry will decentralize itself. If the city were to decline, no one would rebuild it according to its present plan."[8]

As he had in 1944 with *The New City*, Hilberseimer used empirical evidence of the spatial reordering of the city as support for his own, more radical vision of a fully reimagined Chicago. The publication included drawings of various sites across Chicago's South and West Sides that were being considered for radical urban renewal.[9] Characteristically, rather than draw a new illustration of his idea, Hilberseimer reprinted his 1944 diagram for replanning the city, adding the caption "Chicago: Diagram of its proposed replanning" along with a new scheme for replanning the metropolitan region titled "Chicago Area: Diagram for its proposed replanning, Variation" (see "Visuals", p. 303, fig. 51). In addition to these plans for redesigning his adopted city, Hilberseimer also proposed the radical replanning of Detroit (see "Visuals", p. 302, fig. 50). Six years before he would begin work on Lafayette Park in Detroit, Hilberseimer declared in *The New Regional Pattern* that the "structure of the city is wrong. [...] Only a structural change of the city could bring about the necessary order" (Hilberseimer 1949, 171, 174).

In 1955 Hilberseimer published his third major English-language book on planning, *The Nature of Cities: Origin, Growth, and Decline; Pattern and Form; Planning Problems*. Relative to his previous two books, *The Nature of Cities* was both the most extensive in terms of documentation, texts, and case study examples as well as the most applied in terms of its relevance to Chicago. It presented the most eloquent articulation of Hilberseimer's long-standing conception of city planning as a social project and his most pointed critique of the capitalist city: "Cities are an expression of particular spiritual and material, social and political conditions, influenced and modified by the forms of production and the means of communication. [...] The cities of our age are dominated by industry and commerce and ruled by interest. Some day, perhaps, cities and regions will be planned and developed according to the needs of man and ruled by reason" (Hilberseimer 1955, 13–14).

Following *The New Regional Pattern* in 1949, Hilberseimer continued to advocate for the replanning of Chicago and was increasingly engaged in individual projects throughout the city. These undertakings were primarily although not exclusively associated with sites on the South Side that were being developed in the wake of urban renewal. They were characterized by Hilberseimer's interest in deriving an incremental approach to his transformational replanning. In contrast to his urban, and territorially scaled planning diagrams of a totalizing spatial order, these projects were more tactical and measured. Presented in discrete stages of work, they are best described as processes of editing extant portions of the nineteenth-century street grid. Two examples of this kind of experimental incrementalism can be found in Hilberseimer's projects for Marquette Park (1949) (see "Visuals", p. 306, fig. 54) and his involvement in the South Side Planning Board's *Community Appraisal Study* (South Side Planning Board 1952; see also Harrington 1988, 81–88).

The Nature of Cities describes how incremental projects might grow toward something more holistic in scope as the city evolves toward a spatial order more aligned with the modern industrial economy. As with both *The New City* and *The New Regional Pattern*, the publication was followed by a spate of planning projects evincing Hilberseimer's principles. Among these, Hilberseimer's contributions to urban redevelopment projects in Detroit (1955–56) and Chicago (1956–59) offer a compelling pair of contrasts.

In 1955 Mies van der Rohe and Herbert Greenwald invited Hilberseimer to collaborate on the planning of an urban redevelopment project in Detroit.[10] By the time Hilberseimer agreed to join, the site had sat empty for years, ridiculed as "Mayor Cobo's Fields" in reference to the Detroit mayor who supported a racist regime of urban renewal and forced removal of the neighborhood's predominantly African American population.[11] City planners had designated Black Bottom (as it was formerly called) a slum, adjudging it the site of not only substandard housing and building stock but also countless social pathologies.[12] As a result, the city displaced several thousand residents, primarily African Americans, through federally underwritten urban renewal. While this forced removal occurred years before Hilberseimer became involved in the project, his decision to plan a new mixed-race, mixed-class neighborhood for the site further implicates him in the racist practices associated with urban renewal.

The site remained empty for lack of a local real estate development partner, an eligibility requirement for federal funding in support of urban redevelopment projects. In 1955 Greenwald contacted Detroit planners to express interest in taking over the foundering project. The developer enlisted the design services of Mies. Mies brought on Hilberseimer to plan the site, as well as landscape architect Alfred Caldwell. The now-canonical project came to be known as Lafayette Park (see "Visuals", p. 310–311, fig. 61–63). The project proved to be the most significant realization of Hilberseimer's settlement unit of mixed-height housing and the most important built project of his career. Following upon the success of Lafayette Park in Detroit, Greenwald claimed that he would build a Lafayette Park–style project in every American city, realizing Hilberseimer's vision of mixed-race, mixed-class urban projects set within verdant public landscapes. Shortly before his untimely death, Greenwald invited Mies and Hilberseimer to work on a comparable project for Chicago's Hyde Park neighborhood.[13]

The 1956 Hyde Park plan directly followed Lafayette Park, but with a significant difference from the Detroit project. Hilberseimer's plan for Hyde Park was an alternative to a more aggressive plan of nearly complete erasure already put forth by the city's Land Clearance Commission, the government body authorized to clear urban land for redevelopment by eviction and eminent domain. Hilberseimer's Hyde Park plan had more in common with the approach developed for Marquette Park in Chicago several years prior. As in that case, Hilberseimer proposed removing half of the east–west access roads in Hyde Park, thus reducing automobile traffic and improving pedestrian access to an enlarged network of green spaces (see "Visuals", p. 306, fig. 55). As a planning tool, this incremental editing of the street grid was far easier to argue for than expensive new construction or, worse yet, the displacement of residents (South Side Planning Board 1956; see also Hilberseimer 1956–59; and Spaeth 1988, 64–65). It is no coincidence that Lafayette Park, Hilberseimer's greatest professional achievement, occupied a site where the racist removal of thriving African American communities had already happened years before his involvement. By contrast, Hilberseimer had virtually no impact on planning projects in Chicago, where the racist practices of slum clearance and urban renewal were active and ongoing instruments of urban erasure.[14]

In his last years of active research, Hilberseimer authored the German-language publication *Entfaltung einer Planungsidee* (Development of a Planning Idea). Hilberseimer returned to Germany in 1963 for a public lecture to launch *Entfaltung* (see Hilberseimer 1963, 98–99; and Spaeth 1988, 66–67). The book presented one of his final projects, a proposal for replanning the vast Chicago metropolitan region. Hilberseimer's "New Plan for the City of Chicago" imagined a regional pattern of settlement units stretching from Lake Michigan across the river valleys to the western suburbs (see "Visuals", p. 313, fig. 66). The diagram reprised perennial themes in Hilberseimer's planning theories and applied them with extraordinary fidelity to the existing hydrological structures of the city, rendering a decentralized urban order commensurate with the region's mature industrial economy. With characteristic consistency, his last proposal reiterated his earliest projects, using the city of Chicago as a vast canvas for outlining a radically revised order appropriate to contemporary economic, ecological, and societal conditions.

Hilberseimer rightly recognized the brutality of societies built in the image of economic speculation. While he failed to recognize the inherent injustice of racist planning practices, his work offers a model for a more socially just and environmentally emancipatory form of city planning. Our current challenges with respect to structural racism, climate crises, and economic inequality dramatically reveal the continued urgency of planning according to our needs and ruled by reason.

I can't think of a better framework for reconceiving the design of the city today.[15]

Notes

1   See, for example, recent publications by Richard
    Anderson, Pier Vittorio Aureli, Scott Colman, Daniela
    Fabricius, Marcus Kilian, Plácido González Martínez,
    Daniel Köhler, and Philip Oswalt, among many others.

2   Phyllis Lambert, a former student of Hilberseimer,
    found him motivated by ideas rather than projects,
    with little regard for authorship or attribution. Rather,
    Lambert remembers, Hilberseimer was committed to
    socialist ideals of fairness and equity. Interview with
    the author, November 27, 2019.

3   Detlef Mertins (2013, 197), for example, described
    Hilberseimer as a "rationalist with deep communist
    convictions." Hilberseimer's intellectual and cultural
    commitments in the late 1920s included a faith in the
    arts as an element of autonomous individual expres-
    sion tending toward anarchism.

4   George Danforth remembered Hilberseimer refer-
    ring to himself as his own autonomous state: "I am a
    republic unto myself." (Danforth 1988, 11, 14).

5   Scott Colman's excellent work on this articulates the
    access that Hilberseimer enjoyed in the 1940s, and
    his unsuccessful attempt to synthesize the work of
    the Chicago School into his model of The New City.
    See Colman 2014; see also Hilberseimer 1944.

6   The New Regional Pattern included a full-page map
    prepared by the Social Science Research Committee
    of the University of Chicago, under the direction of
    Louis Wirth, with the heading: "Do Slums Make
    Criminals? This Map . . . Answers in the Affirmative."
    See "Sub-Communities based on Census Tracts of
    Chicago," in Hilberseimer 1944, 50.

7   "You can't take a little bit of Hilbs and a little bit of
    someone or something else and put it all together.
    With Hilbs you take everything or nothing. And these
    people [i.e., planning groups and developers] don't
    want that." Ludwig Mies van der Rohe, as quoted in
    Danforth 1988, 13.

8   Ford's precise formulation was: "Industry will decen-
    tralize. There is no city that would be rebuilt as it is,
    were it destroyed—which fact is in itself a confession
    of our real estimate of our cities." (Ford and Crowther
    1922, 192) Hilberseimer's slightly amended version
    was published in Hilberseimer 1945.

9   See for example Hilberseimer 1949, 147: "Chicago:
    Status of a City. Future Planning Areas of Chicago."

10 The press release by developers Greenwald and
    Katzin announcing the Gratiot (Lafayette) Redevel-
    opment promised that the project would "transform
    the cleared 50-acre slum area [...] into a flowering
    residential community which will help rehabilitate the
    core of the City" (Oscar Katov and Company 1956).

11 For a detailed account of race relations in post–
    World War II Detroit, see Sugrue 1996; especially
    pertinent to the discussion of race and housing is the
    section "Urban Redevelopment" in the chapter "De-
    troit's Time Bomb: Race and Housing in the 1940s"
    (47–51). For a thorough accounting of the urban re-
    newal process in Detroit, see Montgomery 1965.

12 On urban renewal and the erasure of African American
    neighborhoods, see Davis 2018; and Herscher 2020.

13 In his presentation of the Gratiot project to Mayor
    Cobo and the Detroit Common Council, Greenwald
    argued "The Gratiot development offers a major
    challenge not only to Detroit, but to the entire nation.
    [...] The city must be liberated from its confinement
    so that it may be linked to the open space of the land-
    scape." (Oscar Katov and Company 1956)

14 George Danforth quoted Hilberseimer on receiving
    an award from the Chicago Plan Commission: "They
    have never done anything I told them to do; and there
    is nothing in this city that reflects my planning. They
    always have been against what I proposed." Dan-
    forth 1988, 12.

15 Thanks to Dr. Florian Strob and the Bauhaus Dessau
    Foundation for convening the conference "Hilbers-
    eimer: Infrastructures of Modernity" in October 2021
    and for his excellent editorial advice. This essay and
    my reading of Hilberseimer have been supported by
    the work of a wonderfully talented research assistant,
    Philip Denny, PhD candidate at Harvard. Portions of
    this argument were published in Philip Denny and
    Charles Waldheim, "Reconsidering Hilberseimer's
    Chicago," Urban Planning 5, no. 2 (2020): 243–48.
    We remain indebted to Michelangelo Sabatino at Illi-
    nois Institute of Technology for the invitation to de-
    velop that chapter in relation to Hilberseimer's work
    on the South Side of Chicago. Thanks also to Phyllis
    Lambert for the generous recollections of her experi-
    ences as a student working closely with Hilberseimer
    at the Illinois Institute of Technology. Our research on
    the topic was supported by the extremely helpful staff
    of the Ryerson and Burnham Libraries and and Ar-
    chives at the Art Institute of Chicago.

The Red Bauhaus and CIAM: Contexts of Ludwig Hilberseimer's Teaching in the early 1930s

Magdalena Droste

The subject of this essay is the most important planning project at the Bauhaus Dessau under Mies van der Rohe, the Fichtenbreite housing estate and its later integration into the CIAM analysis for Dessau 1933. Both projects have received little attention in the Bauhaus historiography to date. The text illuminates the different resonances these two radical left-wing projects experienced: While the Fichtenbreite planning and its protagonists were thwarted at the Bauhaus, the students of the Dessau analysis team received diverse benevolent support via the CIAM.[1] This exemplifies how Ludwig Hilberseimer influenced the debate of the day through his teaching and personal contacts.

Fichtenbreite was a fictitious planning assignment for a workers' housing estate for the local Junkers aircraft factory in Dessau (Selmanagić 1976; Winkler 2003, 119–20; Bauhaus-Archiv 1968, 57; Wingler 1979b; Hahn 1981, 203). Accordingly, it was located to the west of the factory facilities and the airfield (fig. 1). The Fichtenbreite project was developed in the winter semester 1931/32 (October 1, 1931–March 31, 1932) as a collective planning project with seven participants under the direction of the teacher for urban planning, Ludwig Hilberseimer, for students of the fifth semester. On the one hand, the Fichtenbreite project was a typical classroom project of Ludwig Hilberseimer.[2] At this time, Hilberseimer was working intensively on the new plans for Dessau, which he subsequently published in 1944 in *The New City*, without identifying the location. On the other hand, the authors formed a Communist-oriented collective.[3] Before the end of the semester, three students took over the project in order to expand it and work on it as a comparative cartographic analysis of the city of Dessau after consultation with CIAM officials for the Athens Congress in the summer of 1933. These three students were Wilhelm Hess, who had already participated in the first project; Hubert Hoffmann; and Kees (Cornelis) van der Linden.

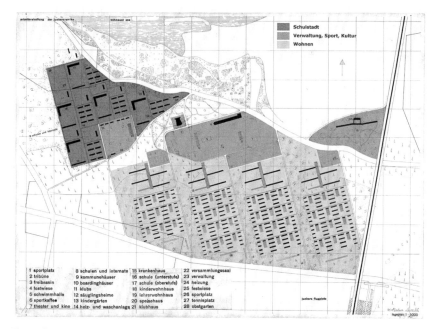

Figure 1: Students of the Bauhaus, arbeitersiedlung der junkers-werke, kühnauer see
(Workers' housing estate of the Junkers works, lake Kühnau, from the lessons of Ludwig
Hilberseimer at Bauhaus Dessau), 1931/1932

Phase 1: Bauhaus

What were the aims of the planning when it started at the Bauhaus? Here we
only have the text that one of the architecture student authors at the time, Selman Selmanagić, published in the GDR in 1976. He combined the description
with a commitment to Soviet-style Communism, as it was officially advocated
in the GDR at the time. "We wanted to plan our ideas of a future Communist
society," Selmanagić (1976) had written about the Fichtenbreite. The basis
was the "Marxist-Leninist theory" for a "socialist residential area" in order
to give shape to a "future Communist society in terms of urban planning and
architecture. […] We students took up new urban planning and architectural
ideas, such as community buildings."

Figure 2: Students of the Bauhaus, kinderstadt zur arbeitersiedlung der junkers-werke
(Children's city for the workers' housing estate of the Junkers works, from the lessons of
Ludwig Hilberseimer at Bauhaus Dessau), 1931/1932

Dwellings

In fact, the settlement for 20,000 residents offers only two types of houses. The
first type comprises four five-winged, twelve-story communal houses; one of
the lower wings (only visible in a bird's-eye view) is an attached infant home
in each case. The very designation as a commune house points to this alternative, Russian-oriented form of housing. The commune houses (with the direct
connection to the infant homes) are intended for "bachelors and pensioners."
"On the ground floor, the walking-impaired." The commune houses contain
"club-dining and social rooms, post office, chemist, pharmacy, savings bank,
hairdresser, laundry, repair workshops." South of this we find four three-story
housing complexes of boarding houses on pillars, arranged in rows with a
west–east orientation. These houses are connected to clubs via passageways.

Each of these housing complexes has a kindergarten to the south. Boarding houses form the second type. "They contain small apartments with compact kitchens (most dining is done in the clubs)" (Selmanagić 1976). According to this, families would have been accommodated here.

Children's town: The special features include a children's town with two schools, boarding schools, teacher housing, and sports and tennis courts (fig. 2).

Recreation: The housing complexes are embedded in green areas. The boarding houses are raised on pillars to allow for through traffic. To the north of the communal boarding houses and again embedded in a green corridor are administration, further clubhouses, an assembly hall, a theater, sports facilities, tennis courts, and a swimming pool. A hospital is located far out.

Traffic: It is kept out of the residential areas. A transport planning innovation is a new transport line east of the settlement from Junkers to the waterfront. This settlement has two important characteristics. Firstly, it is built up like a Russian "rayon," a district in which working, living, and industry are closely connected. In addition, the estate has its own infrastructure. The second important attribute is the collectivization of housing and life; collective ideas are planned in housing, education, culture, and leisure. What are the sources of these ideas of the students?

Russian Influences: References to almost all of these ideas can be found in the illegal KPD-affiliated student magazine *bauhaus* of the Kostufra (abbreviation of Kommunistische Studentenfraktion [Communist Student Faction]), whose first and second issues were still published under Bauhaus director Hannes Meyer in 1930.[4] Issue number 3 contains the first reference to housing. "In reality, the housing question cannot be solved without revolution, because it is itself a part of the revolution" ("Architektur, Soziologie oder Klassenkampf" 1930). At the same time, the authors distanced themselves from the then new director Mies van der Rohe, but also from his predecessor Hannes Meyer.

Meyer was an example of a bourgeois architect "who wants to fight his way out of his class" ("Architektur" 1930). It was a question of "fighting on one front with the revolutionary workers for a Soviet Germany" ("Aus Boudoiren und Amtszimmern" 1930). Mies van der Rohe said the "how" was important. Kostufra, on the other hand, argued that it was only the "what" that mattered ("Der neue Direktor—der neue Kurs" 1930). For the students, this "what" was to be housing.

The following year, 1931, offered particularly many ideas for left-wing architecture students. In the summer of 1931, not only did the great *Deutsche Bauausstellung* (*German Building Exhibition*) take place in Berlin (May 9 to August 2, 1931), whose section *Die Wohnung unserer Zeit* (*The Dwelling of Our Time*) was headed by Mies van der Rohe. As a counterevent, the left-wing architect Arthur Korn had organized the *Proletarische Bauausstellung* (*Proletarian Building Exhibition*, June 2 to July 1, 1931) in the Berlin working-class district of Wedding (Kollektiv für Sozialistisches Bauen 2015).

Important suggestions for the students came from two German architects and urban planners who had been working and planning in the Soviet Union and who gave widely acclaimed lectures that summer of 1931: Ernst May and Kurt Meyer.

The Frankfurt architect Ernst May gave his first German lecture after moving to the USSR in Berlin on June 5, 1931, which met with an enormous response ("Sozialistischer Städtebau in der UdSSR" 1931; and May 1931). In issue 6 of the magazine *bauhaus* of the Kostufra, the students reported at length on his speech. Among other things, Ernst May described the planning of the new factory towns. Primary for the planning was the city as a place of production. Therefore, the distances between home and workplace had to be shortened. In order to include women in production, families were dissolved, and child-rearing and cooking were outsourced and collectivized. The magazine goes on to say: "the most progressive type of housing is the community building, residents of which spend most of their time in communal spaces" ("Sozialistischer Städtebau" 1931). The students' text emphasizes two topics—the satellite town or city complexes; and three housing types: community buildings, boarding houses, and single-family homes.

The students also heard the former Cologne city planner Kurt Meyer, who also worked in the USSR and spoke about the reconstruction of Moscow ("Über den Vortrag von Stadtbaurat Meyer" 1931; Meyer 1931). This lecture left an impression with the students, too. Every worker should reach his workplace in fifteen minutes, he said. Individual quarters were to be rebuilt as "rayons." These would be separated from one another by greenbelts, "each rayon should form a unit in itself, contain workplaces, housing, hospitals, cultural facilities. [...] In the USSR, cities are production sites" (*bauhaus*, no. 6, 1931).

Another important source was the book of the Russian author Milyutin (1930), in which various proposals for rayons were evaluated (fig. 3). His illustrations show the residential zone, the industrial zone—separated by a greenbelt, the school town, and the hospital located on the outskirts. The railway is connected to the industrial zone (Milyutin 1930, 68)?

In the summer issue (no. 6) of the student magazine *bauhaus*, there was another demand that evidently found an audience at the Bauhaus. Students wrote: "it is thus all the more important that the bauhaus masters be required to address this problem and that serious sociological studies, which must be firmly related to this, are offered in the higher semesters" ("Sozialistischer Städtebau" 1931). This already reads like an announcement for the seminar on Fichtenbreite, which began a few months later.

End of the Red Bauhaus

In 1932 Mies van der Rohe put the brakes on the "Red Bauhaus." Many of the students associated with the project were expelled in the spring of 1932 for political reasons or graduated and left the school. Left-wing urban planning went hand in hand with left-wing commitment at the school level—and often led to expulsion or termination of studies (see Hahn 1985, 47–70). These "problematic students" included the three students who took on the project even before the end of the semester on March 31, 1932. What do we know about the three participants in the Dessau analysis, who we can call the CIAM team?

Wilhelm Hess, called Peggy, wanted to become an architect. Following Selmanagić he belonged to the communist students (Selmanagić 1976, 31). Hess

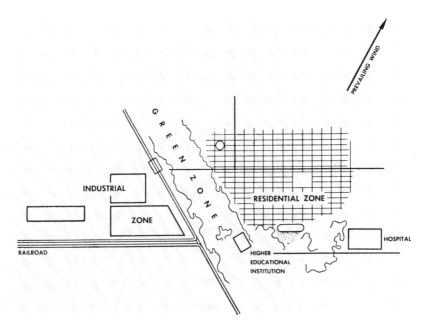

Figure 3: Illustration from: Miljutin, Nikolai A. 1992 [1930]. *Sozgorod: Die Planung der neuen Stadt*. Basel, Berlin: Birkhäuser.

was expelled from the school in December 1932 because he had opposed Mies van der Rohe (Hahn 1985, 101).

Hubert Hoffmann had studied for three semesters under Walter Gropius and Hannes Meyer and had a short period of professional practice with Fred Forbat.[5] In 1931 he had worked at the *Proletarische Bauausstellung*, through which he became very familiar with Milyutin's ribbon city concept (Kollektiv für Sozialistisches Bauen 2015). In March 1932, he was asked to stay away from the Bauhaus.[6] In December 1932, he was banned from the building (Hahn 1985, 101).

The focus was on the student Kees van der Linden, who came from a well-off Dutch household. He was strongly interested in anthroposophy. He just had finished his third semester (Bax 1991; Divendal 1991). In March 1932, Kees was expelled from the school as a "ringleader" because he had "damaged the interests of the Bauhaus" as a students' representative. He never completed his studies (Hahn 1985, 50, 56).

Phase 2: CIAM Commission and Protection

How did it happen that a completely unknown Dutch student in his fourth semester was able to carry out the cartographic analysis of the city of Dessau for the fourth CIAM congress in Moscow (which then took place in Athens and on the ship *Patris II*; see Somer 2007b)? The CIAM was an association of the most important international modern architects who had been meeting annually since 1928, among them Le Corbusier, Gropius, Oud, and so on (Mumford 2000; see also Harbusch et al. 2014).

Probably some earlier connections helped Kees van der Linden, and his Dutch origins also played a role. Kees and his twin brother, Jan, had heard a lecture by the architect H.P. Berlage about the CIAM in The Hague in May 1929 and then decided to study at the Bauhaus.

In January 1932, Van der Linden came into contact with the Dutch urban planner Cornelis van Eesteren. He was chairman of CIAM from 1930 to 1947 and had taught urban planning in Weimar until 1929. But exactly how the contact between him and the student Kees van der Linden came about remains to be clarified. The letter confirmed to van Eesteren on January 25, 1932, that he had received the CIAM guidelines for the presentation (Divendal 2019, 129n25). This was the earliest date for the CIAM cooperation to date.

We learn from a letter that Gropius wrote on February 3, 1932, to the Bauhaus director Mies van der Rohe that Van der Linden was the speaker of the three students. Gropius wrote "a group of bauhaus students, whose spokesman is van der linden, has offered to work on the urban development of the city of dessau in the sense of the attached questionnaire via van eesteren, who recommended van der linden. of course, we in the group must welcome any initiative. as a result, i have informed the group that there is nothing to prevent the young dessau group from cooperating. however, i think it would be good if you, as a member of the congress, were to take care of this matter in dessau […] i would perhaps ask you to think through the matter with hilberseimer, who also stayed away from the meeting, and ask you for a proposal soon."[7] Gropius's skilfully drafted letter asks Mies and Hilberseimer for support and at the same time makes it clear that he himself will support the project. Thus, after CIAM president van Eesteren, the highest-ranking German CIAM representative, Gropius now also became a supporter of the student team. It can also be assumed that Gropius encouraged the students, because Hess, who was involved, later wrote that Gropius had suggested expanding the project in the sense of the CIAM (Divendal 2019, 129n21). None of the three Bauhaus students was, of course, a CIAM member and therefore dependent on contacts and protection.

Further supporters of the team besides van Eesteren and Gropius are Hilberseimer and Arthur Korn. Wilhelm Hess met with Hilberseimer in Berlin and wrote about it to Kees van der Linden: "I've spent four hours discussing every single page with him. He says that every one of us has done excellent work on it and passes on his good wishes to you" (Somer 2007a, 171).[8] Hilberseimer also promised further protection. Hess also contacted Arthur Korn: "herr korn has looked at the work; he would also "like to meet" you face to face for a proper talk."[9] All in all, it can be said that the team, which had to leave the Bauhaus for political reasons, did receive support from there and had prominent international protection from day one.

On time, the team submitted the requested three maps of Dessau. In addition, the students submitted a leporello with 48 sheets in the size of 31 × 30 cm, in which endless research and planning work was invested.[10] The last sheets of the leporello were new proposals.[11] In summary, the team proposed the following: They took over the Fichtenbreite, which had already been planned through at the Bauhaus, and proposed three more new settlements. Two of the four settlements remained nameless. Only the settlement, west of Gropius's Törtensiedlung, was planned through. This southern settlement was the work of the architecture student Ernst Mittag (diploma 10/32) and was also created in the Hilberseimer seminar.[12] Mittag was considered a member of the KPD (Mittag-Fodor 2014, 124). The design was intended for 10,000 people. In the explanatory text, similar to the Fichtenbreite, it says: "the construction method is mixed, single-story flat buildings and ten-story high-rise collectives" for 10,000 inhabitants.[13] All buildings follow a strict east–west orientation. In addition, "clubhouses, theaters, libraries, swimming pools, hotels, old people's homes, administration buildings. to the north-west are the schools, followed by the sports fields."[14] Like the Fichtenbreite, Mittag's plan was designed as a Soviet rayon (fig. 4). The plan also shows wide greenbelts; as in Fichtenbreite, the hospitals are located on the edge, as demanded by Milyutin (1930). Amazingly, a low-rise collective was to be built here. This was the third housing type, which the students in the Kostufra had emphasized in a lecture by Ernst May (Selmanagić 1976).

These four settlements were then interpreted as a ribbon town. On sheet 4, "Tendencies of Development," the authors explain that Dessau has two industrial lines in a north–south direction, to which the residential areas are connected. Thus, the "tendency towards a ribbon town" is present: "the two southern satellites, the Gropius settlement and the Törten, reinforce the tendency toward a ribbon town" (Harbusch et al. 2014, 170; and Somer 2007a, 157). In the future, these two industrial lines are to be connected. A port and railway lines are being designed to optimize traffic and transport routes. On leporello sheet 11, it is explained: "the alignment of the residential areas parallel to the industrial line allows for short working distances." In addition, it says: "high-speed rail transport connects the satellite towns with industry" (Harbusch et al. 2014, 170; and Somer 2007a, 157). The author may have been Hubert Hoffmann, who as a collaborator on the *Proletarische Bauausstellung,* had investigated the linear city based on the Russian model.

The team also revised the population figures. While Selmanagić (1976, 31) gave the figure of 20,000 for Fichtenbreite, the CIAM team calculated for only 10,000 residents per settlement (Harbusch et al. 2014, 170; Somer 2007a, 157). So there has been a change in the density of the development. Wouldn't the children's town then be far too large for the children of only 10,000 residents? The CIAM team ignored such details (Kegler 2016, 143).

The radical left planning for the Dessau Fichtenbreite was lost in the political unrest and the pacification of the Bauhaus from March 1932. The school's move to Berlin in October 1932 also deprived the planning of its topical references. Moreover, Mies had not taken up the offers of collaboration with CIAM members Sigfried Giedion and Walter Gropius. We can only speculate about the reasons; they, too, will be political. As an institution, the Bauhaus was

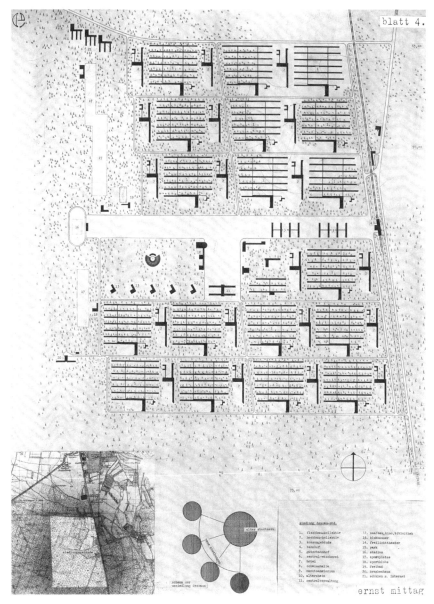

Figure 4: Ernst Mittag, Südliche Siedlung Mosigkauer Heide (Southern housing
estate Mosigkauer Heide), before 1932

dependent on the city's financial backers and had to keep a low political profile. Mies had promised the mayor, Fritz Hesse, that he would run the Bauhaus in a nonpolitical way. In May 1931, Mies had commented "that perhaps town planning was fundamentally a political problem" (Mumford 2000, 65; and Kollektiv für Sozialistisches Bauen 2015, 163).

The three students who took over what used to be the Fichtenbreite planning proposal for CIAM could rely on three advantages: Firstly, the CIAM team benefited from the protection of van Eesteren, Gropius, Hilberseimer, and Arthur Korn. All supported them in many ways. Secondly, the group benefited from a completely different framework. The Bauhaus as an institution depended on political decisions of the city. But CIAM was an international, independent organization financed by its members. It had been founded in Switzerland (Mumford 2000). The political conditions in the individual member countries receded into the background at the meetings.

And this brings us to the third advantage: The presentation of the project on the ship *Patris II* took place extraterritorially and among friends (Harbusch et al. 2014, 165–75). The discursive field on urban planning and architecture in the late 1920s revolved around rationalization in both East and West. Left-wing planning instruments were discussed equally in the Soviet Russian and German contexts. The great interest in the USSR was also shared by Sigfried Giedion, the Swiss secretary general of CIAM. "Like many of his fellow campaigners, Giedion believed that the Soviet Union offered European modernism suitable conditions for the realization of its architectural and urban planning ideas." Especially with regard to the implementation of functionalist urban planning, they promised themselves "grandiose possibilities" (Weiss 2010, 222).

The three students traveled with the *Patris II* and presented their project. Ludwig Hilberseimer did not travel to Marseille. During these months, he acted as a discreet diplomat unscathed between the Leftists and Mies van der Rohe. Hilberseimer's involvement probably did not cause any conflicts of loyalty between them. When he advised the team, the Bauhaus was closed; a little later, he himself was jobless and working as a freelance architect. Hilberseimer rarely exposed himself publicly; he never appeared as a speaker at congresses or conferences, but preferred to work as a publicist and book author through his writings or as a teacher in small circles.

Eric Mumford has stated that in 1932 "the first phase of CIAM had ended" with the imposition of new reactionary architectural policies in Germany and the USSR "though this was not immediately evident" (Mumford 2000, 90). In the following years, CIAM moved in an apolitical direction. There is agreement about this in the body of literature: the radical projects were put aside.

Hilberseimer successfully emigrated to the United States in 1938. Between 1933 and his emigration, a common space of discourse had once again emerged between Hilberseimer and some of the Bauhaus actors, but this time in private. It was the Friday Group, in which a number of left-wing architects met in Berlin. From the older generation, these were Hans Scharoun and Hilberseimer; from the younger generation, Selman Selmanagić from the first Fichtenbreite plan and Hubert Hoffmann from the CIAM team—among others. "After all, we had all taken part in the meetings of the 'degenerate' architects," Selmanagić recalled (Kunsthochschule Berlin 1985, 23). Wilhelm Hess and Hubert Hoffmann became German CIAM members in 1934.[15] On emigrating to England, Gropius asked Hilberseimer to take over as head of the German CIAM group. However, the organization remained marginal in Germany until after 1945. Hess was able to work for CIAM from Switzerland until 1935 (Mumford 2000, 94). However, he never advanced to the premier league of urban planners and architects. Hess's career, like that of Hubert Hoffmann, suffered during the years in the Third Reich. Hoffmann became a professor in Graz in 1959. Kees van der Linden became a member of the Dutch CIAM (Harbusch et al. 2014, 165). He returned to the Netherlands in 1938 and worked as an anthroposophical architect and teacher (Bax 1991, 83).

Notes

1   With thanks to Anke Blümm, Regina Göckede,
    Christa Kamleithner, Winfried Nerdinger, Thomas
    Steigenberger, Florian Strob, and Paul Weber; and
    to Uli Nickel for the translation and Marie Anderson
    for the editing.

2   On Hilberseimer as a teacher, see Winkler 2003 and
    Oswalt 2019b.

3   Selmanagić names as Communist participants
    Waldemar Alder, Isaak Butkow, Wilhelm Hess, Hilde
    Reiss, Selman Selmanagić, Isaak Weinfeld, and the
    Social Democrat Wils Ebert.

4   The Bauhaus Dessau Foundation is planning an edi-
    tion of the magazine.

5   See „Hoffmann, Hubert," from the database of the
    Research Center for Biographies of Former Bauhaus
    Members (BeBA). URL: _https://bauhaus.commu-
    nity/gnd/119197294 (access date: 20.05.2022).

6   Beiratsprotokolle Bauhaus Dessau. Author's copy.

7   Walter Gropius to Ludwig Mies van der Rohe, Feb-
    ruary 3, 1932. Library of Congress, Washington,
    Ludwig Mies van der Rohe papers Box 2, CIAM
    1932.

8   Hess to van der Linden. Letter, May 28, 1933,
    ETH Zürich, Giedion Archiv, Nachlass Hess.

9   Hess to van der Linden. Letter, May 28, 1933,
    ETH Zürich, Giedion Archiv, Nachlass Hess.

10 See Maps I, II, III in Harbusch et al. 2014, 188–91;
    images of the 48 sheets of the leporello in Somer
    2007a, 169–70 and 156–57: and dimensions of the
    leporello in In Simon Thomas and Brentjens 2019,
    131.

11 See the image of the leporello in Harbusch et al.
    2014, 191; and Somer 2007a, 157.

12 See the first sheet of the leporello in Harbusch et al.
    2014, 169; and Sommer 2007, 156.

13 For the text on the figure, see Harbusch et al. 2014,
    157, bottom row, last sheet.

14 Harbusch et al. 2014, 157, bottom row, last sheet.

15 Archiv ETH Zürich, 42-K-1933-Gropius-
    Giedion-21, gta-Archiv / ETH Zürich, CIAM.

Through the Lens of Colonization:
The New City as a Heritage of Modernism

Plácido González Martínez

The consideration of *The New City* (1944) as a heritage of ideas constitutes one of the pending questions around the legacy of modernist architecture and urban planning. This essay aims to advance in this direction by means of a double contextualization: first, within the wider theoretical production developed by Hilberseimer throughout his career, both in the shape of designs and of texts; and second, within a wider process of colonization, which would link Hilberseimer's work to an array of international planners and designers committed to the reform of ways of life and to the occupation of the territory according to the modernist mindset.

An assessment of the links between *The New City* and the rest of Hilberseimer's production requires research on a variety of materials dealing with the same topics of housing reform, low urban density, and infrastructural efficiency that traverse his career in Germany and the United States. This inquiry starts from the roots of Hilberseimer's inspiration, which can be found in his formative reading of authors like Patrick Geddes, Ebenezer Howard, and Arturo Soria y Mata. It continues through a selection of texts and designs by Hilberseimer, both published and unpublished, which may be considered crucial course changes in his career.

The relationship between *The New City* and the modern purpose of colonization is understood both in relationship to the external and internal definition of such a concept. Particularly considering that Hilberseimer's career remained within the borders of the United States since 1938, my inquiry will be directed toward an analogy with similar phenomena of internal colonization in other geographies. I will also aim to ponder the reasons the implementation of Hilberseimer's theories can be deemed either a failure or a success. I argue that even if the real possibility of

43

influencing official planning in the United States was scarce, Hilberseimer trusted in the long-term effect of education as key for the permanence of his vision.

Sources for this research are Hilberseimer's manuscripts (both published and unpublished); books; personal correspondence; legal documents; and his students' thesis graduation projects from the Illinois Institute of Technology (IIT). My research was completed through semistructured interviews with people related to Hilberseimer's career in Chicago.[1] By means of the interpretation of this data, this essay will aim to connect *The New City* with Hilberseimer's own oeuvre and with the wider historical process of colonization, with the final goal of enriching the interpretation of Hilberseimer's theoretical legacy as a heritage of modernism.

Colonization as a Modern Enterprise: The Roots of Hilberseimer's Colonization Principles

Colonization is a historical process that characterizes modernity and relates to purposes of territorial domination, implementation of institutions, and economical exploitation based on unequal relations of power. Hierarchical by nature, colonization traditionally has been understood as an external process in terms of expansion beyond one's borders, yet it can also have an internal orientation within national borders with identical purposes. In recent years, the study of colonialism has aimed to address the crimes of modern imperialism, advocating for the decolonization of knowledge and the assumption of its lasting effects. Conceived by colonizers as an enterprise of civilization, the roots of colonization date back to the origins of human sedentarism and the establishment of the first urban centers far away from mother cities. To the eyes of modernist designers, colonization was blindly identified as the transmission of progress, originating from the cities to the suburbs, from the metropolises to the colonies, from affluent regions to poor areas, from "advanced" societies to what were pejoratively classified as "backward" communities.

Pursuing a shared transformative goal, I find a key difference in modern design approaches to colonization, namely between "closed" and "open" models. This difference lies in their consideration of time and is linked to the availability of resources determined by political will and entrepreneurial opportunity. Accordingly, the definition of *closed models* of colonization would apply preferably in cases when changes happen at overwhelming speed and momentum. They would aim to recreate the functioning of utopian societies, based in a strong spatial determinism, with Walter Burley Griffin's Canberra and Lúcio Costa's Brasilia as models of their immutable character. On the other hand, *open models* would be preferred in situations where development was seen as a long-term goal, and the construction of a community as a lasting process, with examples like Candilis–Josic–Wood's Carrières Centrales in Casablanca, and Hassan Fathy's New Gourna settlement.

Based on the analysis of the references that he used to inform his work, I argue that Hilberseimer adhered to the definition of an open model. The selection of seven titles that Hilberseimer mentioned in an interview with *Der Aufbau* (1959) as core references for his work included three works related to planning. The three of them are explicitly about open approaches to colonization.[2] Patrick Geddes's *Cities in Evolution* (1915) develops a 'natural' interpretation of city growth and development, widely shared by modernist planners and designers,[3] which yet omit any principle of agency nor question any power discourses. Ebenezer Howard's *Garden Cities of To-Morrow* (1902) advocated for the production of a hybrid urban-rural settlement merged with nature, as well as alternative ways of life; it was interpreted as elitist by his contemporaries. Arturo Soria y Mata's Linear City, proposed in 1882, was a novel attempt to imagine the end of a whole history of concentration in traditional settlements and a new era of soft distribution of the population along transportation lines; yet it was deemed daydreaming by planning practitioners. Sharing a deep pragmatism, the three references purposely developed a series of principles rather than any predefined model. As I argue, the means by which Hilberseimer appropriated these principles marked a turn in his career in Germany, and is a key for the assessment of his work.

In 1924 Hilberseimer's work on the organization of high-density urban models culminated in the two famous images of the Hochhausstadt (High-Rise City). Thereafter, his interest shifted from the analysis of the metropolis in its traditional definition as "mother city" to the imagination of its "colonies" in their metaphorical characterization as "daughters" of the metropolis. This turn happened in two stages, related to two building exhibitions happening in the short time frame of less than five years. The first one was *Die Wohnung*, curated by Mies van der Rohe and materialized in the Weißenhofsiedlung in Stuttgart in 1927 (see Llobet i Ribeiro 2007). Hilberseimer's contribution took shape both in building and in writing (see "Visuals", p. 280, fig. 13) (fig. 1). He authored one of the new model homes of the Weißenhof, with the modesty and dignity of a bourgeois retreat for a metropolitan dweller. His theoretical essay, published in the exhibition catalogue as "Die Wohnung als Gebrauchsgegenstand," was far more radical and ambitious for Hilberseimer's later work. Dealing with low density as the new goal to be achieved by modern urbanism, it manifested a shared concern with his contemporary fellow planners. Yet, this text also points toward the key role that the definition of the house as the minimal urban unit would have in this challenge; a germinal condition that *The New City* would later develop to its full extent.

The second decisive turning point rests on the definition of this germinal condition and happened in the context of the Great Depression. A tendered competition, *Das wachsende Haus*, curated by Hans Poelzig in December 1930, attracted more than a thousand entries from German architects, many of them unemployed, who aimed to define new fundamentals for postcrisis construction. So great was the impact that in fall 1931, Martin Wagner organized the exhibition *Sonne, Luft und Haus für Alle*, held in Berlin Charlottenburg and featuring a selection of proposals from the competition. Hilberseimer contributed again both with the construction of a housing prototype and a short theoretical reflection for the exhibition catalogue (see Wagner 1932). The modesty of Hilberseimer's building is of the utmost interest. Far from a bourgeois residence, Hilberseimer's house was deemed a *Hauskern*, a shelter

for a germinal stage of colonization, ready to be transplanted to any location. Solar orientation was the only guiding design principle, aiming to maximize the beneficial interaction with the sun. Construction methods used in the "seed" were also simplified, enabling a do-it-yourself approach, potentially standardized for mass production.[4] Furthermore, Hilberseimer's design laid out an open courtyard, which was the first and immediate part of the land-scape to be appropriated by settlers as a departure for a complete territorial rearrangement.[5]

Cultivating these concerns, Hilberseimer aligned with wider contempo-rary purposes of internal colonization in Europe. Intended to be applied as a low-density urban pattern, scattered with minimal housing seeds to re-form German cities, the early principles that Hilberseimer defined in his turn aligned with the radical aims of deurbanization in the Soviet Union. This is the case in Moisej Ginzburg's 1927 "Green City" plan, which proposed the massive relocation of population from Moscow's city center to a new ring of garden cities; or the alliance with industrialization that inspired Milyutin's proposal for the new settlement of Magnitogorsk in 1929. Not coincidentally, Hilberseimer owned an original volume of N.A. Milyutin's *Sozgorod: Die Planung der neuen Stadt* (*Sotsgorod: The Problem of Building Socialist Cities* [1930]), which he brought from Germany to the United States in 1938. In these examples, the references of Geddes, Howard, and Soria y Mata blended and manifested an irresistible zeitgeist for Hilberseimer and his contemporaries, and reached the classrooms of the Bauhaus to plan "socialist cities."[6] This refers to the overarching ambition of defining a territorial change starting from the design of its minimal habitational cell: true modernization could only reach society from the appropriation of modern life that started from domestic experience.

The Difficult Reception of Hilberseimer's Ideas in the US Context

The design of the housing "seed" and the study of possible arrangements to form communities to colonize the territory became a long-term enterprise for Hilberseimer's career that he took to the United States. This transfer happened in a tangible way: the catalogue *Das wachsende Haus* was among the few books that traveled with Hilberseimer. The preparation for introducing his ideas on colonization in the new American context required further studies of how such process evolved in the United States. Consequently, the first theoretical text that Hilberseimer produced in English after his arrival in Chicago was an unpublished manuscript entitled "The Settlung [*sic*] Americas" (which can be translated as The Colonization of America), dated 1940. Analyzing the European occupation of North America, Hilberseimer delivered a full declaration of intentions, as he identified the United States as an optimal setting for a revolutionary reorganization of the territory that could extend its principles universally.

Nevertheless, the United States was not an easy testing ground. Hilberseimer's simple principles could, indeed, be particularly adapted to the extraordinary changes in American society in the postwar era. The weak point was not the theory but the means to implement it. Basically, the strong state that was present in European experiences of internal colonization did not exist in North America, although Franklin D. Roosevelt's New Deal policies to revert the situation of crisis during the Great Depression could have given Hilberseimer some hope for an interventionist political context, similar to what he experienced during the Weimar Republic (1919–33). Given his thirst for knowledge, it's possible to speculate that Hilberseimer knew of the work developed by the Resettlement Administration (RA, 1935–37), later reformulated as the Farm Security Administration (FSA, 1937–42), though no documents or notes in Hilberseimer's archives refer to an analysis of such policies.

Yet they must have been of interest to him. The Greenbelt Towns initiative, promoted by the RA, was an exceptional approach to public housing by the United States government. To a certain extent, it followed the phenomenal enterprise of the construction of *Siedlungen* that German municipalities led during the Weimar Republic, which Hilberseimer knew about firsthand. Indeed, the goal that Rexford Tugwell, head of the RA, was aiming for in terms of urban redevelopment coincided with that of the Soviet disurbanists and Hilberseimer: to empty the core of the city, sanitize it, and colonize the territory with the relocated population. However, the impact of the RA can be deemed as minimal due to lack of funding and its short life amid suspicions of Tugwell's "socialist" orientation (González Martínez 2015, 70).

The agricultural colonization promoted by the FSA, which succeeded the RA in 1937, also had a negligible effect on the American landscape. Compared with, for example, the ambitious initiatives of the Spanish National Institute of Colonization (NIC, 1939–71), the FSA limited itself to providing emergency solutions to housing shortages in the rural areas hit worst by the Great Depression.[7] Fundamental differences between the American and the Spanish systems, mainly political (democracy versus dictatorship) and administrative (federalism versus centralism in Spain) account for this contrast. Yet, even within the American context, and despite the intervention of significant modern architects like Vernon DeMars in the planning of towns like Yuba City and Manzanar (California), or Chandler (Arizona), the reach of the FSA was insignificant in both population and territorial terms. And it definitely failed in the production of American imaginaries, as the general public preferred to embrace the individualism of Frank Lloyd Wright's Broadacre City instead of any collectivist initiatives.

Considering Hilberseimer's experience of exile and settling in the United States at the same time that the modest initiatives of the RA and FSA were under way, the difficulties in making his ideas take root as part of the New Deal are understandable. Lacking professional connections beyond those of the influential yet limited circle of German émigrés in America, possibilities for a potential contribution by Hilberseimer to federal planning were scarce. Also, the New Deal was not meant to be repeated after the political right-wing turn that followed the war, much to Hilberseimer's regret. The only possibility of cooperation with official policies remained at the municipal level, in the framework of urban renewal promoted by the 1949 and 1954 Housing Acts. Even when Hilberseimer initiated a collaboration with local planning authorities in Chicago for the redevelopment of Fort Dearborn,[8] his intransigent character and highly critical view of official planning rendered any fruitful outcome impossible (González Martínez 2015, 82).

The Intangible Push for Colonization: The Seeds of Education

Hilberseimer was well aware that the reception of *The New City*, both by the general public and specialized readers, was not completely welcoming and that possibilities for direct application were scarce. For this reason, it is my opinion that Hilberseimer trusted the permanence of his ideas to what he considered the longest-lasting vehicle, which is that of teaching (fig. 2). Very much as the "seed" of *Das wachsende Haus*, the cultivation of Hilberseimer's principles was entrusted to their later reproduction by his students, as a message to the future. The fact that the design of a settlement unit already appeared as a teaching assignment in Hilberseimer's course of 1931–32 at the

Figure 2: Ludwig Hilberseimer with students in the classroom, c. 1949

Bauhaus confirms this intent.[9] And not coincidentally, Hilberseimer began to write "Grundlagen des Städtebaus" (Principles of City Planning), which can be considered as the first version of *The New City*, in 1933, right after the Bauhaus was closed by the National Socialists. Seen in perspective, it worked as a syllabus to be implemented after 1938 at the Armour Institute and later at the IIT.

Indeed, the circumstances of American universities after World War II were most suitable for the international dissemination of Hilberseimer's principles. Campuses became melting pots where American students returned from the fronts in Africa, Asia, and Europe, together with international elite students and talents who brought their own cultural backgrounds. Students received instruction from international teachers who, like Hilberseimer, had emigrated to the United States as a safe haven and a land of opportunities. This was the time when Hilberseimer's theories on colonization were, in fact,

Figure 3: Mineral Creek Valdez, Source: *The Great Alaska Earthquake of 1964*. 1968. vol. 1, pt 1. Washington DC: National Research Council.

adapted to a full variety of geographies and cultures. A review of the master theses directed by Hilberseimer at the IIT between 1943 and 1966 shows a total of 18 different nationalities among his students. These students adopted Hilberseimer's invariable method incorporating (1) a historical study of the area; (2) a site diagnosis; (3) the development of an intervention plan based on the four-stage reorganization scheme; and (4) conclusions. By these means, they effectively engaged with the adaptation of the settlement unit to contexts as varied as Japan, India, Canada, Ecuador, France, Egypt, Switzerland, and Azerbaijan (see González Martínez 2013).

Education became the last "soft" and long-term means of transmission left to Hilberseimer. Lacking governmental support for implementation, the outcome of Hilberseimer's teaching during more than four decades did not follow the massive extension of the designs proposed in *The New City*. This research shows how the actual implementation of Hilberseimer's designs and principles happened in very specific situations of crisis. This extent is coherent with the origins of Hilberseimer's *Hauskern*, which effectively happened during the Great Depression, when new beginnings required simplicity of means. A bird's-eye view of the Andes mountain range shows, for example, the project carried out by the Ecuadorian Wilson Garcés Pachano (1948 graduate of IIT), who adopted the "herringbone" arrangement for new towns like Pelileo as part of the reconstruction projects he carried out for the Ministry of Public Works of Ecuador after the 1949 earthquakes. Years later, Paul Finfer (1961 graduate of IIT) implemented a variation of the settlement unit for the new town of Valdez in Alaska (fig. 3), previously devastated by an earthquake in 1964. Far as they may be from the relevance of Letchworth for Ebenezer Howard's theories, or Madrid's Ciudad lineal for Arturo Soria y Mata, these two unnoticed examples share a value: that of representing the material realization of otherwise ambitious proposals for a radical transformation of the territory.

The contribution of *The New City* (1944) to the definition of a heritage of modernism benefits from its contextualization within Hilberseimer's theoretical work. Research on Hilberseimer's production shows how *The New City* is not an episode but the tip of an iceberg extending through a career of four decades in Germany and the United States. The contextualization of *The New City* in a perspective of colonization supports this. Hilberseimer's acknowledgement to the references of Patrick Geddes, Ebenezer Howard, and Arturo Soria y Mata is also revealing. It establishes strong theoretical links to a constellation of planners who developed their proposals with the aim to radically transform housing and territorial occupation, both outside and within national borders, throughout the twentieth century. Having focused mainly on theoretical writing and teaching, I argue that the direct implementation of Hilberseimer's designs was very limited in reach, meaning that their influence relied on the power of education and remains to be circumscribed in the field of ideas. Far from constituting a handicap, an appreciation of Hilberseimer's contribution goes back to the words of Mies van der Rohe. As he declared, the value of Hilberseimer's ideas would be only understood in a situation where they would match the ideals for a harmonious interaction with the environment claimed by contemporary society.[10] Reduced to simple principles and soft as that may be, Hilberseimer's contribution constitutes an outstanding proof of a massive effort for rationalization that deserves full consideration as a heritage of modernism.

Notes

1   The research for this essay was conducted in prepa-
    ration for my book *In Light of Hilberseimer: The Gen-
    esis and the Legacy of The New City*. Seville: Vibok
    Works (2015). The sources can mainly be found at
    the Ryerson & Burnham Library of the Art Institute
    of Chicago and the Graham Resource Center of the
    Illinois Institute of Technology.
2   In addition to the works discussed here, Hilbers-
    eimer also refers to Bücher 1893, King 1911,
    Kropotkin 1907, and Ratzel 1882; see Der Aufbau
    1959.
3   Modernist planners and designers shared a fascina-
    tion for natural processes, which inspired analogies
    and design approaches. See Anker 2005.
4   With this, Hilberseimer was connected to the Ameri-
    can bricoleur tradition of the balloon frame system.
    This system enabled rapid construction since 1833,
    and characterized the internal colonization of the
    United States throughout the nineteenth century.
5   An attempt to materialize the L-shape model took
    place in the planned extension of the Dessau Törten
    Settlement under the second Bauhaus director
    Hannes Meyer. See the essay by Andreas Buss in the
    present volume.
6   See Magdalena Droste's essay on Hilberseimer's
    Bauhaus course and the CIAM in the present volume.
7   The only evidence on Hilberseimer's knowledge
    about the NIC initiatives in Spain is an article from
    the *Reader's Digest* kept in his personal working
    documents (Littell 1961). There is no evidence of the
    impact of Hilberseimer's theories in the architects
    and planners of the NIC.
8   Alison Fischer's essay in the present volume refers
    to the racist aspects of urban renewal projects and
    the highly problematic framing of so-called slums.
9   Drawings from one of Hilberseimer's students, Pius
    Pahl, appear in Achilles, Harrington, and Myhrum
    1986, 84.
10 "Perhaps the importance of his work will be revealed
    one day. The current concerns about saving energy,
    solar orientation and environmental control, etc.
    were common in Hilbs's work." Mies van der Rohe,
    cited in GRAHAM FOUNDATION. 1987. *Ludwig
    Hilberseimer. The Man and the Work. A Concordia.*
    Chicago: Graham Foundation, 21 March, 47.

Ludwig Hilberseimer, the Slum, and Urban Renewal in Chicago: From *Großstadt* to Fort Dearborn

Alison Fisher

Soon after producing one the most compelling, if controversial, set of texts and images about the architecture of the metropolis in the mid-1920s, Ludwig Hilberseimer abandoned the center city in pursuit of a decentralized urbanism based on low-rise housing set in green space.[1] Yet, in the 1950s, he made one brief return to the model of the vertically integrated city for an unrealized project in Chicago's central business district and Near North Side neighborhood, which was later published as part of his landmark book *The Nature of Cities* (1955). By placing this project in the context of Hilberseimer's career in Chicago, this paper analyzes his complex attitude to so-called urban renewal development, which reshaped historical neighborhoods across the United States as part of a broader movement of urban planning as a political, economic, and ideological tool in postwar America.[2]

The Origin of the *Großstadt*

Much of Hilberseimer's career in the United States was spent advancing his model for the settlement unit, a cohesive, walkable neighborhood structure that was meant to replace both the historical fabric of cities and the sprawling, car-focused landscape of American suburbs.[3] While the settlement unit was his near sole preoccupation between the 1930s and the 1960s, Hilberseimer's ideas about the replanning of the historical city began in a very different context with his *Großstadtarchitektur* or Metropolis-architecture project of 1927. Richard Pommer (1988) and others have pointed to Hilberseimer's new metropolis as a dramatic rejection of history. Indeed in his book of the same name, Hilberseimer explained that the *Großstadt* would not resemble any existing urban organization or structures: "Our concept of the city is […] still founded on an ideology attached to the historical past. Although walls and gates have long since fallen, their memory haunts our minds" (Hilberseimer 2012, 133).

Similarly, Hilberseimer's striking drawings for the High-Rise City or Hochhausstadt created in 1924 that illustrate his theory of the *Großstadt* can be seen as a kind of emotional and physical tabula rasa that rejects any trace of the materiality, cultural elements, or even traditional ways of representing the historical city. In the place of the dense and disorganized urbanism of existing cities, Hilberseimer depicts the *Großstadt* (see "Visuals", p. 278, fig. 9) as a seemingly endless landscape of high-rise slab residential towers in moody grisaille, perched on top of large plinths accommodating offices and stores and a dizzying network of elevators, elevated walkways, subways, commuter trains, and subterranean roads.

Hilberseimer's *Großstadt* project was not created ex nihilo, of course, but instead responded to and adapted many principles he observed in existing and visionary cities, including the skyscrapers and transit of New York City, full-service Chicago apartment buildings, and Le Corbusier's monumental Paris Plan Voisin of 1925. Late in life, however, Hilberseimer revealed that the origin of his idea for the *Großstadt* was not one of these fashionable and forward-looking references, but, in fact, the compact and layered structure of the medieval city. In an unusually personal reminiscence, Hilberseimer describes a casual conversation in the late 1920s with friends in Berlin discussing the problems of this rapidly growing city, including traffic and lengthy commutes. He muses, "could not modern cities be built like medieval towns? In the ground floor of the houses were workshops or offices and in the upper floors living and bedrooms. Everybody lived above his place of work" (Hilberseimer 1967, 43). So instead of turning away from historical models, Hilberseimer's new metropolis proposed a return to the compact, multiuse, and vertically integrated organization of the medieval towns which still form the core of many cities in Europe.

This paradox flies in the face of commonly held understandings of Hilberseimer's theories of urban planning, beginning with the *Großstadt* and continuing with his settlement unit schemes of the 1940s and 1950s, many of which proposed the complete replacement of historical city patterns with highly organized, zoned urban landscapes. Importantly for this essay, it also suggests that Hilberseimer understood the value of the layered and interpenetrating functions of the historical city, the very messiness and disorganization that was targeted for elimination by programs of urban renewal in the United States, including Hilberseimer's own proposals for Chicago.

Chicago and the Slums

As Hilberseimer was developing his theories of the *Großstadt* in Berlin, Chicago professor Harvey Warren Zorbaugh was working on the 1929 study *The Gold Coast and the Slum*, which would become a landmark in urban sociology. Zorbaugh was the product of the so-called Chicago School of sociology, which studied the interaction between individuals, social groups, and the urban environment. Founded at the University of Chicago in the early decades of the twentieth century, this group of sociologists, including Zorbaugh, Robert Park, and Ernest Burgess, saw the city as a living laboratory and created new research methodologies based on interviews, fieldwork, and firsthand experiences with population groups, including the working classes.[4] For this reason, the Chicago School also had close ties to social workers and other civic reformers like Jane Addams, the activist who founded the Hull House on Chicago's Near West Side in 1889, a famous settlement house created to support the health and education of immigrant families and others newly arrived to the city (see Bryan and Davis 1990).

Zorbaugh's study was sited in the Near North Side of Chicago, an area that in much of the twentieth century was marked by profound social, economic, and physical disparities between the Gold Coast, an elite strip of mansions, fine apartment buildings, and hotels stretching along Lake Shore Drive, and the adjacent "gray neighborhoods" (Zorbaugh 1976 [1929], viii) which were home to deteriorating and overcrowded immigrant tenements, factories, street gangs, rooming houses, and unsavory bars (1976 [1929] 1–16). His work was an immediate sensation—and remains of scholarly interest today—for offering an unprecedented degree of detail about the lives of local residents, and for Zorbaugh's nearly cinematic descriptions of the area: "The Near North Side is an area of high light and shadow, of vivid contrasts—contrasts not only between the old and the new, between the native and the foreign, but between wealth and poverty, vice and respectability, the convention and the bohemian, luxury and toil" (Zorbaugh 1929, 4).

Much of Zorbaugh's book focused on the social disintegration of these diverse neighborhoods. Importantly, he pointed to the active role the physical environment played in this process, including the unchecked, unplanned expansion of the city and a process he described as "succession," whereby established areas were transformed into a slum by the arrival of successive waves of new residents, be they Sicilians, African Americans, or bohemian artists (Zorbaugh 1976 [1929], 230–35)—and later by Puerto Ricans and a sizable enclave of gay residents. The physical manifestation of succession included residents' adaptations of existing buildings to serve a great variety of functions, including commerce and entertainment. Ultimately, Zorbaugh argued that these alterations and subdivisions created a troubling kind of mixing that resulted in promiscuity, vice, and ruthlessness, much like German sociologist Georg Simmel's observations about the shifting identity of the modern city dweller in his 1903 essay "The Metropolis and Mental Life" (Simmel 2002).

Undifferentiated urbanism was also one of Hilberseimer's primary targets for criticism in *The Nature of Cities* (1955). For Hilberseimer, the industrial or "paleo-technic" city was rife with this kind of disorder, from its "cramped and interdependent" living quarters to the "indiscriminate conglomeration of industrial, commercial, and residential sections" (Hilberseimer 1955, 112, 110). Hilberseimer's claims about the dangers of the disordered city, however, often fail to make a specific connection between physical and social disorder, moving directly from observations about traffic congestion to the emergence of slums in the "worst and unhealthiest parts of the city" (108). At times, Hilberseimer uses the term *slum* to refer to the whole of the historical city, whose darkness and smog stands in stark opposition to the sunshine and vigor in his descriptions of the new decentralized city.

Hilberseimer is emphatic that slums are one of the greatest problems in the contemporary city, yet his concentrated observations about these areas in the book are confined to just two paragraphs in a nearly 300-page text and consist largely of rhetorical questions about the biological or environmental origins of crime and delinquency. His conclusion is clear: "Slums, eating into the city like a cancer, have spread until they now contaminate the countryside. There are many reasons for the growth of these slums. The most basic is unrealistic planning—or no planning at all. Uncontrolled growth has inevitably resulted in social disorder" (Hilberseimer 1955, 242).

On one level, it is surprising that *The Nature of Cities* treats the slum in such vague, journalistic language, first because Hilberseimer would certainly have been aware of the sophisticated—if misguided—research on the urban poor that had been undertaken by Zorbaugh and other sociologists of the Chicago School.[5] Second, by the 1950s, Hilberseimer had spent more than a decade working at the Chicago Illinois Institute of Technology (IIT), an urban university located in Bronzeville, a once prosperous African American neighborhood that by the 1940s had been identified as one of the largest areas of "blight" in the city (Whiting 2001, 652). Beginning in 1947, he worked for over five years as a participant in planning studies funded by the South Side Planning Board for an unrealized urban renewal project near the school that would have razed more than four square miles of residential and commercial areas and displaced nearly two hundred thousand residents.[6] Hilberseimer was also intimately involved with a project led by architect Ludwig Mies van der Rohe in the 1940s to expand and modernize the IIT campus and to insulate the white institution from its lower-income Black neighbors (see Whiting 2001; and Haar 2010). In short, Hilberseimer had a wealth of firsthand, personal exposure to living conditions in the so-called blighted areas of Chicago's Near South Side, both as a daily commuter to IIT and as a professional planner. Consequently, it is hard to understand how he could set aside this substantial and nuanced understanding of low-income neighborhoods to discuss the slum as a timeless and placeless abstraction.

But this willful blindness and erasure is also part of the history of modernism writ large. Mies's S.R. Crown Hall on the IIT campus, one of the most celebrated pieces of modern architecture in the United States, was built on the former footprint of the Mecca Flats, a nineteenth-century apartment building that had been home to many generations of Black Chicagoans. Located in the heart of Bronzeville, the Mecca had a prominent cultural presence, having been featured in jazz hits of the 1920s and a book-length work by Pulitzer Prize–winning poet Gwendolyn Brooks (see Bluestone 1998; and Dyja 2014). The apartment building made the national news in the 1950s when a group of vocal and press-savvy residents unsuccessfully fought IIT to preserve their homes in the Mecca.

This battle jumped from local to national news with a photo essay in *Life* magazine published less than a year before the building's demolition (Kirkland 1951). The haunting photographs highlight the graffiti, broken windows, and weary faces of the Mecca's remaining residents. It is tempting to see these photographs as evidence of blight or even as a justification for institutions like IIT to engage in urban renewal for the good of the community—and perhaps, for the good of the residents themselves. However, we now know that these photographs were taken after nearly a decade of disinvestment by IIT administrators, who had intentionally deferred maintenance after purchasing the property in 1941, callously allowing the building to fall into disrepair in order to ease the path for its future removal.

We should be equally circumspect of Hilberseimer's photograph of the "city slum" in *The Nature of Cities* (fig. 1). This image appears in a section of text and images describing the rise of the capitalist, industrial city and its "serious deficiencies" (Hilberseimer 1955, 108), including air pollution and traffic congestion. Hilberseimer's slum is an unidentified image of a back alley, presumably in Chicago, framed by a jumble of dilapidated outbuildings, strewn trash, an overturned garbage can, and utility poles casting long shadows on the unpaved street.

Echoing the use of urban photographs by modern architects in the early decades of the twentieth century, historian D. Bradford Hunt (2005) has described the powerful role of photography in the political arguments made for slum clearance and urban renewal projects of the 1950s, whether undertaken by public housing authorities or private companies. In Chicago and elsewhere, enterprising housing administrators and developers martialed photographs of

Figure 1: City slum, published in: Hilberseimer, Ludwig. 1955. *The Nature of Cities: Origin, Growth, and Decline, Pattern and Form, Planning Problems.* Chicago: Theobald, 109.

unkempt alleys and children playing in trash in low-income neighborhoods in planning documents as a justification for urban renewal and as an argument for the necessity of federal and private funding to support new building projects. These photographs appear documentary in nature, but were in fact carefully scouted, framed, and sometimes deliberately misidentified in brochures, including instances where one perfect image of the "slum" would find its way into reports covering many different areas of the city.

In these pamphlets, designed for administrators, politicians, and high-minded citizens alike, disturbing images turned attention away from the failure of city government to exercise basic sanitation and building regulation, as well as the greed of absentee landlords, to frame the slum as an unwholesome and largely ahistorical environment that was beyond repair. In short, photographs allowed the idea and image of the slum to operate autonomously, removed from general economic forces. These photographs echo the language used by housing officials and planners of the period that describe slums in medical or ecological terms. Hilberseimer himself describes slums as the "cancer of the city" (Hilberseimer 1955, 110), while Elizabeth Wood, the head of the Chicago Housing Authority during the 1940s and 1950s, wrote that urban renewal projects must be comprehensive or risk creating "islands in a wilderness of slums beaten down by smoke, noise, and fumes" (Wood 1945, 13–14).[7]

While the first two sections of *The Nature of Cities* are dedicated to a vast historical account of the origins and decline of cities from the Neolithic era to the present, the third section, "Planning Problems," includes Hilberseimer's analysis of the state of the contemporary city and his proposed solutions for its replanning. Hilberseimer's goal is nothing less than the complete rebuilding of cities:

> Traffic and parking restrictions, smoke abatement, slum clearance, and other strongly urged reform measures are palliatives only. They can never solve the problem that faces us. This problem concerns the total city. Its solution requires the rearrangement of the city's constituent parts, and the relating of these parts to each other properly. It requires the integration of the city with its environs. (Hilberseimer 1955, 192)

Hilberseimer offers examples for the comprehensive replanning of neighborhoods, cities, and regions based on his settlement unit, many of which are presented in abstract, neutral fields of application, much like earlier visionary plans for the modern city, including Le Corbusier's Ville contemporaine of 1922 or Frank Lloyd Wright's Broadacre City of 1932. Yet Hilberseimer also integrates his own projects for specific sites, including the new IIT campus plan, and speculative plans for the replanning of nearby cities, including Rockford, Illinois, and Elkhorn, Wisconsin. While images in *The Nature of Cities* vary widely from schematic plans to aerial photographs of models, it is telling that even Hilberseimer's site-specific projects are presented through abstracted plans and generic perspectives.

The singular exception in *The Nature of Cities* is an illustration toward the end of the book (1955, 248) captioned "Chicago, commercial area replanned" (see "Visuals", p. 307, fig. 56). This perspective line drawing shows a series of urban blocks with low plinths surmounted by high-rise towers in a number of different configurations, including slab or X-shaped towers. The buildings are drawn with highly detailed facades and a plan demonstrating how one superblock would replace eight existing, smaller-scaled blocks. The level of detail in this drawing is unusual, both when compared to other illustrations in the book and also to the work Hilberseimer produced in his later career more broadly, which includes very few architectural drawings. It also seems to break with Hilberseimer's own claims about his illustrations, which were meant to function as "diagrams" or "frameworks" for possible solutions rather than as specific examples (1955, 276). In fact, to find any comparable treatment of architectural detail or use of perspective in Hilberseimer's work, one has to reach all the way back to the 1920s and 30s, namely to his Hochhausstadt drawings of 1924 (see "Visuals", p. 278, fig. 10).

Hilberseimer subsumes the exceptionalism of this image with text that describes it as part of his larger project of replanning the city of Chicago. However, this section of the book also retreats from his claim for the necessity of holistic transformations, stating that "the commercial area has been left in its present position." Instead of offering a realignment of urban functions according to new planning principles, Hilberseimer (1955, 247) proposes to remodel the Loop business district with superblocks to improve congestion and parking conditions.

So what explains the anomalous nature of Hilberseimer's drawing and planning proposal for the Chicago Loop? Important clues can be found in a cache of little-known plans and design sketches in the collection of the Art Institute of Chicago, three of which were previously published as part of the portfolio section of the museum's 1988 catalogue *In the Shadow of Mies*. Identified in the catalogue as drawings for "Chicago Near North and West Loop development" and misdated to 1960–63, the formal elements of these studies are nearly identical to the illustration for the replanning of the commercial area of Chicago in *The Nature of Cities* (see "Visuals", p. 307, fig. 57).

This group of more than forty drawings encompass a variety of drawing types, from plans showing the Loop area replanned with superblocks, sketches of different configurations of the tower and plinth buildings, and beautifully rendered perspectival drawings in ink showing the spatial relationship between these new building types and the surrounding urban landscape. And although the Loop commercial district appears in many drawings, the majority focus on an area of land just north of the Loop and the Chicago River known as the Near North Side. It is clear that Hilberseimer spent a great deal of time working on this group of drawings, not because they were intended to illustrate an abstract scheme for his book but, I would argue, because they were created for a real project.

Fort Dearborn

In the early 1950s, Chicago's Near North Side was still widely considered to be plagued by many of Hilberseimer's "serious deficiencies" including over-crowding, dilapidated housing, and other conditions that allowed Zorbaugh to identify this area as a slum in 1929. I use the term *slum* here polemically, because this area was not entirely or even mostly derelict, crime-ridden, or blighted. It was a slum because it was a mixed-use area with light industry, warehouses, diners, bars, and aging housing stock that was home to recent immigrants, people of color, artists, Communists, and members of the gay community, which is to say the full roster of undesirables, both for main-stream society as well as for the office of the powerful Chicago mayor Richard J. Daley.[8] It was quite simply a neighborhood that had been identified as economically underperforming, outdated, and dangerously close to the high-est-value real estate in Chicago. The redevelopment of the Near North Side had the potential to shore up the then shaky prospects of downtown Chicago in an era of a massive middle-class exodus to the suburbs and to create a firewall of sorts between the Gold Coast to the east and the now infamous Cabrini Green public housing project to the west.[9]

Beginning in 1949, Chicago real estate impresario Arthur Rubloff focused on this area as his next major redevelopment project. Remaking the faded Near North Side offered him the opportunity to add value to his properties in the Loop and nearby Michigan Avenue shopping district and to protect these am-ple investments from any threat of the "slum". There he hoped to create a new, modern residential area that might be marketed to the middle class and pre-sumably to younger white people who were not ready to move to the suburbs and begin the grueling commute downtown each day.

Figure 2: Mildred Mead,
"Down Some Alley,"
Fort Dearborn Project,
Chicago Land Clearance
Commission, Near North
Side Survey Area, 1953

To market his plan to funders and lobby city hall, Rubloff turned to the standard playbook. He worked with a city agency, the Chicago Land Clearance Commission, to create a survey of the nearly 150-acre area to deem it eligible for slum clearance, with carefully chosen photographs demonstrating the neighborhood's "blight" (fig. 2) (Banfield 1961, 133).[10] He came up with a name for the project, Fort Dearborn, linking the project to Chicago's frontier history. Finally, he hired the solid and opportunistic architecture firm of Skidmore, Owings & Merrill to create a vision for the new community, complete with high-rise towers containing 4,500 apartments, parking, a shopping center, schools, office buildings, and most importantly, a new civic center containing offices for all city, state, and federal agencies (Fort Dearborn Project 1956). The resulting brochure for the Fort Dearborn project follows all of the conventions of a midcentury urban renewal planning document, including the use of photographic collage to show the area's future transformation, a neighborhood excised cleanly and without any human cost.

With endorsements from the governor, mayor, and many municipal leaders, Rubloff demonstrated his exceptional talent for working the system—except this time, his plan didn't work. Rubloff was banking on the relocation of Chicago's federal court buildings to his development as an anchor for private investment; however, Mayor Daley wanted to keep government buildings in the Loop. The mayor was also not keen on the development's focus on small units designed for singles and young couples, which might exclude the families that were so important to his image of the city and reelection (Banfield 1961, 148). But as these things tended to go in Chicago, Rubloff did not go home empty-handed. Just a few years later, he broke ground on Carl Sandburg Village, a large middle-class housing development also in the Near North Side, which was planned in cooperation with the Land Clearance Commission and displaced hundreds of Puerto Rican families from an area known as La Clark (Fernandez 2012, 132–41).

Hilberseimer and the Near North Side

So what is the relationship between Hilberseimer and Fort Dearborn? One possible explanation for his large group of drawings for the Loop and Near North Side is that Hilberseimer was trying his own hand at a solution to the Fort Dearborn redevelopment project. In the years leading up to Hilberseimer's book, Fort Dearborn was one of the city's most prominent urban renewal projects; it was heavily, even sensationally, covered by local newspapers in articles like "How Chicago is Winning the War Against Slums" (Manly 1954). Hilberseimer would have been privy to conversations about the project among city planners, would have read Plan Commission reports on Fort Dearborn, and lastly, he would have been aware of the project as a resident of the Near North Side, with an apartment on Dearborn Street, just two blocks away from Rubloff's Sandburg Village.[11]

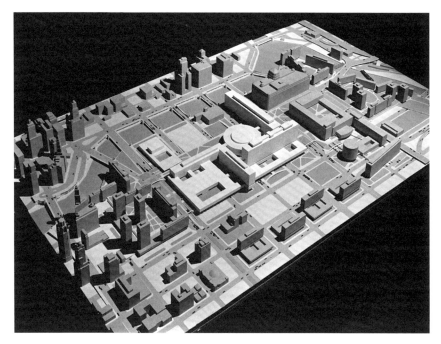

Figure 3: Skidmore, Owings & Merrill, Architectural model for a civic center,
1954, photo: William C. Hedrich for Hedrich-Blessing

Further evidence can be found in a close analysis of Hilberseimer's drawings
for the Loop and Near North Side. In addition to the more general application
of his superblocks across the Loop, other drawings introduce new building
types that break with the plinth-and-tower model. In sketch after sketch, Hilberseimer shows a complex labeled "civic center" on the north bank of the
Chicago River with a dramatic configuration of buildings that includes a low,
round structure, a sloping, wedge-shaped building, and a pair of slab towers or high-rise U-shaped buildings defining an open plaza (see "Visuals",
p. 307, fig. 58). These designs recall the combination of volumes deployed by
Oscar Niemeyer, Le Corbusier, and Wallace K. Harrison for the United Nations complex in New York, completed in 1950, a fitting reference for the nature of this project in Chicago.[12] Closer to home, Skidmore, Owings & Merrill's
own scheme for Fort Dearborn included a circular building framed by two

perpendicular slabs, the centerpiece of the complex's landscaped esplanade area, designed to house the government and cultural components of the project (fig. 3).

As a response, perhaps, to his longstanding frustrations with failing to have an impact in his adopted home town of Chicago (see Danforth 1988, 12), I propose that Hilberseimer seized on Fort Dearborn as an opportunity so potentially transformative that he was willing to return to his earlier focus on the architecture of the metropolis, repurposing the complex vertical layering of one of his most fully elaborated architectural schemes to fulfill a new generation's need for master planning in postwar Chicago. It is intriguing to think about how this project could have disrupted Hilberseimer's trajectory, perhaps troubling his simplistic view of low-income neighborhoods or allowing him to diversify his rigid, abstract model of decentralized planning to include a more complex grappling with the historical city, including its interpenetrating civic, cultural, and social spaces.

After all, by the late 1950s, a simple slum clearance project was not enough to win over politicians, neighborhood leaders, or even architects. The new era of urban renewal was all about selling the dream of prosperity, the idea of a new Chicago rising phoenix-like from the ashes of white flight, much like the origins of another project executed in the Near North Side at the very same time, Bertrand Goldberg's Marina City. Ironically perhaps, Goldberg's dynamic project—including nearly 900 apartments in two towers perched on top of a multiuse plinth of stores, office space, and recreation—not only mirrors the vertical integration of the large buildings in Hilberseimer's Near North project and his *Hochhausstadt* of the 1920s, but shares an uncannily similar inspiration. Throughout his life, Goldberg spoke about his best-known project as a modern form of "living above the store,"[13] like the medieval craftsperson living above his or her workshop, completing the transformation of this model from Hilberseimer's "necropolis" to a realized wonderland.[14]

Notes

1 Anna Vallye has traced Hilberseimer's work on decentralization back to a 1928 review by Edgar Wedepohl. For more see Vallye's essay in the present volume.

2 Although taking shape in different political and social conditions, urban renewal-style projects were also undertaken in many European cities in the nineteenth and twentieth centuries, beginning with Georges-Eugène Haussmann's transformation of Paris in the early 1850s. Relevant to this essay are questions about the modernist transformation of the historical city that emerged through the Congrès internationaux d'architecture modern in the 1930s, namely the 1933 CIAM congress on the Functional City, and efforts to rebuild German cities after World War II. For more on CIAM see Mumford 2000; and for planning in postwar Germany, see Urban 2004.

3 For more on the settlement unit, see Spaeth 1988; Constant 2004; and Waldheim 2016.

4 For an overview of the history of the Chicago School, see Bulmer 1986.

5 The Chicago School sociologists produced many books on Chicago's neighborhoods, which they understood as "one of the most complete social laboratories in the world." Key works include Thrasher 1927; Wirth 1928; Zorbaugh 1976 [1929]; and Frazier 1932.

6 For more on the South Side Planning Board, see Harrington 1988; and Hirsch 1983.

7 For more on the description of slums by urban reformers, see Mayne 2017, 40–88.

8 Redevelopment plans for the Near North Side began under Mayor Martin H. Kennelly and continued the development-focused Mayor Richard J. Daley. For more on Daley's his active role in redeveloping areas around the Chicago Loop, including new highways, public housing, and the University of Illinois at Chicago, see Cohen 2000.

9 For more on this transformation, see Marciniak 1986.

10 See also records of the Chicago Land Clearance Commission, Near North Side Survey Area, 1954–55. Chicago Department of Urban Renewal Records, Chicago Public Library, Harold Washington Library Center, Special Collections, Collection Number: N00096, Box 18, Folder 24.

11 See Hilberseimer's copy of the Chicago Plan Commission, *Report of Activities, 1955* (Chicago: Chicago Plan Commission, 1955), in Ludwig Karl Hilberseimer Papers, Ryerson and Burnham Archives, The Art Institute of Chicago, Series VI, Box.FF 2.8.

12 The United Nations building in New York was also created through a slum removal project on the East River. See Zipp 2010, 33–72.

13 This description of Marina City was quoted widely in the popular and architectural press, see for example, Liston 1963.

14 Hilberseimer (1963) condemned his High-rise City or Hochhausstadt as "more a necropolis than a metropolis, a sterile landscape of asphalt and cement; inhuman in every respect." Cited in Anderson 2012, 20.

Grid and Cell: Inhabiting Hilberseimer's City

Robin Schuldenfrei

Chicago in Berlin

Chicago played a unique role as both an earlier inspiration for a generation of German architects and planners and an eventual landing place for them, where they impacted the teaching practices and domestic design environment—in both built and unbuilt work. Ludwig Mies van der Rohe and Ludwig Hilberseimer arrived in the United States in 1938 to teach at the Armour Institute of Technology (today, the Illinois Institute of Technology, or IIT); previously they had been close colleagues at the Bauhaus in Dessau, Germany. Even before the move of so many modernists—Mies, Hilberseimer, as well as László Moholy-Nagy and Walter Peterhans—to Chicago, Berlin had enjoyed a special relationship to that US city (see James-Chakraborty 2012). Walter Rathenau, politician and heir to the AEG industrial empire, wrote that "Berlin was transforming from 'Athens on the Spree' to 'Chicago on the Spree'" (Hilberseimer 2012, 64).[1] While Weimar Republic Germany looked to the ideal of ordered, gridded North American cities such as Chicago, it would only be upon emigration that these architects might truly engage with a grid, as well as the steel and economic infrastructure that allowed them to build at these scales.

The assimilation of European modern forms and ideas with American circumstances was perhaps inevitable. Prior to World War II, key figures had been developing ideas in their own institutional and national contexts and also in international dialogue with one another, but modernism coalesced most significantly when national borders were abandoned in a process of emigration and resettlement in the years leading up to World War II, during wartime, and in its aftermath. Avant-garde ideas came together and emerged as mainstream modernism in the vibrant postwar period, thereby securing a future for modern architecture and its originators alike. Raw, open possibilities in the US gave some of the émigrés unique opportunities to build in a manner that had merely been a photomontaged dream in Europe, for their pedagogies would be well received at America's highest echelons—at Harvard, Yale, IIT, and the New Bauhaus in Chicago.

Even before his emigration to the United States, from the early 1920s while based in Berlin, Hilberseimer, like many architects of his period, had a long-enduring enthusiasm for the built environment of America and especially the architecture of the Chicago School. He greatly admired Burnham & Root's Monadnock building and was particularly enthusiastic about the scale of American hotels, publishing images of McKim, Mead and White's Pennsylvania Hotel and Chicago's Surf Apartment Hotel (Hilberseimer 1927b, 39, fig. 75). Designed at the turn of the century for both short- and long-term stays, these massive, block-long edifices were conceived as alternatives to apartment living. The hotel room, if well serviced, reasoned Hilberseimer, was the perfected individual cell for inhabitation. He even published a projection and plan of his own version of this typology, though he termed it a "boarding-house" rather than "hotel," thereby suggesting that it might be appropriate for longer-term stays.[2] Hilberseimer thus was seemingly primed for his American experience when still in 1920s Berlin. In particular, he was interested in using the techniques of mass production for housing, focusing on the dwelling unit as a measure of expandable habitation.

In the pre–World War II period, Hilberseimer had put forward radical visions for the future. While also working as a preeminent critic, theorist, and prolific writer, he presented startling ideas of mass-produced towers as an urban workplace and living solution for the core of historical Berlin (see "Visuals", p. 278, fig. 9–10). Workers would live—and shop—adjacent to their places of employment, lightening congestion and shortening commuting times. This was a practical and expedient solution, if uncompromising and unrelenting. Life, it seemed, in this vision, could be contained within—if not embodied by—the superblock structure. As Hilberseimer himself would frame it in his important book, *Metropolisarchitecture*, "Like every building, the high-rise is but a cell, a component of the urban organism, and it must be systematically connected to the latter" (Hilberseimer 2012, 203). It will examine the complementary relationships, as theorized by Hilberseimer, between dwelling units, housing typologies, urban patterning, infrastructural systems, and the institutional, economic, and political frameworks of the period. Against this backdrop, this essay will focus on the work of Hilberseimer, examining his ideas for housing across his career. It will argue that from the individual cell of habitation to the large-scale metropolis, Hilberseimer's scalable unit and the grid onto which it was projected provided a template by which citizens could dwell individually and thrive collectively.

Weimar Republic Germany

Housing was the key economic, social, and political issue for architects in 1920s Germany. Cities suffered from overwhelmingly crowded dwelling conditions as the populace shifted from rural farm labor to factory work. The tenements that sprang up to alleviate the onslaught of new urban dwellers were overcrowded, resulting in subdivided, damp, and dark spaces, often several courtyards deep into the block, with many informal arrangements such as kitchen floors being rented out to boarders. Unhygienic, the bathrooms were located off the central staircase and shared among many apartments.

Large, repetitive, totalitarian-looking urban interventions such as Hilberseimer's proposal for Berlin's city center or his 1922 entry for the *Chicago Tribune* competition, seem more ready-made for the American grid, where, unlike in Europe, a historical medieval or nineteenth-century core would not be in the way of "progress" (see "Visuals", p. 275, fig. 3). Quite quickly, however, Hilberseimer moved away from the urban tower to the row house and then to the single-family home as an ideal living arrangement. The grid, so crucial to this vision of growth, remained integral to this new way of housing the masses. Mies's courtyard houses are much better known and much more expansive in scope. They include amenities such as a garage for an automobile—still a luxury in this period—as well as rich, wooden room dividers. Hilberseimer's single-family houses, on the other hand, are less well known, but folding as they do into a radical vision of future living, they deserve more attention. His shift to these designs for single-family dwellings seems at first glance to be at odds with this period of architecture, in which the tower block in the garden took on new urgency as a potential solution to a housing crisis across Europe. Hilberseimer would always retain a few high-rise apartments in his plans, but the real place of mass production and economies of scale lay in his L-shaped houses and their seemingly infinite reproducibility (see "Visuals", p. 290–291, fig. 28–32). This housing was designed against the backdrop of the Weimar Republic's accelerating technological advances and social upheavals, an era which closed with the emigration of Mies and Hilberseimer, among the last of the avant-garde architects to depart Germany before the war.

The totalizing vision of Hilberseimer's proposals found in his designs for Berlin's city center did not entirely disappear in the United States. There are projects for tall buildings, dominant and repetitive, designed for the urban grid of downtown Chicago. But his Berlin towers relate to his concept for the single-family home, because the same totalizing impulse is there, too, as a vision for mass-produced housing. Hilberseimer's basic design tools are also his theoretical tools, that is, the unit and the grid, and they remain consistent.

The formal language, materiality, and detailed design of the buildings were not his primary concern (in contrast to his peers, such as Mies or Erich Mendelsohn), nor was creating an enticing marketable object, nor were larger ruminations about space and what it might mean to dwell in a modern manner, formulations with which his contemporaries concerned themselves. Hilberseimer's mixed high-rises soon gave way to a separation of the functions of working and living. Only when urban planning was conceived together with a building plan, Hilberseimer argued, could the city function well as an organism (Hilberseimer 1925b, 188). His urban theory depended on the formulation of a relationship between an elementary cell and their dispersal in an urban whole. He envisioned centrally located commercial business districts and factory work, with the surrounding areas made up of residential cities consisting of rows of rental apartment blocks tied to local amenities: schools, shops, hospitals, and train lines. In the residential area, Hilberseimer designed plans in which apartment blocks shielded green courtyards, family houses had small gardens, and the surrounding streets were only for local traffic and shopping, separated from larger throughways designated for heavier traffic.

He was most concerned, however, with two extremes: the macro and micro, namely, with the large-scale planning of the metropolis's overall functioning and with the single room. At the heart of this vision is this object—the room— which can be understood as both a dwelling space and a calculated unit of measurement (see "Visuals", p. 276, fig. 6). Beginning with permutations of beds—often four- and six-bed units for the smallest dwelling—Hilberseimer worked outward to determine the number of rooms. Built-in furniture made the calculation more precise—and, in fact, Hilberseimer depended on specific furnishing plans. His floor plans were thus often very detailed and included the furniture layout that he envisioned would allow so many family members to dwell in a compact space. He argued against building speculators' "schematization" (*Schematismus*) of fixed floor plans that maximized profit; instead he called for "typification" (*Typisierung*) (Hilberseimer 1926b, 480). *Typisierung* was a term popular at that time for the conception of standardized but well-designed objects (usually discussed in relation to the development of furniture, in which a prototype would lead to the mass production of goods). Here, as applied to architecture, Hilberseimer meant identifying basic dwelling needs and devising the floor plans based on optimizing those functions—eating, sleeping, hygiene—while also allowing for a multitude of adaptable apartment configurations to accommodate a range of family sizes, from a single dweller to a seven-member household (1926b, 480–81). Typification in the future, he writes, "will have to extend beyond individual construction details to embrace spatial units" (1926b, 481).

Using unit measurements, Hilberseimer sought an incrementalized solution that could scale up in size, while the main components of kitchen, bathroom, and living/dining remained the same. His insight—and part of this essay's argument—is that in this way he could move away from multistory, looming towers by redeploying the unit in single, stand-alone houses that were as readily scalable in terms of their mass production. Hilberseimer's houses were just one part of a larger vision for the design of future urban communities. With the room as the smallest unit, moving exponentially outward, multiple rooms (each hardly differentiated) made up the house; the houses were aggregated to form a community adjoined to schools and leisure centers. This dwelling community was then situated within a gridded infrastructure network comprised of through roads and rail lines, as well as places of work, including light industry, with heavy industry and agricultural work in the greater distance (see "Visuals", p. 298, fig. 45).

K. Michael Hays has observed the death of the aura in Hilberseimer's highly reproducible architecture, noting that "the auratic architectural object is systematically and utterly defeated by techniques of reproduction now radically rationalized and expanded" (Hays 1992, 173). This was key in booming mid- to late-1920s Germany—both the material concerns for mass production and in cultural and theoretical critical discourse. It is why Hilberseimer's L-shaped housing is compelling (see "Visuals", p. 291, fig. 31). The L-shaped house's aura is one not of uniqueness, as Walter Benjamin (and Hays) would desire; rather its allure is its reproducibility, its aestheticization of rationality, as well as its efficiency and affordability as minimum housing (see "Visuals", p. 293, fig. 36). The unit almost becomes the auratic object.

In Between

It takes Hilberseimer a few maneuvers, however, to translate this vision from his last years in Berlin to his early years in Chicago. In Germany, a typical vision by Hilberseimer was his 1926–27 Welfare City project, designed for 500,000 inhabitants (Köhler 2016, 123). This model city was composed of fifteen-story, "comb-like" high-rises, four-story horizontal slab buildings, and single-family houses, with the density decreasing from center to periphery (2016, 124). Hilberseimer's point of entry into low-density housing was the row house, which represented a design transition for him between his dense high-rises and his eventual repetitive and identical single-family dwellings with gardens. Into his compact row house layout, he allowed for a double-height living room, sleeping accommodations for six individuals (a master bedroom and two bedrooms with two single beds each), a terrace, and a grassy yard. In the 1930s, Hilberseimer began to experiment with what he called a "mixed-type development" that encompassed ten-story buildings and individual L-shaped houses with six beds.[3] Although he doesn't directly reference mass-production techniques, an economy of scale would have been necessary to affordably execute such designs.

Around 1932, just prior to his emigration to the United States, Hilberseimer participated in a group exhibition and book centered around the idea of *Das wachsende Haus* (the growing house). All the participants, of which Gropius was also one, designed houses with a small core but which came with plans so that the house could "grow" as the family expanded in number. Hilberseimer's entry begins with a master bedroom, living/dining room, bathroom, and kitchen. The house could next be expanded, according to his plans, by adding a terrace and a second bedroom with two single beds. Subsequently, a third and fourth bedroom could be added to the basic unit (see Wagner 1932, 72–75). The final house could potentially accommodate a family of six to eight people. Two reasonable prices were offered to the public, envisioned as if they were to be put into serial production: 2,500 Marks for the starter size, rising to 4,500 Marks for the house at its fullest expansion, about a year's wages for a white-collar worker (Wagner 1932, 72).

At first glance, Hilberseimer's design for housing appears to be mind-numbingly the same house; but formalism doesn't have to be fixed, and for Hilberseimer it wasn't. The Growing House illustrates this point. Modernism itself, in housing and urbanism, as originally intended by its protagonists, was less fixed and more anticipatory of growth and change than modernism's chroniclers have acknowledged. To return to Hilberseimer's differentiation between schematization and typification once more; his work might be seen in light of a formalized informality. Typification, in Hilberseimer's articulation, did not mean a cookie-cutter, one-size-fits-all solution, but rather flexibility within a given set of constraints and ideals. He was interested, as both theory and practice, in issues of seriality, scalability, multiplicity, and mutability, organized around what he called typification. The unit and grid allowed for this.

The Growing House is an example of this in practice: it bestows growing space—and along with it, economic breathing room—to its inhabitants. It thus gives them agency and autonomy. It shows a deep respect for the dwellers and their changing needs, as did his inclusion of a few high-rises in every settlement project to cater, he said, to childless couples or the elderly, or to those who didn't want their own yard. Although it sometimes appears that he planned from 10,000 feet above, in reality, he planned from the field. And sensitively, with the potential dweller in mind. He was above all a humanist.

In the 1930s, Mies, too, took up the issue of the small house, often an L-shaped courtyard house, regularly setting the task of its design to his Bauhaus students and subsequently to his IIT pupils. But Mies approached the design, as his sketches show, via loose, expansive drawings that suggest ideas of space and free-floating walls, an entirely different manner from Hilberseimer's constrained and delineated designs—units carefully set out to be reproduced.

Hilberseimer's Chicago

When they reached Chicago in 1938, both Mies and Hilberseimer began translating their ideas for the local environment; the campus of IIT provided an early opportunity. There were many proposed solutions for housing among the institutional buildings that they envisioned in the master plan. These included student dormitories and stand-alone, L-shaped faculty houses that were never realized—but they connect the duo's European ideas to the US situation and its grid.

Mies was also interested in utilizing techniques of mass production for housing. His McCormick House in the Chicago suburb of Elmhurst, made of factory components, was a vital early step in the production of housing in the US.[4] Mies's first genuine foray into designing for mass production was his proposal for the 50 × 50 House, a potentially reproducible design of factory-made steel frame walls and glass.[5] And in 1954–55, he developed a further prefabricated steel prototype—a large, stand-alone house with a carport. Designed as a seven-room house with two baths, it was above the mean in size and amenities, and thus more expensive than the norm; it was advertised for $35,000 (Chicago Sun Times 1955). Neither of these prototypes by Mies, nor Hilberseimer's full-scale community projects, was ever built. While they share commonalities, a key difference is in their approach. Mies carefully focused on structural systems and construction methods for eventual mass production, whereas Hilberseimer's attentiveness was on the unit, its floor plan, and an overall image of how a future settlement of small structures might be dispersed—and might function—in a gridded community.

Hilberseimer had been experimenting in combining both single-family homes and apartment towers. By the time he reached the United States, he had mainly given up his visions of a city of towers. He was trying to find, in his words, "a more human urban environment and a human scale for the community" (Hilberseimer ca. 1960, 112). As Charles Waldheim has noted, in the US, Hilberseimer became increasingly interested in placing his settlements in a landscape that was rural.[6] Hilberseimer was against expanding the city core by multiplying city blocks or housing density, which he argued would only increase traffic toward the city center. Instead, he envisioned new satellite settlements, especially around Chicago (see "Visuals", p. 298, fig. 44). In trying to solve the problem created by the speeding car, especially the dangerous intersection, he proposed that eight—or even more—blocks be put together, reducing streets and limiting intersections to four instead of fifteen junctions, and then creating a large park area in the center, with a school and a playground, reachable by children without ever crossing a street (Hilberseimer 1944, 100).

Hilberseimer's renderings are highly detailed, with furnished floor plans, perspectives, and an overall site plan with the houses set in a repeating pattern (see "Visuals", p. 293, Fig. 36). Thus, much in the same manner that he designed his earlier high-rises, Hilberseimer envisioned for his houses an undifferentiated, scalable typology that implied serial production and its economies of scale. Yet, in contradistinction to Mies, he remained silent on specifics such as materials (whether wood frame, brick, or steel might be most cost-effective), construction methods, or finance structures.

In Hilberseimer's first book published in the United States following his emigration, he identified the single-family house as the urban ideal, writing: "The one-family house is generally regarded as the type which best fulfills the social, psychological, and hygienic requirements of life. It will always be the ideal type of dwelling for families because it connects the house with a garden, a playground for children, and provides the privacy necessary for relaxation and recreation" (Hilberseimer 1944, 75). Taking the design of the single-family house and replicating it outward, the house can be understood as a unit, one made up of rooms acting as expandable cells (and, in the case of the Growing House, designed to actually function in these practical terms). Returning to Hilberseimer's earlier visions for the city, these units can be understood in a consistent manner across his oeuvre, whether stacked in a high-rise or evenly spread in the landscape. Hilberseimer is consistently concerned with the relationship of the individual cell to the urban plan, especially at large scales. The unit, with its infinite scalability, was reproduced by Hilberseimer in many different forms—cell, room, dwelling, block. He also calls his whole postwar urban community a "settlement unit" to indicate that these cities could be dropped down in multiple locations, effectively decentralizing the metropolis.

Hilberseimer's expansive ideas, scaled from a single-room unit to an entire urban community, are perhaps best seen in his ambitious plans for the redesign of Chicago itself (see "Visuals", p. 298, fig. 44). He envisioned that Chicago's lakefront would become an unbroken park; within this large wooded area would be spacious residences, apartment houses, hotels, playgrounds, even gardens, farms, and camps (Hilberseimer 1944, 147). Heavy industry was to be consolidated and moved to a canal inland to the south, with a commercial area to the north, both with nearby residential districts. A new system of highways and railway lines was to connect all of the parts. The land between these scattered settlements could be used for farms and woods. Heavy industry, with its smoke and fumes, was modeled according to the prevailing winds and sited furthest away from citizens. He placed light industry—which did not produce noxious fumes—parallel to the commercial area, also separated by a park strip. In writing about his plans, Hilberseimer concluded that the design would address modern-day demands and that once merged with the landscape, Chicago's old motto, "the city set in a garden"—*urbs in horta*—could become a reality again (1944, 149).

Therefore, the project that most fully circles back to the ideas of Hilberseimer and Mies, and which did come to fruition, is Lafayette Park—located not in Chicago, but in Detroit. Designed and built by Mies and Hilberseimer, this mixed development combined steel-framed high-rises and single-family homes in a 17-acre landscape set just outside Detroit's downtown business district, a gridded neighborhood known as "Black Bottom." Large in scale, it was planned for 1,700 families. Although the row house ultimately prevailed, Hilberseimer's early drawings included a series of L-shaped houses accessed by car, but without through roads, to limit traffic (see "Visuals", p. 310, fig. 62). Set in a lush landscape dominated by trees and shrubbery, his design for Lafayette Park displaces the grid while celebrating it.

As built, the row houses, with their buff-colored brick ends and glass curtain walls, connect well to the McCormick House and Mies's ideas for mass-produced housing; while their siting in a landscape protected from car traffic shows Hilberseimer's influence. In place, at last, were standardized parts and reproducible forms, along with the economic structures necessary to build them. Verdant yet situated within reach of the city, with its community facilities and walkable, non–through streets, Lafayette Park takes much from Hilberseimer's plans for an ideal settlement, one that was engaged with infinite reproducibility conceptually as much as materially, yet which was still concerned with creating a scalable, potentially mass-reproducible living situation for the postwar citizen.

Hilberseimer utilized the grid to offer his dwellers a house with a garden, and he proposed to use it to protect the populace from atomic attack. For Hilberseimer, the constituent element of habitation was based on the unit—which, in his vision, ran from the single bed in the cell-like bedroom to a grid of the whole of the American Midwest. Hilberseimer's arc speaks to contingencies and continuities between his architectural theory and his architectural practice. Here and elsewhere, Hilberseimer's projects' radical rationalization and repetition had in fact been aestheticized, even as they made claims to the contrary. In his process sketches, he aestheticized a deeply rational thought process and put reproducibility on display. It is easy to assume, especially in this period of high modernism, that the rational is not meant to be aestheticized, but it is precisely this pristine aestheticization, not of production but of reproducibility, that was deployed by Hilberseimer: an aesthetic meant to sell a theory of housing. This scalable, reproducible housing unit, along with a projected grid, connects well with Chicago's growth in this period.

Notes

1   Richard Anderson notes that Rathenau uses "City" in English as shorthand for financial city, like City of London, to distinguish it from the rest of the city, *Stadt*.

2   The Boardinghouse was first published in Hilberseimer 1925, 21 and 27, figs. 18 and 30; and later in Hilberseimer 1927, 39 and 40, figs. 76 and 77.

3   See "10 geschossige laubenganghäuser mit wohnungen für 1, 2, und 4 betten, dachgarten und gemeinschaftsräumen und erdgeschoss – einfamilien – L – häuser mit 6 betten und kleinem garten." Photograph, ca. early 1930s. Series X, Box FF 2.13a, Ludwig Karl Hilberseimer Papers, Ryerson and Burnham Archives, The Art Institute of Chicago. See also Hilberseimer 1931b and Hilberseimer 1963, 24–26. See the essay by Andreas Buss in the present volume.

4   Detlef Mertins, Mies (New York: Phaidon, 2014), 367.

5   Also known as the Square or Core House

6   For key insights into Hilberseimer's ideas on the urban in relation to landscape (agrarian urbanism), see Waldheim 2016.

Housing

The Hilberseimer Model House for Kleine Kienheide in Dessau

Andreas Buss

The Hilberseimer model house is a typology that is originally generic but in its manifestation relates explicitly to the expansion of the Dessau-Törten Housing Estate. The building department of the Bauhaus Dessau designed the latter in 1930 as an urban housing estate with green spaces based on the mixed development principle as propagated by Ludwig Hilberseimer. Here, in urban development terms, apartment blocks imposed a structure on a matrix of flat-roofed buildings.[1] A selection of model houses were envisaged for test purposes in Kleine Kienheide, deputizing for the construction site in Dessau-Törten. However, only the Houses with Balcony Access were built there up to 1930. Recently revealed sources suggest that Hilberseimer's contribution sought a design unity with the Houses with Balcony Access, which sets it apart from the other types available.

Building Types for Dessau-Törten

The extension of the Dessau-Törten Housing Estate was developed under the directorate of Hannes Meyer, who appointed Ludwig Hilberseimer to teach at the Bauhaus in 1929 (see Oswalt 2019, 154). Studies for single-family homes and apartment buildings (Houses with Balcony Access) were drafted under separate job numbers by the building department of the Bauhaus, although plans for various "model houses" or "experimental buildings," as the prototypes for single-family homes were also described, date back as far as the winter semester of 1927.[2] But early designs for row house models drafted by various students contain no information about the organization of the estate. The first known depiction of the organizational form as regards urban planning is a sketch by Hubert Hoffmann dating from April 1929 (Hoffmann 1930).[3]

This shows extended construction areas flanked by long rows of both detached and adjoining one-family homes with flat roofs. A House with Balcony Access stands at the southern end wall of every second area. This sketch almost completely omits site-specific characteristics and emphasizes the structural character of the development plan. The axonometric perspective is characteristic of the work of Hilberseimer and his students. Hilberseimer describes the mixed development thus in the essay "Großstädtische Kleinwohnungen" (small metropolitan apartments): "By forgoing closed courtyards and by mixing blocks of buildings facing north–south and east–west or flat-roofed and multistory buildings as they are configured in these development schemes, the urban layout is opened up and structured spatially as dictated by the requirements and has no need of decorative makings" (Hilberseimer 1929a, 514). All these studies were ideal-typical. Only the ground plan "Stadtsiedlung Dessau Törten Bauabschnitt 1930" (Dessau-Törten Housing Estate, construction phase 1930) places the mixed development in the local context (fig. 1).[4] This final but ultimately only partly realized plan is distinguished by its rigid orthogonal road system. It departs from the curved roads set out by Gropius and becomes totally uniform south of the Peterholzstraße.[5] It ranks high in the hierarchy as a so-called access road from which the north-south-oriented residential roads, on which the flat-roofed buildings are located, branch off.[6] This produces parcels of land oriented east–west. The entire block's view of the green space is also shared by the residents of the Houses with Balcony Access.[7] The aforementioned ground plan showing the 1930 construction phase of the estated and the related isometric view indicates three different flat-roofed building types—row, sawtooth, and comb structure—each of which has a specific spatial connection to a garden.

The architectonic design for the depicted row type is not known. The distinctive sawtooth structure comprises freestanding oblong building parts rotated through 45 degrees and connected by projecting roofs. The comb structure, by contrast, results from the multiplication of L-shaped building parts, which may be attributed to Hilberseimer. Their spatial effect is reminiscent of his earlier works (see Hilberseimer 1925, 17, fig. 12) on the row house theme, which features distinctly structured elevations, which he

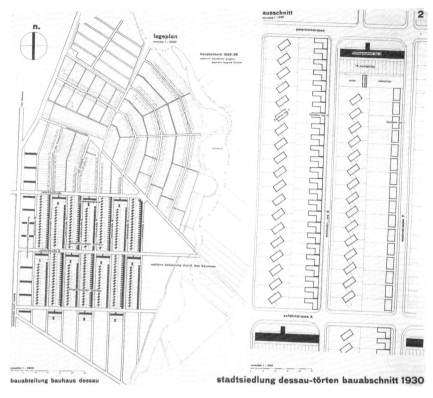

Figure 1: Bauhaus Dessau, building department, Dessau-Törten Housing Estate,
construction phase, 1930; the contextualization of the mixed-use development
is shown on the left, and its smallest unit on the right: two construction fields
with pergolas and three types of low-rise buildings.

reduces here to a minimum: The building mass appears two-dimensional,
as if die-cut.

Unconnected from the flat-roofed buildings, the planning for which was
firmed up in June 1930, the Dessauer Spar- und Baugenossenschaft commissioned to design, plan, and construct the Houses with Balcony Access. This
was a collective project involving students of the Bauhaus's building department, which advanced to the implementation planning stage (see Stengel 2019,
138–39). While it is difficult to ascertain authorships here, central figures involved in the planning and execution of the Houses with Balcony Access have

been identified. In addition, the Bauhaus workshops were involved in workmanship on the buildings. The Bauhaus students were remunerated for their work.

The design and development of the flat-roofed buildings initially progressed based on drafts by students (e.g., Walter Köppe, Hoffmann, and Ernst Göhl; see Stengel 2019, 140). The later model houses, which were intended as precursors to the realization of larger series, were—except for a design by Göhl—designed by Bauhaus teachers. The commissioning for these model houses, which according to Meyer repeatedly reached an impasse, was promised by the municipal authorities or, respectively, by Mayor Hesse himself (Stengel 2019, 140). Nothing is known about potential developers for a proposed large-scale realization—above and beyond the experiment—of at least 500 flat-roofed buildings.[8]

The research project on the Houses with Balcony Access in Dessau-Törten implemented in the department of architectural theory and design at the University of Kassel investigated the planning and construction process and the structure of the Houses with Balcony Access, which are now UNESCO World Heritage sites.[9] Relevant archive materials are found in several public and private archives. A significant portfolio of documents that enable a picture to be made of the final development status of the model houses was discovered in the estate of the Danish architect and Bauhaus teacher Edvard Heiberg (1897–1958), who taught at the Bauhaus in 1930.

The Planned Experimental Setup

In early June 1930, the construction of five Houses with Balcony Access in Dessau-Törten was at an advanced stage. At the same time, utility lines were being laid along part of the road system that encompasses the construction sites for the flat-roofed buildings. Plans were simultaneously being drawn up for model houses grouped in a short row for the experimental Bauhaus test site on the northern periphery of Kleine Kienheide (fig. 2). The set of plans includes the planning application signed by Hannes Meyer for the plot on

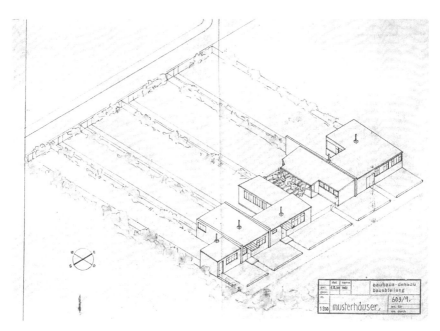

Figure 2: Bauhaus Dessau, building department, isometric view of the four
model houses on the Bauhaus test site in Kleine Kienheide, 1930

Kiefernweg, just a few minutes' walk from the Bauhaus, which was owned by
the city (fig. 3). The corresponding site plan elucidates that the houses were to
be oriented along the same lines as others on the Dessau-Törten estate, with
access gained not directly from Kiefernweg, but parallel to that by means of
a service road to the rear. This is set out as an objective in the surviving construction specifications: "The four model houses will be built as a cohesive
group of flat-roofed buildings in various constructions. The reproduction of
individual types that prove to be especially economical between the existing
houses with balcony access on the Törten estate is being considered."[10]
In addition, the houses are individually rendered in horizontal and vertical
sections and described. Both the costs and building physics aspects were estimated in advance based on the respective construction methods. Due to the
high number of flat-roofed buildings envisaged at the Törten estate, their economics played an important role.

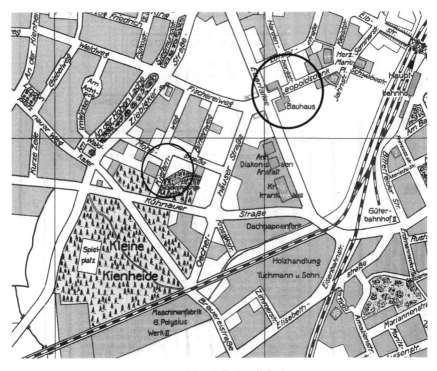

Figure 3: Kleine Kienheide is only a few minutes walk from the Bauhaus. Hofbuch-druckerei von C. Dünnhaupt, G.m.b.H. Dessau, Dessau city map (detail), n.d.

Layout of the Hilberseimer Model House

The facade lengths of the various model houses ranged from just 6.60 meters (Heiberg) to a maximum 10.30 meters (Meyer). Hilberseimer's L-type was midrange at 9.30 meters. It offered a living area of 54 square meters for four persons and may thus be described as a small house. The largest opening in the facade, the parlor window, faces the street (fig. 4). A small front garden strip forms an intermediate space. This is present in both the plan for Dessau-Törten and the layout for the Bauhaus test site. The relationship between house and garden was thematized and specifically realized in all the model houses. According to Hilberseimer (1929a, 511–12), one motive for the

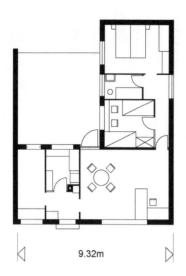

Figure 4: Ludwig Hilber-
seimer (design), Andreas
Buss (drawing), the isometry of L-types in a row was
reconstructed on the basis
of the plan documents of
the time of their creation,
1930 (design), 2021
(drawing)

9.32m

comb structure is the interconnection of the angular ground plan shape and the open space around it, and the associated creation of a private domain. "Through the L-shaped arrangement of the layout, an especially complex problem of the small house estate is furthermore resolved: to be completely isolated in the part of the garden immediately connected to the house, despite the close proximity of other houses."

Hilberseimer had published the ground plan of the L-type, which is referred to in the quote above in the 1929 essay "Großstädtische Kleinwohnungen." Here the ground floor still had a cellar underneath part of it. In the design for Dessau-Törten based on this one, there is no cellar at all: It is replaced by a ground-level utility room. While this increased the facade length from 8 meters in the 1929 version to 9.30 meters, the larger plot benefitted the proportions as well as the utility value of the private part of the garden or terrace. The parlor is situated in the joint between the road- and yard-facing wings. The view to the street is opposite a rear access to the terrace. This is embedded between the garden wing and the fire wall of the neighboring house. The bedrooms in the garden wing faced south and were accessed from a corridor with a skylight.

Variations and Modularity

One variant of the layout for four beds is the type for six beds with an additional room in the garden wing, which is extended for this purpose. This was published by Hilberseimer in the article "die kleinstwohnung im treppenlosen hause" (The Small Apartment in the Stairless House) which appeared in the January 1931 issue of the magazine *bauhaus*, thus six months following the scandal of Hannes Meyer's dismissal without notice from his post as Bauhaus director. The politically left-leaning Meyer was consequently succeeded by Mies van der Rohe. This rupture, but also the wretched economic climate, may have been why the experimental setup had by then long since been abandoned.[11] With both variants, Hilberseimer illustrates the modular layout of his design. Modular in the sense of using building blocks such as the so-called sleeping cabin with two beds, wardrobe, and work surface, which he also implemented, for example, in a design for a "Stairless House" for the Wirtschaftlichkeit im Bau Reichsforschungsgesellschaft- und Wohnungswesen e. V (Reich Research Society for Economic Efficiency in Building and Housing).[12] The modularity is a design strategy. It does not yet explicitly target a capability for extension, but it lays a foundation for it. "The Growing House" of 1932 is the first to equate such modules with actual extension measures.

A single-story apartment designed as a showpiece, utilizing the same room types that were previously used in the four- and six-bed L-type, was likewise created in 1931 in the framework of the exhibition *Die Wohnung unserer Zeit* (see Hilberseimer 1931, 265–56). Structurally, this apartment is nothing other than an L-type, the wings of which are set not at right angles, but parallel to each other.

Compact Kitchen

The kitchen of the model house for Kleine Kienheide corresponds with a type of compact kitchen first shown in 1929. Together with Hugo Häring, Hilberseimer designed the so-called *R-Küchen* (R-Kitchens), the smallest version of which measured just 2.00 by 2.25 meters (4.5 square meters). Hilberseimer was an opponent of the kitchen-diner. As a purely work-oriented kitchen, the type R-1 was designed for cooking only, with space for just one person (see "Visuals", p. 284, fig. 20). It was shown as a 1:1 model in the kitchen exhibition *Die neue Küche* of the architectural association Der Ring. In terms of proportion and size, this kitchen corresponds with those shown in the layout of the model house and its derivatives (four- and six-bed types). The model house would thus also have become the test site for such a kitchen. The R-types do not follow the built-in kitchen concept with made-to-measure furniture, but use typed, standardized units which were available in wood or metal.[13] The cupboards vary in depth and are divided into top and bottom units. The compact working space is only made at all possible by the fact that the cupboards are closed with shutters rather than hinged doors. The design and zoning of the furniture, which is dictated by the process of cooking, lends a particular flexibility to the interior, a spatial interconnection of open work areas and closeable storage spaces.

The modular conception of Hilberseimer's living spaces leads to the paradox that we have available to us illustrations that correspond with individual rooms in the model house without its ever having existed. Photographs testify to the compact kitchen, the sleeping cabin, and the parlor displayed in the 1931 exhibition apartment in *Die Wohnung unserer Zeit*.

The interior of this apartment as well as its preceding studies reveal two of Hilberseimer's preferences: the eschewal of built-in furniture; and the presence of fixed beds rather than folding beds. Hilberseimer designed the dimensions of the rooms in such a way that tenants would be able to install standard furniture. In the construction of small houses around 1930 by contrast, unique solutions enabling spaces to be even further reduced are frequently proposed and realized. This was not the case with the model house.

Contemporary Publications

The Bauhaus model houses designed for Kleine Kienheide were not widely publicized. Exceptions include the aforementioned article in the magazine *bauhaus* (no. 1, 1931) in which Hilberseimer presented his designs, and the Hannes Meyer–designed edition of the Mexican magazine *Edificación* (1940, 25) in which he presented a synopsis of the Bauhaus's work under his leadership. Here, two model houses (Hilberseimer, Göhl) are shown with floor plans. The expansion plans for Dessau-Törten, including the depiction of typical construction areas with Houses with Balcony Access and flat-roofed buildings, were also publicly displayed—for example, in 1930 in the framework of the Bauhaus touring exhibition in Zurich in the category *Baulehre* (architecture theory).[14] Here, the Göhl model house was also shown in greater detail. The same applies to the 1931 exhibition of the Bauhaus's work in Moscow.[15]

Constructive Analogies

Hilberseimer's publications on the issue of small houses contribute to the discourse about urban organization, economy, and type formation. The question of construction is unresolved. With his reduced graphic rendering, Hilberseimer proves to be a master of objectivization. He reveals the bare necessities quite plainly but makes no reference to materials. The published variants of the L-type permit no conclusions to be drawn about building materials or construction, and Hilberseimer offers no suggestions or information about such matters. The quality of these types lies precisely in their generic character, which renders them free of local contexts and universally applicable. Nevertheless, specifications are required to anchor the generic in place in order to enable its construction and, ultimately, its use. For the expansion of the Dessau-Törten Housing Estate, this ascertainment of facts is extrapolated only from the construction specifications, which are fortunately still available to us. As regards the materials for the model houses, it is interesting to note that efforts were made to consider a certain range of contemporary construction methods. With certainty, the aim here was to gain practical knowledge, not least because the construction of the model houses was also addressed in architecture classes, as the drawings made by Howard Dearstyne while studying at the Bauhaus testify. According to these, Hilberseimer's type was to be built from 25-millimeter-thick exposed brickwork with an insulating interlayer.[16] Illustrative calculations for heat transmission and the associated cost of building the wall were completed for this wall structure. The building costs for the whole house were estimated at 9,120 Reichsmark.[17]

While no reason is given in the brief description for the selection of materials, the use of exposed brickwork is an obvious choice: Bricks were readily available in Dessau-Törten because the city's brickworks were located just a few hundred meters away.[18] The building material was thus extracted and manufactured locally. In times of high unemployment, the manual labor associated with brickwork would hardly have been considered a disadvantage. It would thus be incorrect to assume that this indicated a lack of ambition of the kind Gropius showed in Törten with his rationalization efforts and experiments with industrial prefabrication. Rather, the result was a building of solid craftsmanship that continued the local tradition of unrendered exposed brickwork.[19] The same logic was applied at the Houses with Balcony Access, which were already under construction. The utilization of brick masonry, here in the wall thickness of 38 centimeters then typical for multistory residential buildings, is consistently maintained in the reinforced concrete construction of the floors, known as "Ackermanndecken," whose hollow components were likewise brick products. It is hardly surprising that a reinforced brick floor was now also envisaged for the monopitch roof of the model house.

The interior materials for the L-type are entirely consistent with those of the Houses with Balcony Access. The interior wall surfaces (rendered, chalk paint) and the floors (terrazzo, wood cement) are identically finished. One might conclude that these materials were selected for pragmatic reasons based on previous positive experiences. However, Hilberseimer's guiding principle of establishing homogeneity in the mixed development appears more plausible. Rather than assemble the best-suited building methods for the respective forms of housing, which might have been more the obvious strategy given the varied expectations of the residents, attention was paid to a constructional relationship resulting in an aesthetic connection. This levelling strategy is further pursued in the area of comfort: A water-heating system (NARAG) was selected, which was also used to heat the small apartments in the Houses with Balcony Access.

Since the Industrial Revolution, plainly visible brick masonry had carried the connotation of a "proletarian" building material. Hannes Meyer had become familiar with simple workers' estates in the Ruhr area and on his study trip to England. He was also aware of Im Vogelsang (1925), a cooperative housing estate built on an extremely tight budget, designed by his peers Hans Bernoulli and August Künzel of Basel. Jacques Herzog states that this represented "a new type of urban quarter, simultaneously rural and urban" (Architektur Basel, 2018). Its one-story houses were constructed from single-leaf brick masonry (see Bernoulli 1930, 276–79). Hilberseimer for his part again adopts exposed brick masonry in 1930 for the "Stairless House" study for the Reichsforschungsgesellschaft.[20]

A Hypothetical Reconstruction

Of all the Bauhaus's plans for Dessau-Törten, only the unassuming, productively scaled-down architecture of the Houses with Balcony Access was made manifest. For years, these stood on open fields like red block islands. Only when the building work resumed under the National Socialists was the mixed development completed, albeit in modified form. In hindsight, this continued building testifies to the robustness of their structural concept. The existing multistory blocks and the road system determine the matrix of the Junkers estate on which work began in 1935, whose architectural forms and materials convey a conservative vocabulary.

The real form of the housing estate thus reveals connections and ruptures in equal measure. But how would it have presented itself according to the original Bauhaus plans? The known schematic designs provide no answers. Based on the objectivizing, structural depictions of the urban development plans

Figure 5: Ludwig Hilberseimer (design), Andreas Buss (drawing), reconstructed perspective along the housing street with low-rise buildings and House with Balcony Access from south, 1930 (design), 2021 (drawing)

and the isometric views of the model houses and their floor plans, it became possible to model a synthesis from which a perspective image was ultimately gained (fig. 5). While all information is integrated in this hypothetical reconstruction, no attempt was made to depict the materials. This would have inevitably raised questions about details that could not have been answered unequivocally based on the sources.[21]

The perspective along the residential street now showcases the design coherencies between the row of houses and the facade of the House with Balcony Access. The parlor window, divided into four parts and with a low window breast, differs from the other openings and quasi connects both building types for diverse social milieus. It lends both the smallest apartments in the Houses with Balcony Access and the privately owned homes a singular generosity. At street level, this token contrasts with the rather closed facades of Gropius's row houses with narrow ribbon windows dating from the estate's first building phase. As opposed to the first construction phase, even the streets of the estate promise an airier character. The relatively low eaves of the flat-roofed buildings and the building line, which is set back on one side of the residential streets, open up an extensive and green streetscape. The rotation of the houses in every second row, perceptible as a sawtooth pattern, avoids direct face-to-face alignment. The streetscape is animated by the stimulating spatial interaction of the house fronts. All views are of green spaces.

Hilberseimer's L-type is no more and no less than a manifestation of generic architecture, objectively designed and modified by degrees. Such architecture has no genius loci, but it does have local conditions that contribute to its adaption and gradual evolution. The type responds to universal spatial requirements regarding the incidence of light, circulation, living comfort and social interaction, which Hilberseimer explored in classes at the Bauhaus and in his own studies. The proxyship of the model house for the greater whole should serve to ground the ideas behind it. Because it was never realized, it now joins the ranks of unbuilt Bauhaus buildings. The current form of the housing estate is, by contrast, an eloquent testimony to the eventful history of Germany in the twentieth century.

Notes

1 On the mixed development concept, see Hilbers- eimer 1929a, 514.

2 In a class taught by Hans Wittwer. For access to preliminary research findings concerning chronol- ogy, the author would like to thank Anne Stengel, research associate, University of Kassel.

3 Sketch: Building department of the Bauhaus Dessau. "siedlung törten bebauungsschema," dated April 12, 1929, signed Hubert Hoffmann, Bau- hausarchiv Berlin.

4 The plans for the mixed development went through various stages, which are distinguished by the use of different types of single-family and row houses.

5 The Gropius houses were supposed to end here but in reality, they did not continue this far south.

6 The access roads branch off from Heidestraße, the city's north–south link.

7 Hilberseimer preempted the differentiation of the roads and the orientation and proportions of the build sites; see Hilberseimer 1929a, 514.

8 The number is based on the planning status shown in Fig. 1. Other renderings deviate from this.

9 DFG research project The Houses with Balcony Access in Dessau-Törten: Reconstruction and Anal- ysis of the Planning, Construction, and Usage His- tory of the Project of the Bauhaus Dessau under the Direction of Hannes Meyer (Laubenganghäuser in Dessau-Törten). Project leader Prof. Philipp Oswalt, research associates Anne Stengel and Dr. Andreas Buss.

10 Anonymous, "baubeschreibung für 4 zu erbaude versuchshäuser auf dem bauhausversuchsgelände an der kleinen kienheide," estate of Edvard Heiberg, privately owned.

11 There is no known documentation of the actual aban- donment of the project.

12 Twenty-three architects were invited by the Reichs- forschungsgesellschaft to submit proposals for floor plans for compact apartments. "The Stairless House" was just one of the categories. Other cate- gories included the flat-roofed house up to two sto- ries tall and the apartment building with three to four stories. See Reichsforschungsgesellschaft 1930.

13 The wooden exhibition furniture was manufactured by Haus und Hausrat Gildenhall, Berlin.

14 This is revealed by an analysis of photographs of ex- hibits in the Bauhaus touring exhibition at the Kunst- gewerbemuseum der Stadt Zürich (July 20–August 17, 1930). Archiv der Moderne, Bauhausuniversität Weimar, N 54 82 3–5.

15 See photographs with handwritten notes pertaining to the Bauhaus exhibition of 1931 in the estate of Philipp Tolziner, Bauhaus Archiv Berlin, II-15 1 4 1; and II-15 1 4 4.

16 This was a layer of Torfoleum. Multilayered con- struction methods became widespread in the late 1920s. They were also a topic of architecture classes at the Bauhaus.

17 See Howard Dearstyne, *Moderne Baukonstuktion* Dearstyne Class Notes [1928–1933], Harvard Art Museums Archive, Box 1, 2–14.

18 South of cemetery III, between Heidestraße and the rail line.

19 In addition to industrial and public buildings, the Houses with Balcony Access were a housing con- struction project of the Dessauer Spar- und Bau- genossenschaft built in exposed brickwork around the Raguhnerstraße. The use of bricks from the city brickworks for this purpose is documented.

20 The RFG house was publicized in *bauhaus*, no. 1 (1931) together with the L-type. Detailed plans are found in the Art Institute of Chicago.

21 The execution of the window lintels, for example, is relevant to the appearance of the facade. For the un- rendered masonry facades, several options are con- ceivable: A concrete lintel left in its raw state such as those in the facades of the Houses with Balcony Ac- cess or facing the lintel with bricks. Ludwig Hilbers- eimer's drawings for the Stairless House of the RFG, likewise in unrendered masonry, show a visible tim- ber lintel. See "Treppenlosen House, Berlin, Ger- many, Section and Elevations" (Kleinstwohnung im Treppenlose [*sic*]), 1930, Art Institute of Chicago, 1983.1002, and "Treppenlosen House, Berlin, Win- dow Sections and Details," (Kleinstwohnung im treppenlosen Haus Rückfrontdetail M= 1:2), 1930, Art Institute of Chicago, 1983.1790.

Invention of a Metropolitan Architecture: From the Existing City to Collective Housing

Alexander Eisenschmidt

When *Großstadtarchitektur* (Metropolitan Architecture) was published in 1927, it seemed to appear out of nowhere—a dark prediction of an architecture yet to come and an astute observation of a metropolis that was already there.[1] But the seemingly unmediated prophecy was, in fact, a publication long in the making and one that was deeply influenced by previous writings on the existing city and by emerging architectural types that could be sourced from the contemporary metropolis for a new kind of city. The history of *Großstadtarchitektur* begins in 1914. While working as a draftsperson in the Berlin office of Heinz Lassen, the aspiring architect Ludwig Hilberseimer pored over Karl Scheffler's newly published book *Die Architektur der Großstadt* (The Architecture of the Metropolis, 1913). In Scheffler's book, Hilberseimer found a new kind of architectural approach toward the city. Analyzing it with painstaking precision, Hilberseimer partially transcribed it, outlined a fifteen-page article that was modeled on its argument, and then gave it the identical title.[2] Following Scheffler, Hilberseimer's draft attacked the chaos of the capitalist city as well as the answers with which architects and engineers sought to combat it. It already delineated how a new architecture of the metropolis could be formed without yet providing any visual evidence. Hilberseimer's notion of a metropolitan architecture was clearly shaped by Scheffler's early formulation, through which he would eventually arrive at a new kind of architectural urbanism. But understanding Hilberseimer's work as motivated by Scheffler's 1913 publication is not only of historical importance but also offers an additional lens through which the work can be repositioned.[3]

Scheffler based his studies of the metropolis on Berlin—a city whose population had doubled between 1871 and 1895 (from 820,000 to 1.6 million) and where new construction efforts failed to accommodate the influx of people. Population density reached its all-time high in 1900 when an average of 29,750 individuals lived on one square kilometer—making Berlin the most densely populated metropolis in Europe. The enormous urban pressures resulted in rapid construction fueled by developer self-interest. Scheffler rejected the new developments, driven by economic speculation rather than urban consideration, but he also suggested that this kind of hyper-urbanization might lead to unexpected ingenuity in new building forms. And it is this kind of dualism that permeates his work, which constantly oscillates between fascination and horror.

In "Ein Weg zum Stil" (A Path to Style, 1903), Scheffler already viewed urban apartment buildings as a typology that was uniquely attuned to modern life; a standardized floor plan suitable for a more restless metropolitan population was beginning to formulate a new architectural uniformity. His book *Moderne Baukunst* (Modern Building Art, 1907) similarly records new architectural typologies in the newly built districts, industrial complexes, and infrastructural hubs. Three years later, Scheffler reiterated this idea in *Berlin – ein Stadtschicksal* (Berlin: Destiny of a City) by giving historical context to the term *Großstadtarchitektur* (metropolitan architecture), which by 1913 was implicated in the title of his book *Architektur der Großstadt* (Architecture of the Metropolis). In all these works, architectural paradigms were distilled from the modern city as developments toward a modern architecture. As proof of the architectural power of the modern city, he described the uniformity and legibility of the emergent typology of apartment buildings under construction, not yet adorned by ornamentation (fig. 1). This was a reevaluation of a building type that not only dominated the urban landscape but was also widely ridiculed.[4] Viewing these apartment buildings as a raw mass led to the conclusion that the entire urban block should be considered as one.

Figure 1: Bare building frame in Schöneberg, Martin-Luther-Straße, in Karl Scheffler, *Die Architektur der Großstadt*, 1913, 34; original source: W.C. Behrendt, *Die einheitliche Blockfront als Raumelement im Stadtbau*, Berlin 1911.

Figure 2: Heinrich Tessenow, worker's row house for a family in Hellerau, 1909–12, in Karl Scheffler, *Die Architektur der Großstadt*, 1913, 168.

In *Architektur der Großstadt*, he cited works that approximate a close engagement with the metropolis, ranging from the factory buildings of Peter Behrens to the homes of Heinrich Tessenow, which were read as one of the most extreme answers to the tumultuous and inhospitable world around them (fig. 2). While at first Tessenow's single-family homes (all situated at a distance from the modern city) have little in common with a metropolitan architecture, their austere and radical blankness (starved of ornamentation) were also seen as a possible answer to what Tessenow himself understood as the lack of form in the city, a condition that he no longer saw governed by human intention but rather viewed largely as a result of massive metropolitan forces (see Tessenow 1996, 100–101). If Tessenow's homes provided Scheffler with a glimpse of a metropolitan architecture, it was in the work of Alfred Messel and the Wertheim department store that Scheffler found the most vivid expression of architecture's intimate relationship to the modern city and its spatial and commercial pressures. Wertheim represented here not only a new building type for a society of consumers but also a new relationship to the city.

The urban construct of the Wertheim store was viewed as analogous to the city. Its supplementary programs (rooftop garden, library, art gallery, tourist information center, photo studio, theater ticket agency, and several restaurants) all catered to different types of metropolitan individuals in addition to shoppers, making architecture a profoundly urban experience (fig. 3). And, as it grew more massive and uniformly throughout its different building stages, the store internalized the city, adding and assembling a collage of spaces and courtyards behind a regular facade that wrapped its perimeter.[5] Scheffler applauded the way in which the facade had become a continuous element that created a unified building block, an understanding that was informed by Walter Curt Behrendt's *Die einheitliche Blockfront als Raumelement im Stadtbau* (The Street Wall as Unified Spatial Element in City Building, 1911). The latter announced in 1911 the emergence of an urban architecture of large continuous surfaces that would encompass multiple individual buildings and promoted the city block as the new unit for metropolitan space. Here, Behrendt observed how individual buildings were absorbed into a unified urban block, limited only by the surrounding streets. Defining it not just as a conglomerate of different volumes and programs but making it readable as an object through building-surface treatments would make the entire block recognizable as one.

Scheffler's most striking descriptions come with his forecast of a new urban image, where individual shops consolidate into department stores, housing units amalgamate into single urban volumes, and all of these would be expressed in the most rational manner (Scheffler 1913, 130). While he saw these still as entities in themselves and not yet combined into a single form, he predicted a new kind of metropolitan architect who would fully intuit this kind of work. Outlining the characteristics of this new figure, he wrote: "Messel [...] was still too much an academic and child of tradition [...] to entirely solve the mission of our time. For the most valuable characteristics are the impersonal and typical" (Scheffler 1913, 41). In essence, the figure of the architect responsible for a true metropolitan architecture had not yet been invented, prompting Scheffler to call upon architects to rise to the occasion.

Hilberseimer's Project of a Metropolitan Architecture

Hilberseimer took Scheffler's call seriously, meticulously studied his book, and echoed his critique of the "lack of form and rhythm" in the capitalist metropolis. In his notes from 1914, he already stated: "The only possibility to emerge from this chaos" is "the most extreme economy of form [... and the intent] to work toward the essential" (Hilberseimer 1914, folio 11). This, of course, would crystalize at the very core of his 1927 publication. It is therefore no surprise that Messel's Wertheim department store, references to Tessenow's Hellerau, Behrendt's "Einheitliche Blockfront," and housing blocks under construction reappear in Hilberseimer's drafted essay (fig. 4). Building on the typologies that Scheffler had already identified in the metropolis (housing blocks, department stores, and suburban villas), Hilberseimer expanded the catalog of types through a list he started compiling in 1914 and that in *Großstadtarchitektur* would eventually include towers, transportation hubs, and infrastructural and industrial buildings. While studying these different programs, Hilberseimer never lost sight of the way these distinct forms could constitute a coherent urban block.

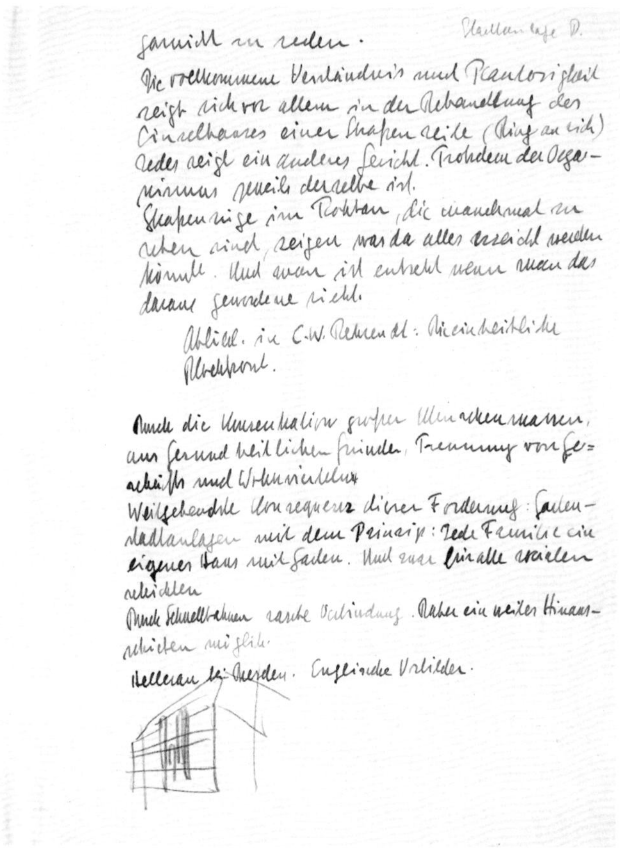

gemischt zu reden. Stadtanlage D.
Die vollkommene Verständnis- und Planlosigkeit zeigt sich vor allem in der Behandlung des Einzelhauses einer Straßenzeile (Ding an sich) Jedes zeigt ein anderes Gesicht. Trotzdem der Organismus jeweils derselbe ist.
Straßenzüge im Rohbau, die manchmal zu sehen sind, zeigen was da alles erreicht werden könnte. Und was ist entsteht wenn man das daraus gewordene sieht.
Abbild. in C.W. Behrendt: Die einheitliche Blockfront.

Durch die Konzentration großer Menschenmassen, aus gesundheitlichen Gründen, Trennung von Geschäfts- und Wohnviertel
Weitgehendste Konsequenz dieser Forderung: Gartenstadtanlagen mit dem Prinzip: Jede Familie ein eigenes Haus mit Garten.
Durch Schnellbahnen rasche Verbindung. Daher ein weites Hinausschieben möglich.
Hellerau bei Dresden. Englische Vorbilder.

Figure 4: Ludwig Hilberseimer, "Die Architektur der Großstadt," handwritten folio, 1914, p. 10

What was already outlined in 1914 would find sharper spatial and programmatic definition in 1923, when he designed the Wohnstadt (a residential city, see "Visuals" p. 276, fig. 4 and 5) and wrote "Der Wille zur Architektur" (The Will to Architecture), in which he described "the room as manifested as an element of buildings linked together in one street block" (Hilberseimer 1923, 136). Conceiving of an architecture that encompassed entire urban blocks gave Hilberseimer the opportunity not only to imagine a new kind of urbanism but also to demand a greater role for the collective. In *Großstadtarchitektur*, for example, he called on unions to invest in housing with the aim to overcome the individualization of parcels. As such, his vision is far from a utopian dream but in fact entails an urban image that invites the participation of collective organizations to invest in larger parcels of land in order to restructure the city and "combine individual parcels into a unified urban block" (Hilberseimer 1927, 22–23).[6] What Scheffler and Behrendt had previously observed as a trend within the metropolis, Hilberseimer now articulates as a design approach and an intentional economic model that extrapolates from the metropolis with the ambition to reorient it—away from individual speculation and toward collective investment.

"The detached house, which transformed the metropolis into chaos, will vanish," he wrote. "It will be replaced by the communal house, which occupies the entire block and includes apartments, work and commercial spaces, and everything else that life requires" (Hilberseimer 1927, 18). Here, the block no longer holds multiple monofunctional residential buildings but instead binds one building that joins different programs on one lot. What Hilberseimer calls "Gemeinschaftshaus" (communal house) is essentially a building of and for the collective, an architectural mammoth that has a dramatic effect on the makeup of the city (see "Visuals", p. 276, fig. 4–5). For Wohnstadt, the shorter ends of the blocks were designated as commercial while the longer sides were configured as residential, which results in an urban formation where all commercial streets would run east–west and all residential streets north–south—creating within the same plan and in close proximity parallel quiet streets for housing and, at a larger distance, more lively streets with stores. Here each block becomes a "microcosm of the city."[7]

One year later, this new type of "superblock" is extrapolated through the Hochhausstadt (High-Rise City) project, for which Hilberseimer produces a single typology that houses all urban functions in one.[8] He described it as a layering of two cities—the city of slabs above the city of perimeter blocks (Hilberseimer 1927, 17). Even as early efforts by CIAM and Le Corbusier continued with a zoned urbanism of designated functional quarters, Hilberseimer created a hybrid urbanism of mixed uses and combined typologies, repeated across the city, each containing all the elements of urban life. The lower city is dedicated to commerce, where each block is a mega office,

Figure 5: Ludwig Mies van der Rohe, Concrete Office Building, Berlin, perspective project, 1923

workshop, and department store, placed squarely on the ground of the city. Here, architecture defines infrastructure, reversing the conventional hierarchy. Of course, this foregrounding of architectural forms relates to his ambition to resituate architecture as a form of urbanism. After all, Hilberseimer was troubled by architecture's retreat into what he called "facade design" and how traffic engineers increasingly dictated the image of the city.[9] In contrast, he saw the role of architecture in its capacity to build the city and to give form to the street. What mattered was not the planning of the city as such, but the forming of architectural typologies that could act as urbanisms of and within the city—a highly spatialized form of architectural urbanism.

At Hochhausstadt, above each commercial block rest two apartment slabs, so as to conflate the commercial emphasis of the Wilhelmine period with the focus on residential buildings during the Weimar Republic (see "Visuals," p. 278, fig. 9). Indeed, Hilberseimer seems to have had particular cities in mind when placing one on top of the other. He especially admired Messel's department store for its corner building that "produced innumerable variations" (Hilberseimer 1927, 55) and the Monadnock building in Chicago by Burnham and Root for its "unmistakable sense of proportion" (65)—building forms that

Figure 6: Burnham & Root, Monadnock building at Jackson Boulevard, Chicago, 1891. Published in Hilberseimer 1927, 65. The proportion and austerity of the Monadnock block seems to reappear in the linear housing of Hilberseimer's Hochhausstadt project (detail on the right, see "Visuals," p. 278, fig. 10).

seem to reappear in the base and slab typology of the Hochhausstadt. When he analyzes these buildings in *Großstadtarchitektur*, little emphasis is placed on the function of the building, highlighting instead its form and placement within the city. The chapter on commercial buildings begins with an analysis of Wertheim and concludes with Ludwig Mies van der Rohe's Concrete Office Building project (1923), which formally clearly resembles Hilberseimer's lower portion of the Hochhausstadt block (fig. 5). And it is telling that the Monadnock is not part of the chapter on commercial building but comprises the longest passage in the chapter on high-rises. At no point does Hilberseimer address the inner workings of the block, fixating instead on how the high-rise can accentuate and direct urban space through its building mass—something Hilberseimer sees unfolding at the Monadnock, which he believes "has nothing to do with banal functionality; but rather with coherence and concentration" (65). It should, therefore, come as no surprise that the proportions of the Monadnock reappear in the slender fifteen-story towers of the Hochhausstadt (fig. 6, and see "Visuals," p. 278, fig. 10).

The two schemes are similar in their seeming solidity, weight, and regularity of window openings. Obviously, the un-ornate facade of the Chicago building was a precursor for Hilberseimer's absolute reduction. Unlike Root, who battled with the idea of a "brick box" entirely stripped of any ornamentation due to economic demands, however, Hilberseimer no longer had any reservations and instead saw the total reduction of the building surface as a necessity.[10] Thirty-three years after Root's hesitant creation of a new building paradigm, produced directly from the laboratory of the metropolis, the building mammoth has multiplied in the perspectives of the Hochhausstadt. The north–south orientation of the narrow Monadnock proliferates now across an unending field of building canyons. Even the photographer's position of the 1891 image of the Monadnock building that Hilberseimer used as an illustration in his book is strangely similar to the viewpoint of the north–south street drawing by Hilberseimer. Both force the viewer to float in midair, "separated from the city," as Sarah Whiting wrote in her analysis of Hilberseimer's drawings, "by a gulf of space" (Whiting 2001, 659).

The course toward a metropolitan architecture here extrapolates existing conditions of anonymity, which recall Scheffler's comments on the dark and gloom of residential buildings under construction that he started to explore in 1903. These notes appear in hindsight as forecastings of Hilberseimer's soberness: "Where buildings are still in their raw form, […] the construction shows itself uncloaked, [and] resulting from consideration of need and dry statistical calculation, there emerges a kind of monumentality. They are gloomy and sad and yet full of character" (Scheffler 1903, 293). Scheffler even described them as "threatening," a characterization easily mistaken for an account of Hilberseimer's Hochhausstadt—a scheme that points toward a radicalization of urban living that follows Scheffler's predictions of metropolitan anonymity.

Collective Interiors from Rooms to Lobbies

Hilberseimer sought as much distance as possible from the image of the single home and instead focused on the program of the hotel, on forms of modern mobility, and on modern work arrangements, with slogans such as "suitcase instead of moving van" (Hilberseimer 1927, 19). For Hilberseimer, housing presented "the actual problem of the architecture of the metropolis"—a problem in which the residential apartment building was primarily derived from the single house, which ignored the multiplicity of units as well as the size of building lots (21). Interestingly, Hilberseimer addressed both issues—the lot size as well as the multiplicity of units—through notions of the collective. For the lots, the involvement of unions and other public collectives was championed while he viewed the abundance of units in housing as a collective in its own right. For the latter, the layout of apartments was instrumentalized by standardizing kitchens, bathrooms, and bedrooms while expanding the living room for family life, dining, and play according to the number of members in the household (see "Visuals," p. 277, fig. 7; see Hilberseimer 1927, 30–33). The size of much larger living rooms is afforded by the minimal dimensions of the bedrooms—intentionally emphasizing the collective within the confines of the apartment.

Movable furniture, sliding walls, and folding elements are imagined as spatial components that may transform the apartments in order to accommodate different uses and users. He admired Mies's apartment building at Weißenhof (Stuttgart, 1927) for its limited use of structural walls and deployment of subdivisions according to the tenants' specifications. "With six to nine such wall components, every spatial variation is possible" (Hilberseimer 1927, 35). To maximize usable space and minimize the dimensions of rooms with the aim to further reduce costs and therefore to lessen the burden on union investments and rents, Hilberseimer proposes that all furniture should be built-in, resulting in apartments in which "beds, chairs, and tables will be the only movable furniture" (24). Hilberseimer effectively provides the building typology and spatial configuration for a new type of metropolitan individual, so poignantly staged in the 1926 "Co-op Interior" by Hannes Meyer (fig. 7). Meyer's rudimentary pieces of furniture (cot, folding chair, and collapsible table) would seamlessly find a place in Hilberseimer's readily inhabitable apartments. While others have differentiated the nomadic furniture of Meyer from the domestic interiors of Hilberseimer, the two proposals should be understood as part of a larger project that rethinks the convention and politics of home in order to structure a metropolitan architecture for the collective (see "Visuals," p. 276, fig. 6).[11]

Figure 7: Hannes Meyer, Co-op Zimmer, 1926

Hilberseimer viewed the high-rise apartment building (or Apartment-Haus, as he named it) as "the future metropolitan way of life," predominantly sourcing from American examples for their extreme compactness and deployment of built-in furniture (Hilberseimer 1927, 38). This led him to imagine an apartment that uses a foldaway bed in the living room with an adjacent dressing room, bathroom, and kitchen alcove. Here the monofunctionality of the bedroom (which remains unoccupied for most of the day) is eliminated, as it is absorbed by the living room. Presumably, the scaling of the apartments according to its users is even more immediate and relies solely on the living room's capacity for foldaway beds. As the programmatic range of the living room seems to expand (from the most intimate to the most communal acts of family life), the trope of minimum dwelling makes room for the collective in the very confines of the private sphere.

In addition, the compactness of the individual apartments is not only justified but encouraged through common facilities that would now take on domestic tasks conventionally (conservatively) assigned to women in the family. The communal, almost cooperative, organization that Hilberseimer imagines becomes most explicit in the 1925 pamphlet *Gosstadtbauten* (Buildings for the Metropolis), where he notes: "The high-rise for living is conceived as boarding house [... where] the single apartments should benefit from the advantages of a collective—with common personnel, communal lounges, centralized kitchen, and maintenance" (Hilberseimer 1925/1926, 28). Metropolitan architecture becomes here a critique of the home and its conventional divisions of labor. In *Großstadtarchitektur*, Hilberseimer quotes a long passage from Meta Corssen's article on "Hausarbeit" (domestic work). Corssen, a fellow socialist and Hilberseimer's colleague at the *Sozialistischen Monatshefte* demands "a systematic dismantling of the total work required within a household, and reassembling it anew" (Hilberseimer 1927, 23). And his proposals for residential spaces seem to do exactly that by evacuating domestic work from the household through services rendered now by the professional amenities of the building. Simultaneously, these new urban architectures were also tailored to a new kind of metropolitan individual who is single, childless, and nomadic.[12]

Clearly, he is taking reference from the Russian avant-garde, which he occasionally cites but rarely illustrates.[13] As Richard Anderson has articulated, Hilberseimer was deeply engaged with and responsive to the work of the Constructivists to whom he also devoted writing as early as 1922 (see Anderson 2012, 46–48; Hilberseimer 1922). In turn, Hilberseimer's project of a Hochhausstadt and his book resonated deeply throughout the Soviet Union's first Five-Year plan. In both works, the compactness of the apartments stimulate the life of the semipublic zones for the collective (lounges, lobbies, and social condensers); both sought to liberate the home from the burdens of domesticity (Ginzburg, for example, cites Lenini's definition of "large-scale socialist housekeeping"); and both aimed to move beyond the parcelization of the city by abandoning conventional land ownership (El Lissitzky associated individual lots with capitalist privatization).[14] But it should also come as no surprise that Hilberseimer's search for a metropolitan architecture does not deploy examples from the rich arsenal of Russian experimentation. Not only were most projects barely underway when Hilberseimer's *Großstadtarchitektur* was published but, more important, Hilberseimer's objective to develop a metropolitan architecture demanded a focus on the very terrain that this new kind of architecture would need to engage.[15] He therefore studied the emerging typologies of the existing metropolis and identified potential ingenuities that could be diverted toward a new kind of metropolis. As Hilberseimer notes in his introduction, "only in a socially ordered society, where production corresponds to the needs of people, not the greed for profit of the privileged, can the metropolis become a purposeful organism" (Hilberseimer 1927, 2). Then he rhetorically asks: "So the end of the metropolis? NO! But the end of the metropolis that is based on the principle of speculation" (Hilberseimer 1927, 3).

Hilberseimer's new metropolis—a place beyond domestic work, individual urban lots, and long-distance commutes—is stimulated by an architectural urbanism that upends the capitalist city through new interior organizations, urban spatial logistics, and economic models. Hochhausstadt identifies the intersection of these realms in the sky lobby, where the ground doubles and one enters into the apartment blocks above and the commercial blocks below. The floor is pulled across the distance between the two slabs—acting not just as connective tissue between above and below but also expanding as an interiorized city of small shops, restaurants, and services (Hilberseimer 1927, 19). The infusion of the city into architecture, so clearly built into the lobby of the Monadnock block and the rooftop garden of the Wertheim store, has no place in Hilberseimer's drawings and can only be found in the descriptions of the scheme. Yet what Hilberseimer avoided drawing is rediscovered several decades later through the super interiors of the Italian avant-garde, the conceptualization of Berlin as nested cities within a city, and the theorization of New York's interior delirium.

Notes

1 I translate "Großstadtarchitektur" as "metropolitan architecture," as it best reflects Hilberseimer's definition of an urban architecture that is both born out of and constructive of a new kind of metropolis. This translation also takes into account the works that influenced Hilberseimer during the writing of his book as much as it considers later iterations of a metropolitan architecture. All translations from German into English are by the author unless otherwise indicated. This essay is based on my lecture at the conference "Ludwig Hilberseimer: Infrastructures of Modernity," Bauhaus Dessau, October 2021. An earlier version of this argument appeared in my recent book *The Good Metropolis: From Urban Formlessness to Metropolitan Architecture*.

2 It is interesting to note that Hilberseimer brought these early notes with him when he emigrated to Chicago in 1938. They can today be found in the Hilberseimer Archive at the Ryerson and Burnham Libraries of the Art Institute of Chicago (15 folios, box 8/3, no. 1/1).

3 On the influence of Scheffler on Hilberseimer, see my chapter "Extrapolation: Urban *Spielraum* and the Project of a Metropolitan Architecture," in Eisenschmidt 2019; Pommer 1988; and Anderson 2012.

4 Berliners would often call their tenement housing "*Mietskasernen*" (rental barracks) because of its monotony and inhospitable living conditions, which comprised the city's most notorious building fabric.

5 By 1906 the Wertheim store had grown from Leipziger Straße toward and eventually into Leipziger Platz.

6 For all quoted passages from *Großstadtarchitektur*, I cite the page numbers from the original text but have relied on the exellent translation by Richard Anderson; see Hilberseimer 2012.

7 I borrow the phrase "microcosm of the city" from Alan Colquhoun's definition of *superblock*. See Colquhoun 1971, 96.

8 Alan Colquhoun coined the term "superblock," which can take the form of a single building, inscribed by the street pattern, or of multiple structures that leap over to adjacent blocks to form even larger units—a terminology that stresses the sheer size of this new economic and formal unity within the modern city. See Colquhoun 1971. More recently, Sarah Whiting revised the concept of a superblock urbanism by looking at Chicago's Near South Side of the 1940s. See Whiting 2009 and Whiting 2001.

9 Against contemporary tendencies, Hilberseimer embraced projects such as Ludwig Mies van der Rohe's reconstruction of Alexanderplatz (1928) because it "attempts to give form to the plaza solely from an architectural viewpoint through individual buildings, and independently of the traffic routes." See Hilberseimer 1929b.

10 When Root inspected a revised drawing of the Monadnock building in 1889, he was "indignant at first over this project of a brick box." See Monroe 1896, 141.

11 See Aureli and Tattara 2018: "Unlike other architects such as Le Corbusier, Walter Gropius, and Ludwig Hilberseimer, who always presented their domestic interiors as part housing typologies, Meyer proposed the Co-op Interior as a universal space for a generic worker."

12 This is not to suggest that Hilberseimer saw the metropolitan nomad as the predominant urban inhabitant (after all, he continued to work on single-family homes during his tenure at the Bauhaus), but he understood it as a growing population for which architecture had not yet found a place to live.

13 I want to thank my fellow conference panelists—Alison Fisher, Robin Schuldenfrei, and Charles Waldheim—for their stimulating questions about Hilberseimer's relationship to the Russian avant-garde.

14 See Ginzburg 1927; Ginzburg 2017 [1934], 138; and El Lissitzky 1929, 50–52.

15 Moscow's first collective housing complex, Mosgubzhilsoyuz, was designed in 1925 and finished in 1928; Ginsburg and Milinis's Narkomfin communal block was designed in 1928 and completed in 1930.

Ludwig Hilberseimer, Le Corbusier, and the Employee

Christine Mengin

This article intends to show that Hilberseimer's urban thinking under the Weimar Republic, while deeply stimulated by Le Corbusier's urban projects, was also rooted in the sociohistorical context of the rise of the social group of employees, whether in his projects for the Berlin business center or in his model housing plans.[1]

Le Corbusier as a prod

It is almost a commonplace to compare the urban visions of Ludwig Hilberseimer and Le Corbusier. In 1927 even a daily newspaper like the *Berliner Tageblatt* ("Wie wird Berlin in hundert Jahren aussehen" 1927), in an exercise of anticipation, has put them opposite, following in the footsteps of Theo van Doesburg[2] and Hugo Häring (1926). Both Le Corbusier and Hilberseimer developed radical urban projects in the 1920s. These projects, which aimed to provide a global solution to the urban question, earned them the reputation of being the main urban theorists of the Modern Movement, one in France and the other in Germany. Strictly contemporary (Hilberseimer was born in 1885 and died in 1967, Charles-Edouard Jeanneret was born in 1887 and died in 1965), they shared a very strong taste for the plastic arts, which dominated their activity during the immediate post–World War I period: Le Corbusier as a visual artist; Hilberseimer, as an art critic. Both returned to architecture in the form of articles and then projects, starting in 1921 with Le Corbusier and in 1922 with Hilberseimer. In their reflections on the great modern city, both of them invoked the American example, which they admired for its chessboard layout but criticized for its lack of planning. In particular, the random arrangement of New York skyscrapers, which steal light from one another,

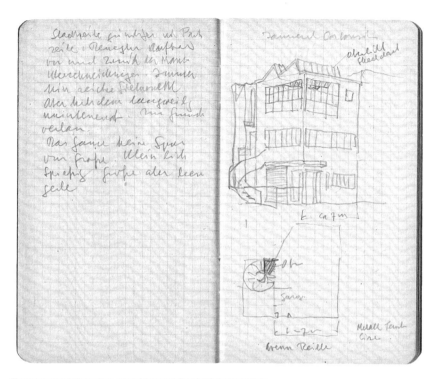

Figure 1: Ludwig Hilberseimer, page of the travel diary for Holland and Paris, with a sketch of the villa Ozenfant, October 1924

congests Manhattan when 20,000 people suddenly invade a narrow street. From then on, their projects sought to remedy these dysfunctions.

Le Corbusier's project for a Ville contemporaine (Contemporary city) for 3 million inhabitants, exhibited at the Salon d'Automne in 1922, concentrated business life in centrally located skyscrapers, surrounded by residential areas and garden cities beyond (Passanti 1993). As for Hilberseimer, in 1923 he initiated his activity as a town planning theorist with articles (notably 1923b) and then with a project for a residential city (Wohnstadt). The principle of this Wohnstadt, which was developed in response to a competition on the theme of housing launched by the magazine *Bauwelt* in December 1923, is that of a central business town surrounded by peripheral satellite towns. The basic

Figure 2: Paul Westheim's buisness card, front and back

structure is the Mietshausblock, designed like the Berlin block surrounded by four streets, but without the enclosed courtyard at its center (see "Visuals", p. 276, fig. 4).

Hilberseimer discovered the Corbusian project the following year. In October 1924, he spent ten days in Paris. There are several indications that he tried to meet Le Corbusier. Le Corbusier's address appears twice in his travel diary (fig. 1): "rue du Cherche-Midi," as well as the telegraphic mention "Sèvres 35," which corresponds to the agency created by the architect and his cousin Pierre Jeanneret in 1922 at 35, rue de Sèvres in the 6th arrondissement. Paul Westheim asked Le Corbusier to receive Hilberseimer during his study trip to Paris (fig. 2).[3] It is not known for certain whether the two men met, but the Fondation Le Corbusier has preserved, in addition to Hilberseimer's business card, half a dozen photographic plates of his projects, dated no later than 1924.[4] Even more than that, it is the development of the Hochhausstadt project that suggests that a meeting did take place—or at least Hilberseimer's discovery of the Le Corbusier's Ville contemporaine.

On his return to Berlin, the shock of the Ville contemporaine project gave rise to the Hochhausstadt (High-Rise City), of which two drawings are dated autumn 1924 (see "Visuals", p. 278, fig. 9 and 10). When he first published the project, Hilberseimer did not say much about the circumstances of its development (Hilberseimer 1925b, 12–14). In his 1927 book *Großstadtarchitektur*, however, he explicitly presented his Hochhausstadt as a response to the Ville contemporaine (Hilberseimer 1927b, 12–17). Commenting at some length on Le Corbusier's project, he concludes that the qualitative improvement is undeniable, his city being well laid out and spacious, far from the "chaos of New York." On the other hand, the quantitative improvement was a failure, as congestion had gone from being horizontal to vertical: the elevators of 60-story buildings were overcrowded at peak hours. In response, his High-Rise City project aims to smooth the flow of traffic by locating housing above workplaces.[5]

While the Ville contemporaine and the High-Rise City have frequently been juxtaposed, the same cannot be said of the Plan Voisin for Paris and the City-Bebauung proposal for Berlin.[6] We sketch a cross-analysis.

Plan Voisin and City-Bebauung

In 1929 Hilberseimer gave shape to his business city in the wake of the publication of *Urbanism* in German. It should be noted that the book in which Le Corbusier published the Plan Voisin had just been translated into German at the beginning of 1929 and seems to have stimulated Hilberseimer's thinking once again (Le Corbusier 1929). The Plan Voisin was financed by the car manufacturer Gabriel Voisin so that Le Corbusier could adapt the Ville contemporaine to Paris. Presented to the Parisian public in 1925, it is described in the book *Urbanisme* and combines two cities: a residential city, composed of apartment buildings arranged in an airy way, and the business district, a set of 18 cruciform skyscrapers, made of glass, containing offices. The complex stretches from the Louvre to the Republic, replacing the Marais district. The photo of the diorama exhibited in 1925 shows this cluster of skyscrapers, each of which can contain 20,000 to 40,000 employees, in a frontal view. In March 1929, in the context of the reorganization of the city of Berlin, Hilberseimer published a "Vorschlag zur City-Bebauung," which he presented as a complement to the Hochhausstadt of 1924 (Hilberseimer 1929f). It has a double function: the homogeneous reorganization of Berlin's commercial heart and the rationalization of the office building. The first version is limited to a single axonometric perspective, very characteristic of the Hilberseimerian design of the 1920s (see "Visuals", p. 283, fig. 18).[7] It is presented as an extract of a device, which seems to be infinitely replicable, and articulates parallel buildings grouped in pairs on orthogonal plots and connected by single-story transverse wings for shops. It suggests the system of underground circulation and parking that allows the separation of car and pedestrian traffic.

In the following year, the project was refined and the second version, published in December 1930, was enriched with several documents, which showed a significant change in Hilberseimer's design (Hilberseimer 1930b). Axonometry, without shadows or illusionist means, accentuates the schematism and abstraction of the representation (see "Visuals", p. 282, fig. 17). Plans and sections document the project on a block scale.[8]

Where Le Corbusier opted for the verticality of the city, Hilberseimer favored a horizontal solution for the Geschäftstadt, the business district that the heart of the capital was to become.[9] For Berlin, the economic and intellectual center of Germany, is also an exhibition city in the sense of the German term *Messestadt*, where everything made in Germany can be seen at all times. The city center must therefore accommodate sales and exhibition facilities (Verkaufs- und Ausstellungsgelegenheiten). Dwellings are removed from the center, and the buildings are used for offices. But unlike the Plan Voisin, Hilberseimer adopted a system of slabs grouped in pairs. In doing so, he confirmed his commitment to the Zeilenbau system (ribbon development), which he believed would allow the ever-increasing traffic toward the city to flow more smoothly.

The buildings, inserted into rectangular blocks, have 8 levels, instead of the 5 levels of the Berlin building, not counting the basements used for parking. The project has evolved: instead of the low buildings connecting the slab towers, the entire center of the block is occupied by shops on two levels. This vast space replaces the narrow courtyards that characterize the Berlin perimeter block. This transformation of the heart of the Berlin block into a shopping mall is one of the highlights of the project. The central space is to house two-story exhibition halls, 40 meters wide and 160 meters long. In these courtyards, which are the same width as the streets, exhibition halls, sales halls, or storage spaces can be housed as needed. Businesses (*Geschäfte* and *Betriebe*) can present their entire production in the immediate vicinity (Hilberseimer

1931d, 130). The city was to become a permanent exhibition, with these large exhibition spaces integrated into the design of the business district, which would replace the function hitherto performed by department store windows.

This is the only case where Hilberseimer integrates the architectural program of the hall into an urban proposal. However, the configuration of these halls is not specified. This disaggregation of the typical hall building, which is very present in Hilberseimer's work, is somehow surprising.[10] While his various projects and publications treat the hall as an autonomous architectural object without integrating it into urban projects, it undergoes a profound transformation in the City-Bebauung project. In fact, in this proposal for the epicenter of Berlin, the hall disappears as an architectural object and its architectural character is dissolved into the functional purpose of these trade-related spaces.

Visualization of the Business City in situ

In addition to the axonometry and the plans and sections, the second version of the City-Bebauung includes a ground plan and a photomontage, which I would suggest are in dialogue with the posterior Corbusian staging. In *Urbanisme*, the Plan Voisin is essentially visualized by a sketch (Le Corbusier 1925, 266), by a (rather illegible) photo of the diorama exhibited at the Exposition des Arts Décoratifs in 1925 (1925, 270–71) and by a very legible plan of the insertion of this double city in the heart of Paris (1925, 272–73). A fourth document contrasts the old urban fabric, where tuberculosis and misery "triumph satanically," with the hold of the blocks housing the skyscrapers (1925, 274).[11] Although the articles in which Hilberseimer presents his City-Bebauung project do not mention Le Corbusier, one manuscript explicitly refers to the Corbusian project for Paris.[12]

The ground plan of the City-Bebauung echoes the Plan Voisin. But whereas the latter completely replaces the existing fabric, the layout of the slabs in Hilberseimer's plan is superimposed on the Berlin plot.

Figure 3: Le Corbusier, model of the *Plan Voisin*, 1930, photo: Marius Gravot

The photomontage showing the insertion of the City-Bebauung in the heart of Berlin is contemporary with the model of the Plan Voisin. This model was made in the autumn of 1930 for the short film *Architectures d'aujourd'hui* by Pierre Chenal.[13] It was photographed from above to create a bird's-eye view. This view was included in the film and was later widely distributed and commented on (fig. 3).[14]

The parallelism, including the chronological one, is striking, since the second version of the City-Bebauung project, in addition to the abovementioned documents, is enriched by a spectacular photomontage situating the project in the Friedrichstadt (see "Visuals", p. 282, fig. 16), the historical heart of Berlin, where the metamorphosis of the Prussian city into the capital of the Deutsches Reich took place. At the time he conceived this photomontage, Hilberseimer had certainly not had access to the periodical *Plans*, whose distribution remained confidential, nor had he yet seen the film, which was screened in Berlin in January 1931 (Boone 2017, 1:96–100 and 2:40).[15] Despite their remarkable synchronism, the two visualizations differ.

Where the elegant axonometric perspective neither locates nor delimits the repetition of the business buildings, the same cannot be said of the photomontage, which precisely locates a group of nine double blocks in the heart of Friedrichstadt: bordered to the north by Unter den Linden and to the east by Gendarmenmarkt, it closes off Friedrichstraße, a high point of Berlin's life and an office/shopping street. One striking difference is the way these two radically new, even provocative, areas are inserted into the urban fabric. Both form a violent contrast, but the skyscrapers of the Plan Voisin overwhelm the preserved historical monuments (from the Louvre to the Sacré-Coeur), or appear only in watermark, while Hilberseimer, on the contrary, accentuates the potential for insertion of the City-Bebauung into the Friedrichstadt. The scale does not overwhelm the clearly identifiable monuments of the twin churches on the Gendarmenmarkt, on either side of the Schinkel theater with their 70-meter-high domes.

Berlin, City of the Employee

Beyond the debates that animated the development of urban doctrines in the interwar period, we argue that Hilberseimer's urban planning vision responds without being formulated to a sociological environment and that his city-building project for Berlin corresponds to the district of white-collar workers.

Berlin is the city of the employee par excellence, as Siegfried Kracauer expressed it in his 1929 report for the *Frankfurter Zeitung*: "Berlin today is a city marked by the culture of employees, by a culture made by employees for employees. Only in Berlin [...] is it possible to understand the reality of the life of the employees. To a large extent, this reality is the reality of Berlin itself."[16]

Employees are a social group that emerged in the second half of the nineteenth century as the need for new skills in industry and commerce became apparent. The standardization of production, the intensification of paperwork, and new business techniques led to the development of a bureaucracy within companies. In Germany, it became an organized social group, with a legal status and specific pension insurance from 1911 onward (Schulz 2000).

In terms of mentalities, employees appeared to be a class without traditions, forward-looking, modern, with a lifestyle impregnated with the technical and industrial world. Living in the big city, the employee adopts a modern demographic behavior by limiting the number of children. He spends a relatively large part of his income on leisure. He goes to restaurants and cinemas rather than concert halls, smokes cigarettes instead of pipes, is concerned about his dietary standards and wants comfortable, modern accommodation that conforms to the characteristics of a middle-class lifestyle. For the employee "sees spending on culture and housing as a symbol of upward mobility" (Oeckl 1935, 154).

Although he did not formalize it, Hilberseimer was part of the rise of the social group of employees in the Weimar Republic. Sabine Hake has shown that modernist architects affirmed white-collar workers as the main protagonists of modern urban life. This transformation of class society was materialized by two types of buildings: office buildings and housing estates: "it was the public housing estate on the periphery and the office building in the center that most clearly symbolized Weimar modernity" (Hake 2008, 107). The corporate office buildings shape the public life and urban identity, the Siedlungen participate in the spatial reorganization of private life. Their architecture forms a homogeneous whole through the use of the plastic medium of repetition and thus gives meaning to the community. Hake sees in the rationalist fixation on structure and order the temptation to control the "mutability, changeability, and sheer energy of the modern masses."

Rethinking the Office

Unlike Le Corbusier, Hilberseimer was interested in office work. While the plans for the Plan Voisin dwellings are detailed, those for the cruciform office towers are not. Le Corbusier merely evokes the sense of power they provide, as Hilberseimer recalls, citing *Urbanisme*: these skyscrapers constitute "the command post of the country" (Le Corbusier 1925, 270) and will contain "the brains of the whole nation. [...] Everything is concentrated in them: apparatus for abolishing time and space, telephones, cables, and wireless; the banks, business offices, and the control of industries; finance; commerce, specialization" (Le Corbusier 1925, 177).[17]

Hilberseimer, for his part, wanted to rethink the office building *(Geschäftshaus)*, which at the time was mostly a residential building that was transformed at random by the development of economic activity and extended erratically into a labyrinthine collection of rooms and corridors. Rationalizing it involved designing on a block scale (Hilberseimer 1931c), which allows buildings to be spaced at the same height as they are so that the offices and work spaces themselves benefit fully from daylight, air, and sunlight.

This environment is designed for the employee who, unlike the worker, works at a distance from production, performing nonmanual work, in a more comfortable, sound environment and with better hygiene conditions. In 1933 the number of employees reached more than 4 million, or 15 percent of the working population. Of these, 7 percent were office workers, or 230,000 employees (Oeckl 1935, 151). The most numerous occupational categories were accountants, clerks, salesmen, and typists. In the office *(Bürosaal)*, employees used pens and pencils to compare, add, subtract, or balance bills of material, stock lists, receipts, disbursements, calculations, and salary lists. Workstations were lined up as tightly as in the army or at school so that the office manager could see everything at a glance. The typewriter became the emblem of this professional world, and the range of equipment includes ink pads, blotters, inkwells, filing cabinets, telephones, and calculators (fig. 4). In terms of furniture, desk lamps and swivel chairs shaped the working environment of the employee, who was strictly dressed in a suit and tie.[18]

This is the population for which Hilberseimer's City-Bebauung is intended. Significantly, the version published in March 1931 in *Moderne Bauformen* equates the fine axonometric design with proposals for the arrangement of office furniture *(Möblierungsvarianten)*, from the large common room to the head's office. The variants include the open space of the time, with rows of employees one behind the other, three by three, lined up in one or even two bays, two-person desks, double desks with a secretarial station—never facing each other (see "Visuals", p. 283, fig. 19). Also envisaged are rooms for metal

Figure 4: The employee's desk: neatly arranged tables, a world of files, typewriters, stamps, published in: Heinrich Helfenstein / Martin Steinmann. 1985. "Eine Deutsche Versicherungsgesellschaft um 1930." In: *O.R. Salvisberg: Die andere Moderne, Dokumente zur modernen Schweizer Architektur,* ed. by Claude Lichtenstein, 130–141. Zurich: Gta-Verlag.

lockers, the superior's office, with a more imposing seat than the simple swivel chair, armchair, and coffee table, plus the meeting room. Hilberseimer's interest in the question of workplace furniture was shown at an exhibition organized by the Deutsche Gesellschaft für Gewerbe-Hygiene (German Society for Industrial Hygiene), whose recommendations he deplored as not being followed up more.[19] A hierarchical world, as indicated by the size of the desks and the design of the chairs, which are more pronounced in the case of the executive chairs. The rounded shape of the swivel chairs designed by Thonet is also evident.

These design options are an expression of one of the characteristics of rationalized work: monotony, which the sociologist Ludwig Heyde has described as an asset: "the monotony of work that is repeated in the same way leaves the mind free for other objects" (Kracauer 1930, 56). Kracauer contrasts this with the statement of a boss to a trade union representative that "the life of a commercial employee, an accountant for example, [is] of an appalling monotony which he would find difficult to bear on his own account" (1930, 57). With the City-Bebauung project, Hilberseimer seems to have put an end to the projection of the modern commercial city, and from then on concentrates on the Mischbebauung and the organization of housing in a green environment.

Housing for the Employee

By contrast, he continued to be interested in housing and developed dozens of housing plans during the Weimar Republic. Although he never socially characterized the inhabitant, we argue that the intended target is the same as the Berlin office building, namely the employee (*Angestellter*).[20]

The layout of the dwellings depends on the number of occupants.[21] But the destination of all the rooms is extremely constraining, revealing a tacit project on the inhabitant. This corpus of plans makes it possible to identify a typology of Hilberseimerian housing.

This typology is part of the white-collar worker's dwelling as it developed during the Weimar Republic. This new type of housing differs from the dwellings of the wealthy strata of society as well as from the traditional structure of workers' housing and from the models developed by employers at the beginning of the twentieth century. This layout, which was developed in response to the needs of the social group of employees, was the work of the trade union building societies, in tune with their members (Mengin 2007; see also Mengin 2011).

This layout is characterized by a number of specific spatial devices. In contrast to traditional tenements and workers' housing without sanitary facilities but with a Wohnküche that can be entered directly, each dwelling consists of an entrance, a living room, a separate kitchen, bedrooms, and sanitary facilities.

The entrance is to preserve the family's privacy. A single living room replaces the plurality of living and reception areas in bourgeois housing (dining room, reception room, family living room, not to mention luxury housing with a music room, boudoir, smoking room, office, etc.). This new living room is subdivided into different "areas" that are reminiscent of the former. A place of intimacy is provided for each member of the family: the marital bedroom brings together those of the husband and wife. The children's bedrooms, which were smaller, became more numerous. The presence of a separate kitchen in each dwelling, close to the living room, was an innovation, as in the tenements, a single room served as a meeting place for the members of the household and as a kitchen: the *Wohnküche*. In late-nineteenth-century rental buildings for the poorer social classes, the kitchen was not always located in the dwelling but rather on the landing; sometimes it was shared by two or more families. Finally, in the middle-class home, the separation of the service areas from the family rooms meant that the kitchen was relegated to the back of the flat or to a particular wing of the house. The kitchen becomes a rationally organized space for the preparation of meals and is connected to the living room, where the dining table is located. Finally, the bathroom and toilet embody the new standards of modern comfort.

This organization of the dwelling is a transcription, on a reduced surface, of the bourgeois dwelling. Typical plans are based on distributive values that give the family a central place. They also show the perspective of social ascension through intellectual work. The clearest indication of this is the almost systematic presence on the plans of a space in the living room for a desk, a sign that the occupant has access to an intellectual activity. The work area appears in all flats, regardless of their size (22, 37, 48, 58 or 70 m²) (see "Visuals", p. 285, fig. 23). This office area is present in all living rooms, whether in a single-family house or a flat. The variations published by Hilberseimer in the Bauhaus magazine in 1929 include it regardless of the size of the dwelling: 22, 37, 48, or 70 square meters and regardless of the number of occupants: one, two, four, or six. Similarly, all children's rooms, however small, are provided with a work surface and seats. These can be seen in the drawings from 1924 as well as in the plans and photos of the flat Hilberseimer designed in 1931. A photo taken at the exhibition entitled *Die Wohnung unserer Zeit* (The Dwelling of Our Time) clearly illustrates Hilberseimer's vision: at the end of the living room, a man dressed in a shirt is sitting in front of a desk with a modern desk lamp. The widely published photographs taken during the exhibition show different arrangements, depending on the orientation of the dwelling (fig. 5).[22]

It should be noted that the sociocultural relevance of this type of housing for the salaried middle classes was to be the usual standard for European housing until the 1980s.

Figure 5: Desk in a living room designed by Ludwig Hilberseimer for the exhibition *Die Wohnung unserer Zeit*, 1931, published in: Alice Simmel. 1931. "Die Wohnung unserer Zeit." In: *Frauenwelt* 8, 20.

Primarily a Planner

Hilberseimer, who claimed to be primarily a planner ("hauptsächlich Planer," Hilberseimer 1963a, 4), puts Le Corbusier back to architecture and characterizes him at the same time as a "great architect." However, Le Corbusier's projects had twice been a stimulus to his vision of the city. In one of his last books, *Contemporary Architecture*, Hilberseimer draws a parallel between their approaches (Hilberseimer 1964a, 149–53). Although their mutual membership in the modernist sphere has repeatedly placed them on the same playing field, from the Weißenhof housing estate to the CIAM, we have concentrated here on the direct stimulation of Hilberseimer's thinking by Le Corbusier's projects on two occasions in the 1920s. Subsequently, Hilberseimer proclaimed his admiration for Corbusian architecture, most notably the Soviet Palace project (Hilberseimer 1930a), and questioned the sculptural turn of the post–World War II works (Hilberseimer 1964a, 210–13). When he returns to "Le Corbusier and city-planning," Hilberseimer places him in a line of thinkers whose fundamental figures are Camillo Sitte, Ebenezer Howard, and Soria y Mata. For

him, Le Corbusier shares with Sitte an architectural approach to city planning. Both are oriented toward the past—Sitte, toward medieval cities; and
Le Corbusier, toward the axial-geometric city—but their patterns do not offer
solutions to contemporary problems. His conclusion is that Le Corbusier is
one of the few great contemporary architects but that urbanism is not architecture (Hilberseimer 1945b).

Hilberseimer's projects are a contribution to the employee's environment,
from work to home. They respond to their imaginary, as they embody the
regularity, uniformity, and repetitiveness of office work, as well as the desire
for equality and homogeneity that was reflected at the same time in the apartment buildings built by Bruno Taut or Otto Salvisberg for the Gehag trade
union building company.

This "Weltstadt" moment in Hilberseimerian thinking faded away in the
early 1930s. After the Great Depression, Hilberseimer found himself in a
very different environment from that of the Berlin metropolis: Dessau was
not very urbanized at the time. Hilberseimer turned away from this global-
izing thinking and no longer produced totalizing urban models. From then
on, he developed urban projects based on the housing unit, surrounded by

greenery and located in satellite towns for which he no longer drew up a plan (fig. 6).

His thinking is part of the historical moment of the cultural response to the aspirations of the newcomer on the German social scene: the white-collar employee. It concerns a more socially characterized recipient than Le Corbusier's inhabitant or user. Hilberseimer, we could conclude, put his work as a planner at the service of the modern employee, for whom his projects were designed, unlike Le Corbusier, whom he considered above all an architect, closer to the plastic arts than to the living conditions of the white-collar employee. During the 1920s, this sensitivity to the social context gradually led Hilberseimer to abandon architecture for planning.

Notes

1. Many thanks to Florian Strob for his help, his encouragement and his patience.
2. In *Het Bouwbedrijf* no. 2 February 1926 p. 74–78, refering to the presentation of the "Ville contemporaine," no. 1 January 1925, p. 32–38.
3. Both Hilberseimer's and Westheim's business cards are preserved in Le Corbusier's archives. Contacts between Hilberseimer and Westheim go back at least to 1922; and in September 1923 an article by Ozenfant and Jeanneret was published in Westheim's *Das Kunstblatt* (Ozenfant and Jeanneret 1923). Thanks to Isabelle Godineau and Delphine Studer, Fondation Le Corbusier (FLC). In the spring of 1928, Westheim devoted a glowing article to two of Hilberseimer's projects, the house in the Weißenhof housing estate and his railway station project for Berlin in the successful daily newspaper *8 Uhr-Abendblatt* (Westheim 1928).
4. Two are related to the Wohnstadt, two show row houses (Reihenhaus 1 and 2), one a Mietshausblock, and the last the Chicago Tribune and Hochhaus projects, FLC, D2-14-159-001 to D2-14-159-012. Hilberseimer does not seem to have spoken French, as evidenced by the basic vocabulary he carefully notes in translation.
5. The criticism that this project is a "necropolis rather than a metropolis" was formulated as early as 1928 by Edgar Wedepohl (1928). Hilberseimer uses this formula again in Hilberseimer 1963, 22.
6. The small exhibition dedicated to Hilberseimer at the end of 2021 in the Bauhaus Museum in Dessau puts them in eloquent contrast.
7. The drawing is dated 1928, AIC 10/2 box 9 folder 6.
8. The plans would be published again with the same illustrations, but in a slightly different organization, in Hilberseimer 1931e.
9. He expressed this opinion as early as 1926, on the occasion of the competition for the exhibition grounds (Messegelände), see Hilberseimer 1926b.
10. Among Hilberseimer's early designs are a covered market (Markthalle, 1914) and a city hall (Stadthalle); see Wagenführ 1919. His large market hall for Berlin 1927 is often reproduced. The most developed and detailed project is the one for the competition for the city hall of Nuremberg in 1929.

It was published in the magazine of the Werkbund, *Die Form* (Hilberseimer 1931c). A chapter of *Großstadtarchitektur* (Hilberseimer 1927b) is devoted to halls and theaters (Hallen- und Theaterbauten); *Beton als Gestalter* (Hilberseimer and Vischer 1928) focuses on the constructive aspects of these wide-span structures; *Hallenbauten* (Hilberseimer 1931d) is devoted to halls, characterized as large covered spaces with a public function.

11. On the different documents elaborated by Le Corbusier to represent the Plan Voisin, see Delbaere 2004; see also Delbaere 2005, which gives a good overview.
12. Typescript entitled in pencil "Citybebauung." AIC, series 8/3 box 1 folder 22, n.p.
13. On this model photographed by Marius Gravot in November 1930 and published several times, see Boone 2017, 32; and Rosellini 2020, 68–69.
14. It is published in Le Corbusier 1931—thank you to I. Godineau. The *Œuvre complète* for the years 1910–1929 does not reproduce it, while the following volume, which covers the years 1929–1934, returns to the Plan Voisin—which it dates to 1922–1930—with four photographs of the model: see Boesiger and Stonorov 2013 [1930], 109–17; and Boesiger and Stonorov 2013 [1935], 91–93.
15. The early 1930s was a time when architectural ideas were disseminated through film. The Liga für unabhängigen Film, founded in Berlin in November 1930, brought together leading figures from film and architectural circles, including Ludwig Mies van der Rohe, Hans Richter, and the lawyer Otto Blumenthal, brother-in-law of Udo Rukser (with whom Hilberseimer had written his first articles and for whom he built a house in 1932). See Robbers 2012, 1–4. Thanks to Véronique Boone for this information.
16. The chronicles he wrote during his stay in Berlin in 1929 are published in Kracauer 1930, here 33.
17. Quoted in Hilberseimer 1945b, 10. Originally intended for a monograph edited by Stamo Papadaki, *Le Corbusier Architect, Painter, Writer* (1948), the contribution was not included in the end, as Hilberseimer refused to accept the cuts made by Papadaki. I am grateful to Florian Strob for providing me with a reproduction of this unpublished manuscript.
18. On the employee at work, see the very well illustrated Lauterbach 1995, in particular Beck 1995.

19 This traveling exhibition was shown in Berlin in 1929 at the Deutsches Arbeitsschutz-Museum; see Hilberseimer 1929a; Hilberseimer 1929b.

20 My various master's theses on LH in the 1980s led me to question the social target of its housing projects, and I finally wrote a thesis showing that the social housing of the Weimar Republic was aimed at employees. Indeed, their powerful trade union centers set up building societies which met the aspirations of this pioneering social group in Germany. Returning to Hilberseimer several decades later, I came across the abovementioned Hake 2008.

21 See Philip Oswalt's contribution in the present volume.

22 In *Die Form, Moderne Bauformen, Stein-Holz-Eisen, Deutsche Bauhütte.*

Housing as Infrastructure: Typological Studies of Ludwig Hilberseimer

Philipp Oswalt

Physical infrastructures are deemed to be systems "essential to enable, sustain, or enhance societal living conditions" (Fulmer 2009, 32). In addition, as public assets they are "usually subject to state regulation in respect of the price and quality of provisions as well as supply security" (Klodt n.d.). While housing does not generally count as infrastructure, it is very much the spatial domain of private life. Ludwig Hilberseimer, however, addresses the question of housing as infrastructure. He sees it as an issue of the spatial organization and structure of a community, across all scale levels, which connects the individual sphere with the city as a whole. "The architecture of today," writes Hilberseimer in 1923, "relies largely on the resolution of two factors: The individual cell, the room, and the overall urban organism. The room as a component of the house consolidated in the street block will define this in its outward form" (Hilberseimer 1923, 138). And: "Only when the city plan and the construction plan are considered collectively is it possible to configure the city as a single entity, as an organism." (Hilberseimer 1925b, 188) While the urban functions are not limited to housing, they make up most of the building mass and are therefore central also to Hilberseimer's deliberations as regards urban development. For him, the "single cell" as a cornerstone of the built environment is the individual room to sleep in and withdraw to.

Over the decades, Hilberseimer seeks to provide precise and fitting answers to what he considers essential questions concerning the spatial organization of human coexistence. The starting point of this development is his 1923 utopian design Wohnstadt (Residential City), in which fundamental ideas on usage, circulation, building construction, use of sunlight, ventilation, and multiplication are combined in a spatial model. He subsequently develops this basic idea step by step in countless studies. In his search for universal answers, he consistently develops new variants based on different parameters to optimize his approach in a continuous evolution.

For the apartments themselves, he begins with an internal structure that clearly distinguishes between individual and communal areas (see "Visuals", p. 277, fig. 7). In doing so, he initially focuses on the apartment block, whereby he considers the housing typology for various access systems.[1] In early 1929, he transfers the organizational principle developed for the highrise to one-story and two-story single-family houses. One notable feature of Hilberseimer's work on housing types is his focus on the capacity for combination and multiplication, both of which enable diverse building typologies and building shapes to be generated from one single housing type. This approach is typical of his specific understanding of design and architecture, which combines the quest for universality with diversity.

For Hilberseimer it is a question of formulating basic principles. Thus, even the 1923 Wohnstadt design does not refer to a specific location but formulates an abstract, ideal-typical solution. The settlement is conceived as a ca. 1,000-meter-wide linear city, the spine of which is formed by a railroad that stops at stations every 1,000 meters and is thus easy to reach on foot. The hierarchical road system distinguishes between main shopping streets running in a north–south direction and residential streets extending in an east–west direction, which are connected by footpaths running perpendicular to these, parallel to the main roads. The settlement structure, which is dominated by residential housing, is punctuated at regular intervals by commercial buildings, schools, and hospitals. The five-story housing blocks extend in a linear way along the residential streets (see "Visuals", p. 276, fig. 4). At the gable ends of the housing blocks, two-story shops and commercial buildings face the streets, framing the road space without depriving the blocks of light, air, and sun (see "Visuals", p. 276, fig. 5). This structure also lends the building masses a sculptural quality, which in the blocks is accentuated by stairwells and housing units that push out of the building line. Hilberseimer develops a flexible system for the apartments. In each case, several minimized individual cell-like rooms stand alongside one another in a row, opposite a generous living space. "The ground plan variants for 3, 4, 5, 6 and 7 occupants are each based on the same spatial elements" (Hilberseimer 1925b, 187). Only the living and dining room varies according to the size of the apartment. Hilberseimer's typology does not optimize single, isolated factors but endeavors to integrate diverse requirements in an overall solution. At the same time, it avoids architectonic specificity to express a universal solution. All apartments are lit and ventilated from both sides. The systemization of the ground plans for the variously sized apartments allows for identical, repeated spatial elements, which their industrial prefabrication is designed to facilitate.

Hilberseimer also attaches considerable weight to the issue of privacy. The residents' psyches are irritated by the stress of the city. By providing spatial isolation, the apartment should therefore serve as a "spatial means of relaxation" (Hilberseimer 1929a, 509). In addition, this principle should apply not only between neighboring apartments but also inside the apartment. Initially, Hilberseimer envisages a minimized bedroom for each occupant (apart from the parents). He contrasts these individual minimal cells with a generously sized communal space: "Because spending time in too-small rooms has an oppressive and restrictive effect, while the contrast between a large room and small rooms is invigorating. With a small apartment, the living and dining room, as the shared space, will always have to be made quite big, while all other rooms can be quite compact" (Hilberseimer 1925a, 289). Hilberseimer thus pairs individuality with an emphasis on the communal-collective. In the development of his basic principles over the following years, Hilberseimer modifies the concept. He now factors in the question of flexibility in the ability to furnish, for "this is not the business of the architect, but of the inhabitants, and it must be possible to vary the furnishing according to the nature of the new requirements" (Hilberseimer 1929a, 512–13). This is still important in small apartments, even if the scope here is limited. To enable this, he now moves away from the idea of a separate room for each child and makes do with separating the sexes (1929a, 510). In this way, the small rooms can be furnished differently and provide a workspace as well as a place to sleep and dress.

Hilberseimer's perspective on the economics of housing construction is likewise holistic. He criticizes the prevailing tendency to focus only on area minimization, which in fact inflates the cost per square meter of an apartment. With a rational construction with standardized, prefabricated building components, as Hilberseimer aspires to with his typology, somewhat larger living spaces can also be economic due to the cost-effectiveness of production.

Hilberseimer increasingly varies the housing typology. While he initially focuses on north-south-oriented buildings divided into two or three apartments, he later also develops small apartments with center corridor access,[2] balcony access apartment blocks, and variations on the ground plans based on different sun paths (Hilberseimer 1931a). Soon, Hilberseimer finds even this spectrum of possibilities too limited. From 1929, alongside the apartment blocks, he makes a case for the inclusion of one-story and two-story flat-roofed buildings in the lexicon of housing types for families. Here, he again varies the building typology between classical row house, L-types, and detached single-family homes and works out the specific pros and cons for each of these. He is partial to the single-story building: Although this requires a longer front facade, its additional cost is offset by the simpler construction and the omission of stairs. He favors the L-type and the detached single-family home over the row house. The L-type not only makes it possible for all living areas to face the garden but also simultaneously offers privacy from neighbors. The single-family home is at first glance the most expensive, but it holds the most potential for industrialization and offers the most scope, not only in terms of the arrangement of the rooms but also for the addition of extensions (the "growing house," see "Visuals", p. 292, fig. 33–34). For the single-family house, Hilberseimer also designs different layouts aligned to different cardinal directions. Here, the interior structure of the dwellings stays true to the principles developed for the apartment block and transfers these to the flat-roofed building.

Hilberseimer reduces the architectonic articulation to a minimum. Windows evenly distributed in the facades provide the required lighting and ventilation. Only the three-dimensional molding of the building parts expresses an explicit design aspiration: "the decisively cubic effect of these buildings negates all details. The overall design of the building mass alone is definitive" (Hilberseimer 1922a, 528). Hilberseimer aspires to "the greatest restraint and concentration at once. Forming large masses according to a universal law while suppressing multiplicity is how Nietzsche understands style in general: The general case, the law, is honored and accentuated; conversely, the exception is put aside, nuance whipped away, the standard becomes master, chaos is forced into shape: logical, simple, unambiguous, mathematic, law." (1922a, 531; also in Hilberseimer 1927b, 103) Hilberseimer reduces the construction to the bare essentials (see Hilberseimer 1923). In his later designs, he even refrains from refining the three-dimensionality of individual building parts—for example, by drawing out the stairwells—and reduces the volumetric composition to an urban aggregate of the simplest construction volumes. While architectonic articulation is avoided wherever possible, Hilberseimer endeavors to avoid uniformity on the urban development level. Here, he seeks contrasts, which he achieves by varying the building volumes, for example, by modifying the numbers of stories. In addition, for lighting and ventilation reasons alone, he aims for an open, flowing space. The "customary density of the enclosed apartment block" (Hilberseimer 1929b, 4) is replaced by open construction.

Hilberseimer sees housing construction as a macrosocial task and therefore believes in the socialization of land ownership and in financing housing construction through taxation. In addition, only centralized planning by the state would enable him to address the reciprocity between the housing floor plan and city planning that he regarded as essential, and thus to arrive at a spatial order that extends from the single room to the city master plan. At the urban benchmark level, Hilberseimer varies not only the building volumes but also the access infrastructures, as is reflected as early as 1923 in his Wohnstadt design. He envisages not only thoroughfares and residential streets but also footpaths for residents. At the city level, Hilberseimer develops multiplicity and variation in the framework of his system, especially in respect of housing typology. He envisages different forms of housing for different accommodation requirements. In addition to the conventional apartment, he develops concepts for hotel-like apartment buildings (Hilberseimer 1929b, 2–4, see "Visuals", p. 285, fig. 23) and balcony-access blocks, which are especially suitable for single persons and childless couples and address the housing requirements of families with single-family homes. By reducing the plot size to barely 200 square meters per house, with low-rise buildings housing more than 300 persons per hectare, he manages to achieve a settlement density similar to that of sunny and well-ventilated multistory residential buildings (Hilberseimer 1931c) (see "Visuals", p. 290–291, fig. 28–32).

In 1928/29 Hilberseimer begins to mix the different house types in a neighborhood to generate synergies: Multistory buildings should benefit from the green spaces of private gardens, single-family homes from the civic amenities of the urban housing blocks. Furthermore, the typological diversity of the concept, which he calls a mixed development, results in a social mix of inhabitants. It enables contrast formation in the building volumes and thus breaks up and structures the urban space. From 1931 Hilberseimer develops his concept more and more toward the settlement unit, which now addresses above all the larger scales up to the regional and spatial planning dimensions—but which exceeds the remit of the study at hand.

No architect or planner of his generation focused as consistently as Hilberseimer on the various requirements of a housing infrastructure or developed models that condense the optimization of these parameters in a variable house and urban planning typology (fig. 1). The closest equivalent would be the floor plan designs of the architect Alexander Klein (1879–1961), which likewise demonstrably optimize the modern housing floor plan through the systematic development of variants. However, these focus more on specific issues of housing use and almost entirely ignore other issues (such as structural design) and other scale levels (such as urban planning). While these studies of Klein's provided important impetuses for the housing of their time, they are confined to the two-dimensional improvement of the housing floor plan. Hilberseimer, however, combines a greater range of factors and scale levels in a spatial-typological model. For him, the main factors are building costs, construction, sun position, utility value, privacy, urbanity, spatial effect, and flexibility. He deliberately avoids the subjective, the arbitrary, and the unsubstantiated, and derives everything from objectively justifiable criteria. He is concerned with universal principles that at the same time enable pluralism (figs. 2–4).

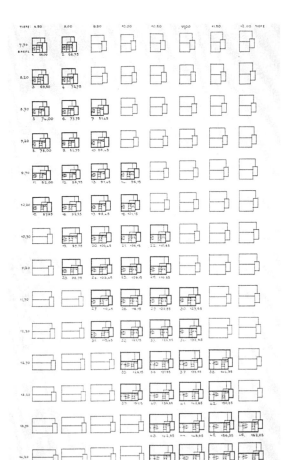

158. Schema der rationellen Grundrißbildung für einen beliebigen
Typ in verschiedenen Wohnverhältnissen (vergl. Text Seite 133)

His is a parametric design method, before the concept even existed. In studies, he repeatedly develops many variants, which he then puts to the test. With this method, he attempts to gradually develop and optimize his concept without presuppositions—and thus also without referring to traditions. Hilberseimer can be regarded as a modern counterpart of the architectural theoretician Jean-Nicolas-Louis Durand (1760–1843), who just a few years

Figure 2-3: Jean Nicolas Louis Durand, *Précis des leçons d'architectures données à l'École Polytechnique,* 1802–1805

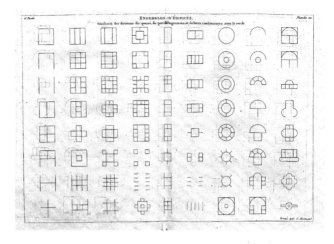

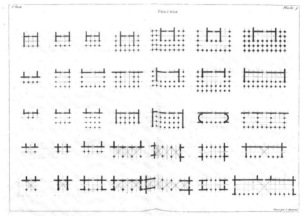

following the French revolution published the treatise on typologies *Précis des leçons d'architectures données à l'École Polytechnique* (1802–05). Durand sought to objectivize the design process and, like Hilberseimer, omitted reference to specific locations. With his typological ideal designs, he aspired to expediency and efficiency and sought universal, timeless solutions free of personal expression.

Unlike Durand, Hilberseimer was able to realize some of his buildings. Their relevance must however clearly take second place to his theoretical work, precisely because they are constructional realizations of his theoretically developed typologies.[3] Conceptually precisely located in his thought model, adapted as required to the specific situation of the building contract (such as to the sloping lot of the Weißenhof Estate in Stuttgart), even here Hilberseimer eschews an architectonic specificity. It was left to his colleague Mies van der Rohe to develop a specific architectural language from his concept. Hilberseimer's influence here is however immense. The transition from the "European" to the "American" Mies may be traced back above all to his impact. In the early 1930s, Mies leaves his still De Stijl-influenced compositional design vocabulary behind and develops, especially from 1938, his renowned, radically reduced, sublimated architectural language. Together with Hilberseimer, he realizes the residential district Lafayette Park in Detroit from 1955 to 1963, which brings to life on a large scale the mixed development concept developed by Hilberseimer from 1928. Hilberseimer's drafts also had a distinct effect on the work of some Bauhaus graduates post-1945. These include the housing estates of Lotte Stam-Beese in the Netherlands (fig. 4), residential buildings and kibbutzim by Arieh Sharon in Palestine/Israel, the Kollektivplan for the reconstruction of Berlin, the Wohnzelle Friedrichshain of 1946–51 (Wils Ebert, Selman Selmanagić, et al. fig. 5), housing blocks with balcony access in Potsdam-Babelsberg by Robert Lenz, and Eduard Ludwig's contribution to the 1957 *Interbau* in the Hansaviertel, Berlin.

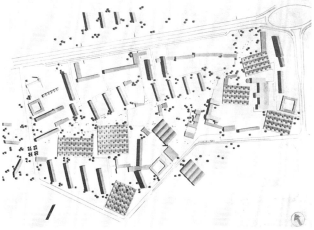

Notes

1   Buildings divided into two or three apartments and
     balcony access housing blocks.
2   Competition entry, Haselhorst model housing estate,
     see Hilberseimer 1929a.
3   These include especially the residential architec-
     tures Stuttgart-Weißenhof, 1927; the Growing
     House, Berlin, 1932; Blumenthal House, Berlin,
     1932; Fuchs House, Berlin, 1935; the Des-
     sau-Törten housing estate, Dessau, 1930, and La-
     fayette Park, Detroit, 1955, also the model kitchen
     R1 with Hugo Häring, exhibition *Die neue Küche*,
     Berlin, 1929.

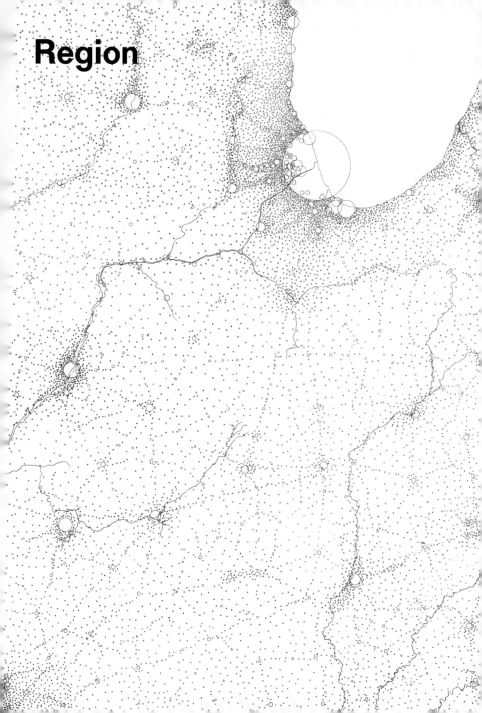

Region

"A Framework for Life": Hilberseimer's Region and Vitalist Urban Theory

Benedict Clouette

In his book *The New Regional Pattern*, Ludwig Hilberseimer defines a region as "an organic entity, an organism [...] which can live and support life" (Hilberseimer 1949, 89). He describes the form of the preindustrial region as the result of a process of organic growth that produces "an even distribution of different kinds of settlement [...] a well-proportioned arrangement of villages, towns and cities, based on traffic distances as well as on conditions of production and economy," where "differences in density and distribution of settlements were due to geographical or topographical and soil conditions" (1949, 98). Hilberseimer illustrates this pattern of settlements with three diagrams by the German geographer Walter Christaller, initially published in his book *Die zentralen Orte in Süddeutschland* (*Central Places in Southern Germany*, 1968 [1933]).[1] The first diagram presents a theoretical distribution of five scales of town, shown as circles of different sizes connected by lines of varying thickness, resolving into a layered hexagonal lattice (see p. 180, fig. 1). The second diagram projects this idealized pattern onto the existing towns of southern Germany, the study area chosen by Christaller in developing his theory, distorting the geometry of the hexagonal lattice into soft circular shapes that deform along their tangents, like bubbles in a foam (fig. 1). The last diagram shows a field of irregular white blotches—clusters of points where "each dot represents 400 people"—against a black background, with the shape of the region delimited by a thin white line and its interior traversed by even thinner lines representing district boundaries (fig. 2). While the first describes a pure geometrical schema—a theoretical and nomological geography—the second and third, despite mapping onto an existing terrain of cities, remain almost as completely abstracted from any sense of locality, lacking place names, references to regional topography, and even indicators of scale and orientation.[2] The status of Christaller's work as a theoretical and

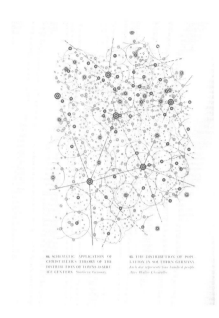

Figure 1: Ludwig Hilberseimer, Schematic application of Christaller's Theory of the Distribution of towns as service centers. Southern German, published in: Hilberseimer, Ludwig. 1949. *The New Regional Pattern: Industries and Gardens, Workshops and Farms.* Chicago: Theobald, 100.

scientific geography, a normative system of spatial relationships rather than an empirical description of particular places and their contexts, no doubt enabled its wide circulation in postwar urban planning discourses, including in Hilberseimer's book, despite the circumstances surrounding its development and its early applications in the National Socialist planning of annexed areas of Poland.

Christaller's book was initially researched and written as his doctoral thesis, completed in 1932 under the biogeographer Robert Gradmann at the University of Erlangen, and was published shortly thereafter in 1933, in the same year that Hitler was appointed chancellor of Germany. Christaller, at that time a socialist and a member of the Sozialdemokratische Partei Deutschlands (SPD), left for France on his bicycle later that year as a political refugee, he would later suggest (Barnes and Minca 2013, 678). But within a few months, he returned to Germany and gradually resumed his geographical work under the new regime, conducting research for the Reichsarbeitsgemeinschaft für Raumforschung (Reich's Association for Area Research) in 1935–37 for its

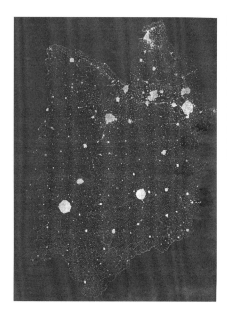

Figure 2: Walter Christaller, diagram, published in: Hilberseimer, Ludwig. 1949. *The New Regional Pattern: Industries and Gardens, Workshops and Farms.* Chicago: Theobald, 101; captioned: "The distribution of population in Southern Germany. Each dot represents four hundred people."

Atlas des deutschen Lebensraumes (Atlas of German Living Space), and founding a subsidiary research group, the Arbeitskreis Zentrale Orte (Working Group on Central Places), in 1937 (Rössler 1989, 431). The methods developed by Christaller in his study of southern Germany formed a theoretical basis of the working group's research, which adopted central place theory as a model for planning the spatial reorganization of German territory, initially focusing on the efficient production and distribution of goods and services within the country's existing borders. After the invasion of western Poland in 1939, central place theory was directly enlisted in the planning of areas newly under German control, when, the following year, Christaller formally joined the party in order to work for Heinrich Himmler's Stabshauptamt für Planung und Boden (Planning and Land Department), under agronomist Konrad Meyer (Barnes 1998, 103). Under the framework of the Generalplan Ost, developed by Christaller and other researchers at the department as a classified project overseen by the SS, the western areas of Poland would become a laboratory for the application of central place theory as a planning tool. The Generalplan Ost was conceived as a geopolitical project of settler colonization aligned with the long-standing German nationalist program of a "Drang nach Osten" (Drive toward the East; Mazower 2008, 599–600). Christaller's work with the Stabshauptamt für Planung und Boden was to translate geopolitical strategy into a spatial system of resettlement, articulated as a network of urban administrative centers organized in a hierarchy of scales, facilitate the political and socioeconomic planning of territories incorporated under the NS state (Preston 2009, 6). In addition to increasing spatial efficiency, the reconstruction of the system of central places, Christaller suggested, was to recreate the character of a German landscape on Polish terrain, "to give the settlers roots so they can really feel at home" (Christaller 1940; Preston 2009, 23).

Why then would Hilberseimer, described by his colleague Hannes Meyer as a "socialist architect," illustrate his most extensive theoretical excursus on regional planning with the diagrams of a state planner for the Reich?[3] The question is particularly troublesome considering that Hilberseimer obliquely conjoins the histories of the war and the writing of *The New Regional Pattern* in a note that closes the book:

> The studies for *The New Regional Pattern* were begun in the early thirties when I suddenly found myself with the leisure time necessary for the contemplation of its problems. As the date of the introduction shows, this book was finished in 1945. Its publication, however, was delayed for various reasons until now. During this interval two things were added; a sketch-map of the western part of eastern Europe and along with it a plan of Warsaw, the capital of Poland.
>
> L. Hilberseimer
> Chicago, January 1949

The book thus describes the arc of the war through Hilberseimer's life, from the closing of the Bauhaus at Dessau and his flight from Germany to America, to his later career in Chicago as an urbanist and professor at the Illinois Institute of Technology (IIT). The specters of war and nationalism similarly haunt his concept of regionalism. He introduces the plan for Warsaw, to which I will return later, as an attempt to resolve the "problems which keep Poland in turmoil," not by "moving border lines and exchanging populations" but by "applying the idea of regionalism" (Hilberseimer 1949, 176–78). The idea of regionalism to which Hilberseimer refers is elaborated in the preceding chapter, "What is a Region?," where Christaller's diagrams effectively answer the rhetorical question of the chapter's title by illustrating the pattern of the region as an organism, both alive and supporting life.

In all likelihood, Hilberseimer would have known few specifics of Christaller's wartime activities, given that the Generalplan Ost was destroyed by the SS at the end of the war; its contents—and Christaller's involvement in its planning—have only been reconstructed in recent decades through archival research. Nonetheless, Christaller's participation in the regime, like that of many scientists and academics who worked within NSDAP-sponsored research institutions, was not a secret during or after the war, given that he published extensively in state-funded journals during the National Socialist period. But Hilberseimer's ignorance of or indifference toward Christaller's biography belies a more difficult problem—that the politics conditioning the development of Christaller's theories are not perceptible in these three images, at least to Hilberseimer, presumably, when he includes them in his book. On the contrary, political antinomies are resolved in these three diagrams through their evocation of the city as a living organism and of its form as the expression of vital forces. In the first decades of the twentieth century, the concept of the city as a living organism, subject to laws of biological growth and form, was widespread in German discourses on urbanism, spanning the political spectrum. In the interwar period, theorists of architecture and planning drew upon philosophical conceptions of life in developing approaches to pressing concerns of mass housing, settlement design, and infrastructure. Vitalist urban discourses were advanced by left-wing architects such as Meyer and Hilberseimer and by the nationalist critic Paul Schultze-Naumburg, as well as by figures with more ambiguous political commitments, such as Hermann Muthesius, and by others, such as Christaller, who worked for the NS government but later denied its politics.

Given the prevalence of concepts of life in these urban theories, despite their presumably divergent politics, what differences might be marked between fascist discourses of life and those advancing a socialist or revolutionary project? Furthermore, assuming that vitalist theories do not inevitably and necessarily lead to racist state violence, nor, for that matter, to modernist bio-functionalism, what potentials might remain in the concept of life for urban theory?[4] Does life still retain the indeterminacy and originality that Georges (Canguilhem, 2001 [1952]) identifies as properties of the living, as opposed to the mechanical, despite its entanglements with reactionary tendencies, whether the racist ideology of the urbanism of National Socialism or the invocations of the health, hygiene, growth, and decay of the city as an organism in modernist architecture and urban planning?[5] And how might such a philosophy of life relate to the biopolitical dimension implicit in these and other theories of urban planning in the first decades of the twentieth century, as well as to the subsequent critiques of those theories?

Lebensraum

The metaphor of the state as organism, which figured in both political and biological debates in the nineteenth century, was extended by Friedrich Ratzel, a biogeographer who first studied zoology under Ernst Haeckel at the University of Jena (Bassin 1987, 487n6). In his seminal work *Anthropogeography*, Ratzel described the struggle for space (*Kampf um Raum*), a concept that became central to his essay "Lebensraum" (1901), in which he sought to subordinate human geography to biogeography by framing human competition for territory as part of the natural world, suggesting that "a people, a race, a species can only migrate by colonizing" (Ratzel 2018 [1901], 66) through the growth of its living area (*Lebensgebiet*). Ratzel drew the term *Lebensraum* from biogeography, in which it designated the geographical extents of the habitat necessary for supporting a population of an animal species, but applied it to human political relationships. Just as competition among animals leads to the displacement or extinction of weaker species, Ratzel describes how colonization of the Americas since the sixteenth century is a process by which the European settlers expanded their living area, leading to the extinction of animal species and the suppression of indigenous peoples (2018 [1901], 73).

Ratzel explored the implications of his theory for urbanization and human settlements in his contribution to the volume *Die Großstadt*, a collection of essays commissioned to accompany an exhibition on cities in Dresden in 1902 (for which Georg Simmel wrote his more enduring essay "Die Großstadt und das Geistesleben" [The Metropolis and Mental Life]). Ratzel's essay, "Die geographische Lage der großen Städte," introduces a theory about the relationship between the natural landscape (*Naturlandschaft*) and the cultural landscape (*Kulturlandschaft*) of human settlements in rural regions, and attempts to specify the particularity of the German people's ties to the land (Ratzel 1903). Ratzel recognized agrarian production, by which human communities adapt to their environments, as key to the bond between cultural and natural landscapes. The metropolis was only able to flourish in relation to the larger region from which it drew its resources, chief among them food and other agricultural goods. Consistent with the dynamic growth implied by the concept of Lebensraum, the growth of the metropolis required a corresponding expansion into new hinterlands to increase agricultural production. Ratzel's conception of the state as an organic entity was based in the relationship between the soil as a source of agrarian production and the patterns of settlement to which it gives rise.

While Ratzel's intellectual orientation is sometimes regarded as nationalist, insofar as he recognizes the origin of nation-states and national identity in natural laws, it would be reductive to wholly identify his politics with reactionary geopolitical theories and their consequences. However, after Ratzel's death in 1904, his work was a key source for more overtly nationalist geopolitical theories. But putting aside the question of the influence of Ratzel on the formation of NS spatial theory, the regime's drive for territorial expansion required the expertise of many other geographers, planners, and military engineers to carry out the integration and development of captured territory. As the historian Karl Schlögel (2016) has argued, through the work of these experts, organized under state-sponsored research units such as Konrad Meyer's Planning and Land Department, space became a key term in NS political theory. In 1937 a speech by Hitler to his generals called for the creation of "empty space" in the East for the resettlement of Germans, ultimately tasking Himmler with carrying out the task of population transfer after the annexation of western areas of Poland (see Giaccaria and Minca 2016, 19). Christaller's work for Himmler's Planning and Land Department was to effect the reterritorialization of captured areas through planned development. Christaller's theory of central places, which sought to establish a "general explanation for the sizes, number, and distribution of towns" according to what Christaller called "special economic geographical laws," became a planning technique for rationalizing the pattern of new settlements in occupied Poland (Christaller 1966, 2–3). According to Meyer, who hired and supervised him, Christaller's work under the NS regime was directly related to his dissertation research, published as *Die Zentralen Orte in Süddeutschland*, the book featuring the diagrams reproduced by Hilberseimer in *The New Regional Pattern*.

The efficacy of Christaller's geography as a planning method derived in part from his attempt to approach geography as a set of general laws rather than a description of existing places. As Christaller wrote in the introduction to *Central Places*, "one can find a certain order in diversity, but the principle of order itself can never be found through historical inquiry" (1966, 2). Similarly, Christaller argued that statistics were of limited use, because while they can suggest patterns, they are merely empirical. Rather, the task was to describe "laws of the geography of settlements" (1966, 3), akin to the laws of other scientific theories, thereby elevating geography from a descriptive technique to a science. Christaller refers to Ratzel as a precedent for his geographical theory, noting that Ratzel first developed a "science of distance" that allowed him to explain the "spatial arrangement of the earth's surface" (1966, 2; Christaller here cites Ratzel 1882, 177). Beyond the "arbitrary" size, number, and distribution of cities and towns considered as individual cases, Christaller sought laws that would give an economic-geographical order to patterns of development (1966, 58). Such laws describe a "normal or ideal" system of central places, representing the optimal spatial arrangement of a territory.

According to Christaller, the aim of state planning is to effectively employ "economic-political measures to influence the present size and distribution of central places so that they approach as much as possible the scheme of highest rationality that we have developed theoretically" (1966, 125). In short, the status of Christaller's theory as a law-giving, normative order implies that actually existing spatial relationships should be encouraged to conform as much as possible to the rationalized system. Planning is understood as a "rationalization of reality" in which the distribution of settlements within a national territory is brought in line with "spatial-economic laws" (1966, 124). He recommends that governments organize their administrations as hierarchies of officials corresponding to the five scales of settlement units identified in his theory, with the administrative boundaries of their jurisdictions aligning with the regions surrounding each central place , and implement transportation infrastructure and tax incentives to promote development in the ideal locations of cities and towns to "enable transformation toward the optimum state" (1966, 124).

To explain the geometrical properties of the hexagonal meshwork of settlements, Christaller introduces the metaphor of the growth of crystals. He describes the relationship of a central place to its surrounding region, referred to in his theory as the "area of distribution," as analogous to the "crystallization of mass around a nucleus," which "is, in inorganic as well as organic nature, an elementary form of order of things which belong together—a centralistic order," which exists not only in the human imagination but as "the inherent pattern of matter" (1966, 14). The crystalline order is an internal logic that unfolds into an outward expression, and Christaller suggests that an "aesthetic pleasure" results from the congruence of the "invisible objective form" and an "outer form [that] is logically correct and therefore can be recognized as clear" (1966, 14). The model for such a visual order is the medieval town, which Christaller suggests contrasts to the "young, modern town," where "we regret the lack of order"; however, beyond these appearances, both the medieval and modern towns functions are the same, as "central organs of centralistic orders" (1966, 15). Visual order is ultimately subsumed as a property of the vital and biofunctional order of the network of cities.

The metaphor of the crystal in Christaller's text unifies a number of apparent oppositions—organic and inorganic life, visible and invisible, social and physical, spiritual and material—in a process of growth according to a natural order, a regional pattern unfolding from the nuclei of cities and towns into a lattice extending across the landscape in a geometry defined by Christaller's economic-geographical laws. Crystals are a recurrent figure in modern architectural theory from Gottfried Semper to the Bauhaus, invoked to describe the vital process of growth through which an invisible inner logic unfolds into a visible outward expression.[6] Hilberseimer and Mies both owned and reproduced images from the book *Der Kristall* (1937) by Johann Killian (see Harrington 1988, esp. 70 and 76; and Killian 1937). The metaphor of the crystal in *Central Places in Southern Germany* participates in this longer history of exchanges between the natural sciences and the constructed environment; but, in shifting the object to which the crystal analogously refers from the building or site plan to the geography of settlements, Christaller establishes a different logic: instead of the building's form as a singular and holistic expression arising from an internal logic or essence, the crystal of the settlement unit is always one of many, not simply an individual crystal but a crystalline pattern of cities and towns of different scales, an intricate lattice that extends from multiple centers where each "nucleus" or settlement is both the center of a "mass" or region surrounding it and one of many center-regions constituted in relation to each other.

The logic of the crystal, as a vitalist figure describing the growth of an inorganic form of life, suggests that Christaller's theory, despite its apparent emphasis on centrality, is finally less concerned with the urban center itself than it is with its multiplication and diffusion, a theory that seeks to rationalize and resolve the centrifugal forces of urbanization in an optimal pattern of regional growth. Implicit in the unfolding of this polycentric crystalline geometry is a logic of territorial expansion, where the relationship between the regional boundary and urban center is key to a dynamic process by which territory is expanded, through the creation and capture of "empty space" beyond its limits, and the interior is reterritorialized through subdivision and internal colonization.

The spatial order of the theory of central places was thus well suited to the task of developing the broad political imperative of German Lebensraum into a modern, rationalized system of urban planning. It translated the reactionary forces of racial theories and conservative appeals to the traditional landscape of the Heimatschutz movement into a scientific method for rapidly resettling German populations on captured land. In moving between a theoretical geography describing existing patterns of settlement and a planning technique for locating new urban centers, the theory was both regressive and future-oriented, at once suitable for reproducing a mythical German townscape for Volksdeutsch settlers to colonize Polish land and for optimizing the economic productivity of a future urbanized region.

In considering why Hilberseimer chose to illustrate *The New Regional Pattern* with Christaller's diagrams, a few resonances between Hilberseimer's and Christaller's theories are salient, following from their conceptions of the regional landscape as a living organism: urbanization is conceived as a process driven by relationships between the cellular unit and the organic whole; vitality is taken as the measure of a system's functional optimization; and the drive for growth and expansion from urban centers is considered as the vital force by which the natural form of the region emerges. Recognizing the alignments between Hilberseimer's and Christaller's theories is not to elide their differences, nor to suggest that Hilberseimer's socialist-modernist project is somehow tainted by reactionary-modernist spatial theory and racist pseudoscience, much less to posit a moral equivalence between their positions. Rather, acknowledging certain ambivalences in their politics of life—in relation to the history of exchanges between urban discourses, nationalist and colonialist ideologies, and the life sciences in Germany—may help to account for the degree of compatibility between Hilberseimer's and Christaller's theories suggested by their enjambment in Hilberseimer's *New Regional Pattern*, and perhaps also for their afterlives in the postwar United States.

Published in 1949, a decade after Hilberseimer had emigrated to Chicago in 1938 to join Mies van der Rohe's faculty at the Armour Institute of Technology (later IIT), *The New Regional Pattern* is Hilberseimer's most extensive treatment of the relationship between urbanization and the social and environmental geography of the region. Among the projects included in the book, Hilberseimer's scheme for a regional network of industrial bands in "part of present-day Poland" situates his later work in the United States in relationship to the devastation of the war in Europe. Hilberseimer introduces the project as a possible European application of an "urban-rural planning system," the last in a series of his projects included in the book, having already illustrated variations sited in the Central Valley of Northern California, the Chicago area, and the Detroit area, along with a diagram at a larger scale showing a proposed network of industrial belts stretching across the United States east of the Mississippi River (see "Visuals", p. 304, fig 52).

Turning to Europe, Hilberseimer's tone is grave, noting that "the disaster which befell Europe is material as well as spiritual," and that the reconstruction of the continent's cities will be hindered if not rendered impossible because the "creative forces of life have been broken" (Hilberseimer 1949, 176). He suggests that planning alone could not have prevented the war or stemmed the spiritual decline, but that today planning "can, if in accordance with life, provide a better framework for life" and release whatever "spiritual vitality" remains in Europe.

The framework for life that Hilberseimer proposes is regionalism, as a system countering and superseding nationalism by aligning patterns of settlement with natural geographies. He speculates that the destruction of the war might have been avoided if Europe "had been able to replace its national states by natural regions and to create a federation of all its people, based on a regional framework" (1949, 176). Hilberseimer's proposal for Poland seeks to transform the area—which he notes in its current form "violates the spirit of the Atlantic Charter"—into an organic unity, to align its future development with the form of a natural region. With a geographic extent similar to

Christaller's map of "the eastern areas" from his 1941 study, the diagram shows sinuous bands of urbanization connecting north–south from the Baltic Sea port of Gdansk to a large urbanized area spanning from Krakow to Brno before connecting northwest to Berlin, crossed by east–west bands intersecting at Wroclaw and Warsaw and leading toward Dresden and Prague in the west and Bialystok and Vilnius in the east (see "Visuals", p. 305, fig. 53). The crisscrossing bands of urbanized areas, which Hilberseimer terms "arterial settlement belts," are composed of a series of alternating residential and industrial settlement units, adjacent to agricultural areas and forests and connected by a system of roads, highways, and railways (fig. 3). Hilberseimer notes that all residential areas are within walking distance of industries and yet are still "in the midst of forests, farms, and gardens" (1949, 178). Consistent with his abiding interest in the model of the garden city, the region is defined by its organic integration of "industries and gardens, workshops and farms," as in the subtitle of the book, echoing Peter Kropotkin's *Fields, Factories, and Workshops*, which Hilberseimer cites.[7] The projects included in *The New Regional Pattern* draw upon Hilberseimer's readings of earlier theories of urbanism and urban projects: along with references to Ebenezer Howard and Siedlung projects in Weimar Germany, the layouts of Hilberseimer's settlement units draw from the street plan of Radburn, New Jersey, by Henry Wright and Clarence Stein, as translated through Hilberseimer's earlier "Fish-Spine" studies of 1931–34 (see "Visuals", p. 299, fig. 46).[8] Hilberseimer also refers to Arturo Soria y Mata's Ciudad Lineal project and N.A. Milyutin's Sotzgorod plan as precedents for linear bands of settlements.

Just as the pure geometries of Christaller's scheme are then adapted to actual topographical conditions, stretching and distorting into an irregular mesh to accommodate landforms and capture existing cities, the arterial bands of Hilberseimer's plans for Poland and American cities arc and bend across the landscape as they link up existing cities and industrial centers. At different scales, Hilberseimer's Fish-Spine studies and his regional plans participate in the same logic as Christaller's hexagons, in which an ideal mathematical description of spatial relationships is inflected and developed as it unfolds in relation to external forces, recalling the evolutionary interactions between

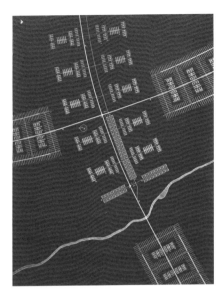

Figure 3: Warsaw, a diagram for its proposed replanning, as part of regional plan for eastern Europe, published in: Hilberseimer, Ludwig 1949. The New Regional Pattern: Industries and Gardens, Workshops and Farms. Chicago: Theobald, 179.

species and environments developed by the naturalist Alexander von Humboldt and Haeckel. The morphology of the region develops analogously to a biological organism, following an internal logic interacting with environmental conditions. The branching organization of Hilberseimer's settlement unit echoes the diagram of crystalline growth in Killian's *Der Kristall*.[9]

Hilberseimer elaborates upon his theorization of the relationship of the city-organism to its environment in *The Nature of Cities* (1955). He describes the relation of urban form to its site as an organic order through which "all things can grow and unfold" in cities conceived as "well-functioning organisms," where "each part develops according to its own law," but must also "have its due place [...] within the whole" (Hilberseimer 1955, 133). The siting of a city, including the topography, available resources, climatic conditions, and transportation routes, constitute an "interaction of forces" (1955, 115) that determines its natural pattern and form. While geometrical planning, represented by Roman and colonial cities, attempts to force nature into its pattern, the organic order "strives [...] to achieve harmony with nature," rather than dominating (1955, 160).

To comprehend these natural determinants, the planner starts with a survey of the region, understood as a "living entity, capable of supporting and maintaining life," including its natural and man-made features: "geography and topography, climate, soils, vegetation, growing seasons, water, mineral and other resources," as well as "the distribution of people and their occupations [...] the existing settlements and transportation routes [...] production, agricultural and industrial" (Hilberseimer 1955, 259). Hilberseimer recognizes soil, water, and sun as the "sources of life," and while he concludes that "man has no power over the activity of the sun," and dispatches with water requirements in technical terms ("the maintenance of the hydrologic cycle, the result of alternating precipitation and evaporation"), he endows soil with vital properties, not unlike those ascribed to it by Ratzel: "Soil is not a mere mechanical mixture. It is the result of the interaction of animate and inanimate forces. Not only is it full of life: it is, in truth, the source of life" (1955, 267). Regional planning must start from the ecology of the region, which is defined by the types of vegetation and agriculture that its soil supports; soil, as it interacts with climate and other environmental variables, is therefore the basis of all land use decisions and the planning of settlements. The conception of soil as a living substance was common to architects, planners, and landscape architects of divergent political commitments, from the Werkbund-affiliated landscape architect Leberecht Migge to NSDAP members Schultze-Naumburg and garden designer Willy Lange (Haney and Sohn, 2011, 113–114; Lange, 1910, 5; Cupers, 2016).

Hilberseimer's theorization of the ecological region is perhaps shaped by his reading of Ratzel's *Anthropogeographie*, a book that Hilberseimer describes as among those that have exercised a "decisive influence" on him.[10] In the book, Ratzel describes the formation of human societies in relation to their climate, environment, and the land that they occupy. Hilberseimer's conception of the region thus participates in the logic of Lebensraum as an organic relationship between a people and their patterns of settlement, not only through his inclusion of Christaller's diagrams, but through Ratzel's more ambiguously nationalistic theories of the vital forces shaping human geography.

The question remains of how to mark the distinctions between the uses of concepts of life in fascist and socialist urban discourses. In the case of Christaller's work for the SS on the Generalplan Ost, the connection to NS geopolitical strategy is relatively direct, and yet the theoretical basis of his work predates his employment in the state apparatus, which is why the continued influence of his theories on urban geography after World War II presents a difficult historical problem. Is a theory with close historical ties to fascism necessarily a fascist theory? How much distance between a theoretical formulation and a historical event is necessary for contingencies between them to be assumed? Even the language of historical closeness or distance depends on an association of degrees of proximity with likeness, suggesting that historical and spatial thought may be thoroughly imbricated. The causal relationships between biological theories and political formations is not always so clear as Haeckel's "republican" or "monarchic" theories of the cell-state would suggest: as Canguilhem argues, even as he attempts to establish correlations between politics and the life sciences, "Who can say whether one is a republican because one is an advocate of the cell theory, or whether one advocates the cell theory because one is a republican?" (Canguilhem 1965, 70) Furthermore, the entanglement of urban theories with the practices of states makes it difficult to establish strict limits between political power and disciplinary knowledge. This difficulty is only compounded by the later translation of these urban theories to very different political contexts, whether the postwar reception of Garden Cities theories in the development of new towns in postcolonial contexts, the rearticulation of Hilberseimer's Mischbebauung (mixed-used development) housing projects of the 1930s in Detroit's Lafayette Park (1959–63), or the influence of Christaller's central place theory on American academic departments of geography and regional planning. These afterlives of vitalist urban theory pose further questions for historians: specifically, since planning is inevitably a political process, and planning theory is not merely technical but rather is concerned with the ordering of a society, how to account for the extent to which the politics of urban theories are conserved, transformed, or left behind in their translation between historical contexts?

The afterlives of interwar German urban theories, such as those of Hilberseimer and Christaller, destabilize familiar historical, geographical, and political terrains in architectural history. While World War II is generally understood as an epochal event—establishing the periodization of the interwar and postwar eras, capping the shift of the geopolitical center from Europe to the United States, and, in architectural history, marking the major turn in the careers of canonical European architects—that historical framing reinforces a schema that has outlived its usefulness: the socialist-radical avant-garde of interwar Europe versus the pragmatist-corporatist émigrés in postwar America, with the rise of fascism and the war years both marking the epochal turn and clarifying the political commitments of major figures (the radical Meyer, the complicit Mies). A genealogy of these vitalist urban theories might trace the concept of life as a relational category that proposes affinities, both historical and conceptual, across these epochal breaks and national scenes, between apparently incompatible politics and ideologies. If life remains viable, so to speak, for urban theory, it is as a troubling and ambivalent concept that always entangles political and biological life with something other than life: immanent spirits and formative drives, species and races, the growth and decline of cultures, and land and territory. The political valences of life, like the concept of life itself, remain unstable.

Notes

1   The diagrams appear as full-page images in Hilberseimer 1949, 99–101.

2   Careful comparison with a map of Germany reveals that the diagrams as reproduced in *The New Regional Pattern* are rotated ninety degrees from their original orientation in Christaller's study, while the other maps in the book are oriented with true north at the top. Given the extreme abstraction of the diagrams from standard geographical conventions, it is entirely possible that Hilberseimer, as well as the editor and book designer, misconstrued their orientation.

3   A letter from Hannes Meyer mentions his appointment of "socialist architect L. Hilberseimer" to the faculty of the Bauhaus at Dessau in connection with Meyer's ouster from his position as the school's director. See Meyer 1980, cited in Anderson 2012, 28–29n20.

4   Scholarly attempts to trace the origins of National Socialist ideology too often assume that the politics of the 1930s develop directly from the German life sciences of the nineteenth century and thereby exaggerate the inevitability of German Darwinism's complicity in genocide. In architectural history, recent literature drawing from Foucault's concept of biopolitics has reframed modernist discourses of hygiene as a set of techniques of governmentality that attempt to impose a spatial order on the city and its population; see, for example, Wallenstein 2009.

5   In particular, see Canguilhem's comments on the "originality" of life as the distinguishing theoretical novelty of Lamarckian vitalism, in relation to the mechanistic theories of Newton and Comte (Canguilhem, 2001 [1952], 12).

6   On the crystal metaphor, see Hvattum 2006, esp. 503 and 506.

7   The subtitle of the book is *"Industries and Gardens, Workshops and Farms."* Hilberseimer includes Kropotkin's book in his bibliography in Hilberseimer 1949, 195.

8   The relationship to the Radburn plan by Wright and Stein is suggested by Richard Pommer (1988, 43).

9   This observation was first made by Kevin Harrington (1988, 70).

10   The reference to Ratzel's book appears in a typescript of Hilberseimer's answers to a questionnaire. In declining to respond to an unknown question (the typescript does not include the questions, only his answers), Hilberseimer writes that he would prefer to "mention a few books that have had a decisive influence on me" ("einige Bücher erwähnen, die auf mich einen entscheidenen Einfluss ausgeübt haben"). These include Bücher 1893, Geddes 1915, Howard 1902, King 1911, Kropotkin 1907, Ratzel 1882, and Soria Y. Mata 1882. See "Biography – Personal information form 1956–1959," Ludwig Hilberseimer Papers, Archives of the Art Institute of Chicago, Series 1, Box FF 3.5.

In Search of Order:
Hilberseimer's Visual Patterns

Christa Kamleithner

Both contemporaries and historiographers have seen in Ludwig Hilberseimer an obstinate mind aiming to order the world according to fundamental principles. When the German architect presented his book *The New City* with an exhibition at the Art Institute of Chicago in 1944, his regular plans formed a marked contrast to the pragmatic view of American planners and sociologists that characterized the accompanying lecture series (Harrington 1988; and Colman 2014). As Scott Colman (2014, 123) noticed, Hilberseimer did not conceive his plans with regard to "vested interests [...], class and racial inequalities, property rights, demographics, municipal governance." But while he was not interested in specific features, he was interested in larger trends. Statistics provided a starting point for Hilberseimer, who generalized demographic developments and transformed them into universally applicable patterns. The idea of the linear city was ventilated by him when Bauhaus students were mapping Dessau for the fourth congress of the Congrès Internationaux d'Architecture Moderne (CIAM); and his later books include population maps justifying the settlement patterns he designed. As idiosyncratic as his approach was, he participated in an epistemic paradigm emerging from statistics which was characteristic for modern urban planning; and like many other architects, designers, and social scientists of the time, he was fascinated by the view from above and the patterns it revealed. In the following, I will explore the role of statistical maps and other media representations for Hilberseimer's designs and show how the urbanism of the architectural avant-garde and urban and regional planning were both interconnected and distinct.

Hilberseimer and the CIAM Analysis of Dessau

Teaching at the Bauhaus Dessau, and Dessau itself as a paradigmatic site of industrialization, left a permanent mark in Hilberseimer's work. Both his plan for Dessau (see "Visuals", p. 288–89, fig. 26–7), which would have transformed the town into a ribbon development, and the smoke map legitimizing the quite brutal proposal date from 1932 (Harbusch et al. 2014, 168) and were published in *The New City* from 1944, Hilberseimer's first book in English, as well as in *Entfaltung einer Planungsidee* (1963), the summary of his planning ideas in German. The two books represent starting and end points of a lifelong preoccupation with urban planning and the definition of the elements and principles of a universal planning system. As in the Dessau plan and numerous other schemes, these were settlement units with housing and schools stretching into the greenery, commercial units along the main traffic axis, industrial units placed to keep the smoke away from housing, and a transportation network to connect the different elements. With them, Hilberseimer seemed to have developed a formula that encapsulates modern life: living and working side by side, but arranged so that both run smoothly. How idealistic or realistic was this formula? On the one hand, the concept of a linear city composed of functional ribbons circulated among CIAM members around 1930 in the version of Nikolai Milyutin's book *Sozgorod* on the future socialist city.[1] On the other hand, the decomposition of the city into functional elements was the subject of mapping in preparation for the fourth CIAM congress on the "functional city," which focused on the analysis of existing, that is, capitalist, cities. The congress that finally took place in 1933 emphasized that the modern city already consisted of zones for working, living, recreation, and circulation, but that these needed to be reorganized. No particular model was preferred. The concentric extension and reorganization of old trading cities like Amsterdam was as welcome as the linear developments that Bauhaus students discovered while mapping the industrial town of Dessau.[2]

What was the aim of mapping more than thirty cities, most of them in Europe, with a few in the United States and in colonial territories? As it was said, the project intended to expose the shortcomings of existing cities. Above all, however, it consolidated assumptions that had been fixed from the beginning, and by representing very different cities in the same way, it created a unity that had not previously existed (Somer 2007a; and Van Es et al. 2014). The maps documented what was considered the urban condition—this is particularly evident in the first of the three maps to be prepared, which depicts business districts, industries, slums, working-class, middle-class, and luxury districts, garden cities, and green areas in colors chosen to form units and divide the cities into functional zones that surpassed the actual more or less mixed state. Then, as now, there is no real business district in Dessau, to give just one example; and where exactly are the boundaries of a slum to be drawn—that is, of an area that can be considered ripe for demolition? The whole project hovered between documentation and design. The amount of available data varied across countries; some CIAM members had to be inventive because they did not receive any data at all. But apart from that, the maps were the result of assessments and decisions that adjusted the different cities to conform to a universal norm derived from a tendency toward spatial differentiation.[3]

As the Dessau example shows, the mapping project was about future figurations. Hubert Hoffmann, Wilhelm Hess, and Cornelis van der Linden—students of Hannes Meyer and Hilberseimer—not only provided the requested maps but also added a study of the entire region, including a settlement plan and housing designs.[4] Urban research had started at the Bauhaus in 1930, when Meyer hoped for a commission to draw a settlement plan for Dessau (Winkler 2003, 67). In the months leading up to his dismissal, he contacted the authorities to obtain data and approached the regional planning association in Merseburg, one of the first of its kind, which was in the process of mapping and planning the Central German Industrial District.[5] As this exchange failed, however, it was not until 1933, when the National Socialists had already closed the Bauhaus, that the students of Hilberseimer—who followed Meyer as a teacher—discovered the planning atlas, on which the association had been working for years (Harbusch et al. 2014, 171). Their 48-page analysis included material from the atlas, but although they gathered a lot of historical and statistical information, very little of it played a role in the replanning of Dessau

(Kamleithner 2021b, 122–25).[6] Turning to Dessau's data was not about details, but about discovering "lines of development," as the title of the analysis's fourth chapter says (fig. 1).

In this map, the Bauhaus students detected Dessau's future as a linear city. All industries had settled near the railroads, garden cities already separated living and working, and the Dessau-Törten Housing Estate south of the town, designed by Walter Gropius and expanded by Meyer, reinforced the transformation of the town into a ribbon development. In particular, the map's design amplified this trend: it dissected the town and gave the impression that the urban fabric only needed to be disentangled and its "functions" placed according to natural development. The wind chart, the most visible item in the settlement plan (fig. 2), gave a hint on how to steer this development: Only the dark-checkered industrial area at the railroad junction and the barely visible core of Dessau, which was perceived as a business district, were to be preserved. The densely populated areas in the southern part of the town were

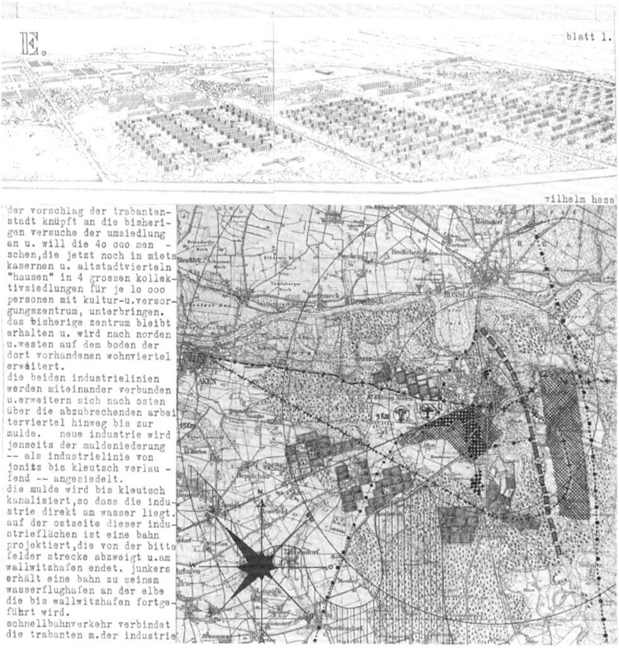

Figure 2: Dessau analysis, 1932/33, settlement plan by Wilhelm Hess

to be demolished. Instead, this area—checkered in a lighter shade—was to be used for industrial purposes, too, and all the housing was shifted to the west in accordance with the prevailing winds.

In Hilberseimer's Dessau plan from the same period, the winds were also key (see "Visuals", p. 288–89, fig. 26–7). Industries were rigorously placed in such a way that smoke was kept away from housing; even more consistently than his students, who would have destroyed most of Dessau but spared the old center, Hilberseimer reorganized the town from this point of view. Yet a second parameter interested him: circulation. When Hilberseimer dissolved Dessau into a linear city, he chose the railroad line to Bitterfeld-Wolfen as a backbone. As a map of daily commuter flows in the planning atlas shows, the railroad was indeed a lifeline for many Dessau residents who commuted daily to the industrial area.[7] Hilberseimer's students included this very map in their analysis, but were not really interested in the topic—their vision was rather static, as they planned only housing for the local Junkers company, which, however, had just filed for insolvency. Hilberseimer instead saw Dessau as part of a larger region, in which transport networks allowed people to commute. Such flexibility had become particularly important after the Great Depression of 1929 and was an issue in the planning atlas.

Mapping and Regional Planning in the Weimar Republic

Hilberseimer and the Bauhaus students did not operate in a no-man's-land. The Dessau Bauhaus was part of an industrial region in which numerous actors had visions for the future (Scheiffele 2003; and Perren et al. 2016). The region was characterized by an enormous concentration of capital: the largest chemical enterprise in the world at the time, the IG Farben trust, had sites in Wolfen and Leuna; there were potash works and brown coal mines, the Contigas company, which produced gas from coal, and large power plants converting coal into electricity. The regional planning association in Merseburg—a voluntary association financed by the municipalities and the industrial enterprises—was to coordinate these endeavors and provide the necessary infrastructure. Compared to the contemporaneous planning association in the Ruhr area, this association is not well known, but its atlas was pioneering work. Rarely was regional planning, which emerged from urban planning in the 1920s, based on such in-depth analysis (see Leendertz 2008, 49–75; and Kegler 2015).

The atlas included topographic, demographic, and economic maps as well as land-use plans. One pie chart map, for example, showed the increase or decrease in population in each municipality. While the municipalities with decreasing population were located in the upland areas, the municipalities with increasing population were the larger cities and industrial areas in the well-connected lowlands. Another map illustrated the traffic volume within the region and its connections to major cities (fig. 3). With only a little imagination, one could see the map as a plan for linear cities—and the general settlement plan in fact envisaged something like this. This plan reflected and promoted the economic and demographic change; it located industrial areas

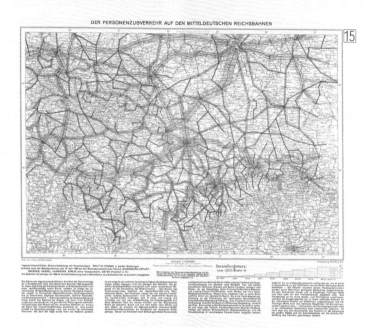

Figure 3: Merseburg planning atlas, 1932, passenger traffic on Central German railroads in 1928

close to the supraregional railways and the residential areas within commuting distance, and thereby created a well-connected future growth zone. The most notable feature of the plan by Martin Pfannschmidt was its intended flexibility: taking into account that people want or need to change jobs without changing their place of residence, the plan allowed for mobility within the region's core area (Kegler 2015, 170; and Kamleithner 2021b, 115–18). This is a planning attitude one would not expect until the 1960s.

Typical topics discussed in the 1920s and the following decades were the dissolution of larger cities, the resettlement of the population, and the mixing of industry and agriculture. But while some *völkisch*-minded German planners sought to restructure the nation as a whole and relocate the population to the rural fringes, a lot of planners took a pragmatic stance and focused on infrastructure planning in the most dynamic regions (Leendertz 2008, 76–104). Pfannschmidt, who took his inspiration from the Regional Planning Association of America (RPAA), was one of the latter. In relating mapping and planning and reinforcing population shifts rather than counteracting them, he referred to the RPAA's New York State plan from 1925, which assumed and promoted linear urbanization in the larger valleys. Hilberseimer must have known both: the Merseburg plan, which was part of the atlas used by his students, as well as the RPAA plan, on which Walter Behrendt had reported, who, like himself, was a member of the avant-garde circle The Ring. Both plans were gray literature and soon after forgotten. Only in the 1960s, when linear urbanization had become an obvious fact, did this figuration become the basis for regional planning (Fehl and Rodríguez-Lores 1997, 44–45, 203). Hilberseimer, however, pursued the concept from the 1930s to the 1960s.

Hilberseimer's Linear Cities, 1930s to 1960s

Between the 1930s and 1960s, Hilberseimer developed a planning system that could be adapted for any scale and location. Within this system, the metropolis of Chicago—to which he emigrated in 1938—could be replanned, just as he had replanned the industrial town of Dessau. The medium through which the system's elements and principles were created was essentially paperwork: Hilberseimer and his students at the Illinois Institute of Technology did get involved in the actual replanning of Chicago in the late 1940s, but as Hilberseimer was rather annoyed by the discussions that planning processes always entail, his ideas unfolded by working with his students—and within the space of the book (see Harrington 1988, 77–87; and Denny and Waldheim 2020). From 1944 to 1963, he published four books in which he presented and elaborated his planning system (Hilberseimer 1944; 1949; 1955; 1963b).

In *The New City* from 1944, three parameters defined his system: wind, sun, and circulation (Hilberseimer 1944, 48–49). Since teaching in Dessau, Hilberseimer had done endless studies with his students on solar radiation, which form a large part of the book; different volumes and positions of both high-rise and low-rise buildings were studied in terms of optimal sun exposure (76–97; see Poerschke 2018). On a larger scale, winds were crucial. Depending on the number of prevailing wind directions, the system provided for a range of settlement types: ribbons composed of industrial plants and tree-like settlement units (as in the Dessau plan), as well as fan-shaped settlement units arranged around a central industrial complex and lined up at varying intervals along a traffic axis (Hilberseimer 1944, 113–22). For replanning Chicago (see "Visuals", p. 300–01, fig. 48–9), Hilberseimer used both: As in Dessau, he preserved the older industrial areas and relocated housing to a smoke-free environment; as an extension of this linear structure, he planned a commercial core that included housing; and for the surrounding area, he proposed fan-shaped industrial settlements, connected by a centerless network of highways and railroads. This parameter, circulation, was not handled in as much detail as wind and sun. The only explanation Hilberseimer used for justifying his preference for linear structures was that traffic can be timed faster in linear cities than in concentric cities—a fact the architect and mathematician Peter Friedrich had figured out (Hilberseimer 1944, 72–73).

Sociological arguments or data are rare in Hilberseimer's books; even when he argued for settlement units, which contemporary planners propagated to strengthen social cohesion (see Schubert 2000), his focus was on circulation—that is, here, the separation of pedestrian and car traffic (Hilberseimer 1944, 110–13). Hilberseimer preferred to rely on seemingly irrefutable facts and designed his plans by means of geometric operations. Nevertheless, political decisions were of course involved. When he designed units in which working and living were within walking distance but which were at the same time loose "clusters" in a network (see Stalder 2009, 46), he opted for a society that allowed for a certain degree of flexibility. The strict separation of working and living, on the other hand, favored large corporations and dependent employment; and the obsession with the sun was linked to the social-hygienic idea that low population densities would ensure better "crime and health statistics" (Hilberseimer 1944, 49). This is where one of the very few statistical maps in *The New City* came into play: between a photo of Chicago's smoky sky and a photo of a traffic jam, Hilberseimer placed a map of juvenile delinquency in

Chicago, which, like the photos, showed a form of congestion—where the city was most densely populated, the crime rate was highest. So why not decongest the city to solve all sorts of social and health problems? Hilberseimer's planning ideas tied in with hundred-year-old reform approaches emerging with disease and density mapping, which identified the "dark" spots of cities and at the same time suggested that nothing more needed to be done than to dissolve them (see Kamleithner 2021a). In the 1940s, attempts of this kind were at their peak.[8] But irritated by the complexity and opacity of current planning dynamics and disgusted by the resulting "disorder and chaos" (Hilberseimer 1944, 53; see Harrington 1988), Hilberseimer gathered abundant material on historical cities rather than current statistics. Aerial photographs and plans of older cities revealed in his eyes an "organic" social and visual order, whose underlying patterns he wanted to identify. His own visions were to be based on the knowledge of such patterns; being primarily interested in a balanced environment and visual harmony, however, he mostly derived his patterns from seemingly timeless factors.

Later books of his, though, addressed the topical issue of the shift of population from rural to urban areas. In *The New Regional Pattern* from 1949, an entire chapter on "Population Problems" drew on the apocalyptic discourse concerned with declining birth rates—especially in cities—and the rural exodus, which had led to national recovery programs in many countries since the 1920s (see Weipert 2006; and Hoffacker 1989). In the United States, a resettlement program intended to help impoverished farmers ran from 1935 to 1946. Besides rural rehabilitation, the program included the construction of new rural communities and "greenbelt" towns; with its procedures for selecting a fit population, the program was linked to both family planning and negative eugenics (Currell 2017). This was far from Hilberseimer's mind, but he seemed blind to these issues, just as he ignored the racist background of the eviction and redevelopment of Chicago's South Side (Hirsch 1983).[9] But he too was worried about fertility rates and a composition and distribution of the population that seemed out of balance. After presenting graphics depicting the aging society, Hilberseimer thus connected this phenomenon to population distribution. Using three hypothetical maps, he explained that the population distribution had changed over the past hundred years, and while the population was evenly distributed at the beginning of the nineteenth century, the rural population subsequently shrank and the large cities grew disproportionately. This was counteracted by his planning system, which now provided for agricultural plots of different sizes and aimed at a more even population distribution. However, Hilberseimer did not intend to go backwards. This is particularly evident in how he dealt with Walter Christaller's central-place theory, which appears to pursue the same goal, but in fact does not.

Christaller's economic geography theory was particularly influential for National Socialist spatial planning, but was also used in other countries; US planners, for example, used it in defining the Interstate Highway System (Thrall 2010). In *The New Regional Pattern*, Hilberseimer presented Christaller's mathematically derived diagram of a distribution of towns, which was to ensure optimal supply throughout the country, and its application on a map of southern Germany without explanation (Hilberseimer 1949, 99–101).[10] Yet the positioning of the two schemes was a comment in itself: since the map shows an early-modern pattern typical for times when traffic was still slow, Hilberseimer inserted it into a paragraph on population distribution in the past. Unlike Christaller's, his planning system did not propose a hierarchical system with declared centers and defined spheres of influence but rather conceived cities and regions as part of an interconnected network. All the plans in the book show linear patterns without center, where agriculture and industry develop along a traffic axis consisting of highways, railroads, and commercial units. As for the combination of industry and agriculture, both the anarchist Pyotr Kropotkin and the capitalist Henry Ford were points of reference for Hilberseimer (1949, 82); Ford had actually experimented with reviving village industries in Michigan's valleys in the 1920s and 1930s.[11] Hilberseimer, on his part, envisioned a network where industry and agriculture were served by an urban infrastructure that would transform large parts of the United States into a kind of network city—with industry developing along traffic axes connecting industrial Chicago and the Great Lakes region with the rural South (see "Visuals", p. 304, fig. 52). Quite probably this kind of map had triggered his fantasies (fig. 4): in 1944, the Interregional Highways

Committee presented several proposals of what was to become the Interstate Highway Network, which would connect major cities. Unlike these proposals, however, which still thought of cities and traffic lines, Hilberseimer envisioned linear agglomerations.

Linear agglomerations, as we have seen, were mapped as early as the 1920s, and the Interregional Highways Report maps made it clear that a megalopolis was already emerging in the Northeast United States by the 1940s—it was, however, not until Jean Gottmann's famous study from 1961 that these patterns became ingrained in the minds of planners (Gottmann 1961; and Fehl and Rodríguez-Lores 1997, 47, 203). At that time, the architectural avant-garde was infected with "network fever," as Mark Wigley (2001) called it. Constantinos Doxiadis, Archigram, the Metabolists, Constant, or Yona Friedman, to name just a few, designed megastructures spanning whole regions or the entire planet, which were meant as infrastructures enabling choice and change. During the 1960s, when linear agglomerations were visible everywhere in the United States, Europe, and Japan, linear urbanization became a matter of course in spatial planning—even in Germany, where Christaller's theory was at the heart of the discipline. This meant concentrating planning efforts on conurbations and neglecting peripheries, thus moving away from the idea of an evenly distributed population, which was a turning point in the history

173

of planning (see Fehl and Rodríguez-Lores 1997, 48, 316, 319–20; Kegler 2015, 413–63, and Kegler 2016). Where is Hilberseimer's position in this history? His maps and plans of the Chicago region, included in *Entfaltung einer Planungsidee* (1963b, 102–13), may provide a clue to us (see "Visuals", p. 312–13, fig. 64–65). His last book on planning once again addressed the shift of population from rural to urban areas. This time, however, the maps did not show hypothetical distributions, but the historic development of the Chicago region, where linear settlements formed around 1900 and developed into urban agglomerations by 1950. Hilberseimer responded to this development with a plan that thinned out the tangled rail network by retaining only the lines in the more populated valleys, but also decongested Chicago and other populated cities by using regular linear structures. For the rural areas in between, he designed a pattern of small and large agricultural areas and thus tried to rebalance industrial development—industrialization was by no means to be stopped, but rather to be brought into harmony with nature and given a stable order, not least visually.

In Search for Visual Order

Hilberseimer's plan for the Chicago region concentrated the population in the main valleys, but distributed these agglomerations evenly. The pattern lies somewhere between Christaller's even distribution of towns and the network city of the 1960s; it resulted from the combination of industry and agriculture, and at the same time it connected part-time farmers to an urban network and turned them into modern consumers. Absorbing various impulses, Hilberseimer's ideas crossed the 1930s and 1960s. As he was only marginally involved in actual planning, his planning system unfolded as a parallel project that dealt with the same issues as the authorities—but within the space of his books. In the abundance of maps, plans, bird's-eye views, and aerial photographs gathered therein, he hoped to find order; all social, economic, and ecological issues at stake were treated from this perspective, that is, as distributional and ultimately visual phenomena. A good order, for him, was a balanced pattern.

In the end, Hilberseimer was in search of beauty, and although the beauty of his patterns was best seen from above, some of the images in his books reveal that he considered them as scenic landscapes. In *The New Regional Pattern* (1949), a photo series explained how the well-ordered landscape of former times was destroyed by man and how it could be restored. For centuries, as the visual story tells us, man cultivated crops, creating an intact landscape in which both fields and trees had a place. With industry and industrialized agriculture, the trees disappeared, the soil began to erode; devastation was the result. The story nevertheless ends well, with man's reclaiming the land (fig. 5). This happy ending, however, apparently is about visual balance: driving by car through the undulating landscape, one would have the impression that industrial scale and aesthetic harmony can be successfully combined. Strip cropping and contour cultivation, which produced the pattern, were promoted by the US Soil Conservation Service, and Hilberseimer did address soil erosion in his book; his patterns, however, created above all a unified visual field modulated by differences and repetitions. This is also what interested the artist and theoretician György Kepes, who in 1956 would publish an aerial photograph of the service in *The New Landscape in Art and Science* (fig. 6). For this book and the 1951 exhibition at the Massachusetts Institute of Technology

Figure 6: Strip cropping
and contour cultivation,
US Soil Conservation
Service, 1956

preceding it, Kepes collected masses of aerial and microscopic photographs that he hoped would provide a new foundation for design.[12] Like him and Hilberseimer, around 1950 many scientists and designers became interested in scientific photography as a means of discovering patterns (see Law Whyte 1951); ethnographers and sociologists used it to discover order, and planners and architects to create it (see Haffner 2013, 72–78). Paul Theobald, who published Hilberseimer's as well as Kepes's books, particularly supported this hype. Around 1960, this hype ended. As the network city became the dominant model, architects and planners cared more about infrastructure as a means of flexible use than about visually ordered patterns. They also began to talk to their designs' users, and by the end of the 1960s, this communicative opening brought to light the violence of the relocation processes inherent in all these patterns seen only from above.

Notes

1   A German copy was available as early as 1931; see
Somer 2007a, 105–7. In the same year, an exhibition
organized by a collective initiated by Arthur Korn
presented the concept in Berlin; see Fezer et al.
2015, 6–9.

2   One of them, Hubert Hoffmann, had designed panels
for the Proletarian Building Exhibition; see Fezer et
al. 2015, 6.

3   On these cartographic operations as well as the longer history of the relationship between mapping and
planning, see Kamleithner 2020.

4   On the Dessau analysis in general, see Harbusch et
al. 2014, 168–72; on the included designs, see the
essay by Magdalena Droste in the present volume.

5   Meyer received material from the census, but the
planning association was rather irritated when it
learned that a student project was running parallel to
its own efforts—see Bauhaus Dessau Foundation
I007473; many thanks to Philipp Oswalt for bringing
this correspondence to my attention.

6   For a reprint of the analysis, see Somer 2007a,
156–57; or Harbusch et al. 2014, 169–70.

7   See Landesplanung für den Engeren Mitteldeutschen Industriebezirk 1932, reprinted in Kegler
2015, which is an online publication.

8   To get an idea of the extent of statistical mapping in
Chicago in the 1940s, see Klove 1948.

9   See also the essay by Alison Fisher in the present
volume.

10   For the schemes and more about them, see the
essays by Benedict Clouette and Anna Vallye in the
present volume.

11   This was, however, a personal project of Ford's,
financed from revenues in Dearborn and Detroit;
see Mullin 1982.

12   On Kepes's idea of pattern-seeing, see Martin
2003, 42–79.

On the Diagrammatic Rationality of Hilberseimer's Planning

Anna Vallye

Founded by Camillo Sitte in 1904, *Der Städtebau* was in the 1920s a leading journal of the German urban planning field, and its book reviews occasionally indulged a delight in witty putdowns. But Berlin architect Edgar Wedepohl's review of Hilberseimer's *Großstadtarchitektur* (1927) was harsh even by those standards. The book, Wedepohl (1928, 161) opened, "links 229 illustrations through a text" (see "Visuals", p. 281, fig. 15). It consists not of "feasible solutions" but rather "theoretical gimmicks [...] capable of causing a fatal confusion about the tasks and possibilities of urban planning." The "theoretical quackery" of Hilberseimer's technical "inventions" is coupled to the "peculiarly cadaverous impression of his urban designs," he concluded, "in which not a tree, not a flower, not a piece of nature is included. [...] This is already more than Metropolis, this is Necropolis, the city of living corpses."[1]

That *bon mot* is well known to Hilberseimer scholarship, but mainly through the architect's own retrospective commentary on his work of the 1920s.[2] "All natural things are excluded," he wrote in 1963, for example, about the studies featured in *Großstadtarchitektur*. "No tree, no grass interrupts the uniformity. [...] The result is more of a necropolis than a metropolis, a sterile landscape of asphalt and cement, inhuman in every way" (Hilberseimer 1963, 22). "'More a Necropolis than a Metropolis,'" Richard Pommer's contribution to *In the Shadow of Mies*, the Chicago Art Institute's influential if backhanded 1988 rediscovery of Hilberseimer, set the tone for a still prevalent reception of the architect's production as an avatar of technocratic rationalism, whether condemned as "inhuman" or elevated as "post-human."[3]

Wedepohl's consequential characterization addressed not so much Hilberseimer's words as his images, specifically the 1924 sketches for a Hochhausstadt (High-Rise City) reproduced in *Großstadtarchitektur* (see "Visuals", p. 278, fig. 9 and 10). In their supreme austerity, the drawings have long captivated Hilberseimer's critical reception. Already in 1926, the architect's friend Hugo Häring observed that the project "subject[ed] man to a geometric principle of order [*Ordnungsprinzip*] [...] and le[ft] no room for the living," and claimed to find it a "little bit frightening" (Häring 1926, 173 and 175). The effect centered for him, in part, on the peculiar way in which Hilberseimer's aesthetics were "neither purposeful nor essential," but rather a "spotless [*blitzsauber*] byproduct of a performance of thought and will," the outcome of calculations conducted "in terms of economics, professional life, industrial management" (173). The images were thus in a certain sense devoid of formal properties. And yet they were also quite potently replete with aesthetic effect: their sparkling inorganic cleanliness startled.

Both Häring and Wedepohl detect in Hilberseimer's work, it may be said, a *Sachlichkeit* in extremis, whereby "theoretical" (Wedepohl 1928) neutrality acquires a deathly affect: rationality pushed to the limit confronts intense emotion and is sublated into an aesthetics without qualities. Hilberseimer's reception is frequently caught up in that dialectical drift when it seeks to identify the work's expressive logic. A paradigmatic example may be located in Pier Vittorio Aureli's post-Marxist reading of the Hochhausstadt as a "generic" image that represents the total abstraction of capitalist alienation—the estrangement of "human nature without qualities" in the metropolis, conveyed by means of "an architectural language that is deprived of any specificity" (Aureli 2011). There is a persistent contradiction in the attempt to attribute representational abstractness and inaesthetic affect to Hilberseimer's work, for all the occasional elegance of its solutions.

I want to consider instead the aspect of the architect's discourse that both Wedepohl and Häring, from their quite different respective positions, subjected to critique: its theoretical reasoning. The Hochhausstadt proposals, Hilberseimer wrote in *Großstadtarchitektur*, "should [not] be considered as urban plans [...] but a theoretical investigation and schematic application of the elements that compose the city" (Hilberseimer 2012, 131). The problem was thus placed in terms of the relationship between theory and practice—the nature and validity of theoretical reflection within urban planning as a field oriented to "feasible solutions," as Wedepohl put it. This was a claim to a

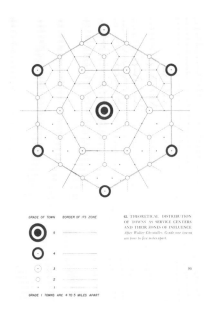

Figure 1: Walter Christaller, Marketing regions in a system of central places, originally published in: Christaller, Walter. 1933. *Die zentralen Orte in Süddeutschland: Eine ökonomisch-geographische Untersuchung über die Gesetzmäßigkeit der Verbreitung und Entwicklung der Siedlungen mit städtischen Funktionen*. Jena: Fischer; as reproduced in Hilberseimer, Ludwig. 1949. *The New Regional Pattern: Industries and Gardens, Workshops and Farms*. Chicago: Theobald, 99; captioned: "Theoretical distribution of towns as service centers and their zones of influence."

different discursive framework than the one we are accustomed to applying in Hilberseimer's case, an invitation to pose to his work questions of knowledge, rather than those of art. "His city planning proposals and their austerity have often been misunderstood, and a formal principle seen in them," wrote Hilberseimer's former Bauhaus student Hubert Hoffmann in 1966. "Hilbs always emphasized that it should only be a question of a scheme, which, when implemented, is modified by numerous influences" (Hoffmann 1966, 215). Within the history of knowledge, there is a concrete way to understand an image without qualities—as a quantitative image. In *The New Regional Pattern* (1949), Hilberseimer reproduced a set of diagrams borrowed from a 1933 book by the economic geographer Walter Christaller, *Central Places in Southern Germany* (fig. 1). They framed the architect's own project for an "urban-rural planning system"—also expressed through diagrams—that would accomplish an "integration of industry and agriculture" within a certain regional "pattern"—a project of "planned decentralization" that dominated his thinking from the 1930s forward (Hilberseimer 1949, 157, 130, 136). Christaller's "schemes" described the territorial distribution of a given population according

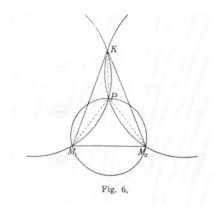

Figure 2: Alfred Weber, Calculation of site location according to transport distance, published in: Weber, Alfred. 1922. *Über den Standort der Industrien.* Tübingen: J.C.B. Mohr.

Fig. 6.

to a "system" of "central places."[4] His thesis was that population settlement follows identifiable patterns, which could be explained by the interaction of trade exchanges and geographic locations. In other words, people tend to settle and form communities at certain optimal distances from centers of trade, at locations that could be calculated based on the type of market, industry, and communication systems. The circles in the diagram defined the "range of a good" (Christaller 1966, 22), the distance a consumer travels to obtain it on the market. The places where many goods could be obtained were the most central, and the rest were distributed around them in descending order.

"We have [here]," wrote Christaller, "only a scheme, a rational scheme of general economic theory," arrived at deductively (1966, 70). Assuming standard economic conditions and a given population size, the circulation of goods could begin to be calculated; a system gradually evolved, plotting the correlation between geographical distance and "economic distance" (1966, 22). Diagrams conveyed the framework of Christaller's deductive method, and not only the results of its calculus. As the 1922 book *On the Location of Industries* by his mentor Alfred Weber made clear, the connecting link between economic theory and its spatial articulation was secured through the analytical procedures and graphic tools of geometry (fig. 2).[5] The ruler and compass maintained the measure set by the economic calculus as it unfolded across space, thus the graphic "schema" enacted the "ordering principle"

[*Ordnungsprinzip*] (Christaller 1968 [1933], 21) that governed the theory. In this, Christaller's diagrams were like the inaesthetic products Häring discerned in the Hochhausstadt drawings, mere "results of [calculating] order creation in terms of economics" (Häring 1926, 173).

Christaller's system demonstrated that the most uniform distribution of central places sustained an "economic harmony within [a] region" (Christaller 1966, 126). The same point was also highlighted by Hilberseimer. Christaller's diagrams, he wrote, showed "an even distribution of different kinds of settlement," which defined a "well-balanced regional economy" (Hilberseimer 1949, 98). The architect provided his own analogous set of drawings, demonstrating historical stages in the distribution of settlements within a theoretically isolated region—an island, "to simplify the problem and in order to be more graphic" (1949, 83). The last of these showed a potential city in the landscape, where an economic "balance between factory work and work on the soil" would make life "truly harmonious" (86–87) (figs. 3–5). The distributive logic of the diagram was then employed to develop three new urban planning systems, one of which, the central system, was most visually reminiscent of Christaller's diagram—but appearance was not really the point (fig. 6).

Christaller sought to combine the then mostly separate fields of economics and geography. Could an ordering principle, he asked, be determined to govern the location and distribution of cities? Geographers rejected such a possibility. They claimed that "nature [was] much too diverse to be ordered into a mathematically constructed scheme" (Christaller 1968 [1933], 12).[6] History and statistics, on the other hand, did seek regularities, but their work was descriptive. They determined "frequencies and averages" and highlighted a "certain order in diversity," but were not able to find the "principle of order" itself, the "logical proof [of] genuine laws" (Christaller 1966, 3). The lens of economics, however, revealed certain "law-like tendencies" [*Gesetzmäßigkeiten*] (1966, 3, translation emended; 1968 [1933], 15). These were not as "inexorable" as natural "laws" (1966, 3), nor did one arrive at them inductively, proceeding from a "descriptive statement [*Darstellung*] of reality," as one did with natural science (1966, 4; 1968 [1933], 15). They required, instead, a "purely deductive theory" (1966, 4).

Figure 3–5: Ludwig Hilberseimer, Theoretical population distribution on an island: past, present, and possible future, published in: Hilberseimer, Ludwig. 1949. *The New Regional Pattern: Industries and Gardens, Workshops and Farms.* Chicago: Theobald, 84–86.

49. POPULATION DISTRIBUTION. *One Hundred Years Ago.*

50. POPULATION DISTRIBUTION. *Today.*

51. POSSIBLE POPULATION DISTRIBUTION.

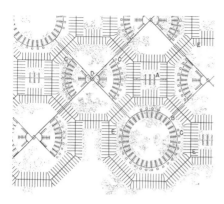

Figure 6: Ludwig Hilberseimer, Centric System. Octagonal units, which can be added to each other— Detail A. Commercial and cultural center. B. Commercial area. C. Industry. D. Air polluting industry. E. Small fams and gardens, published in: Hilberseimer, Ludwig. 1949. *The New Regional Pattern: Industries and Gardens, Workshops and Farms*. Chicago: Theobald, 164.

Crucially, one could not begin with a representation [*Darstellung*] because social reality was replete with any number of "personal, historical, and naturally conditioned 'resistances' [and] deviations" (Christaller 1966, 5, translation emended, quotation marks in the original). For law-like regularities to emerge, such factors had to be held in suspense. The last chapters of Christaller's book "verified" (1966, 5, 190) his system by means of mapping it across the current territory of Southern Germany (fig. 7). Here, the author wrote, the system could be found in general outline, since topography, administrative structures, traffic systems, and other factors modified its regularity. Such perturbations also deformed the geometric precision of the schema, which was understood to maintain only in an imaginative "let us suppose" (1968 [1933], 34) of the mathematical problem.

Christaller's understanding of a constitutive distance from reality necessary for a *gesetzmäßig* social analysis was based on the methodological writings of Max Weber.[7] For Weber, social science was a study of the causes of human actions and, in that respect, similar to the natural sciences, which search for the causes of natural phenomena. But, unlike in nature, "where causality was assessed empirically through observation, which revealed determinate regularities that could be formulated into laws", the causes of human behavior could never be fully known, subject as the latter was to "all manner of irrationalities"—emotions, mistakes, contradictory motives. The social scientist wandered through that morass of "qualitative[e] heterogene[ities]," "diversionary

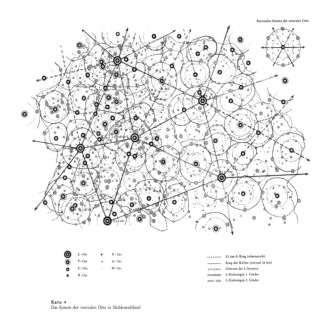

Figure 7: Walter Christaller, Population distribution in Southern Germany analyzed through the central place system, published in: Christaller, Walter. 1933. *Die zentralen Orte in Süddeutschland: Eine ökonomisch-geographische Untersuchung über die Gesetzmäßigkeit der Verbreitung und Entwicklung der Siedlungen mit städtischen Funktionen*. Jena: Fischer.

elements," and other "deviations," equipped only with the blunt instrument of rationality. His conclusions could only hope to reveal the course that "human action *would* follow *if* its purposive rationality were rigorously formulated, its execution undisturbed by error and affect" (Weber 2019, 81, 82, 85, emphases in the original).

The knowledge of society could only ever be an "as if," and could never be mistaken for "is."[8] The "uniformity" that social science discerned in human actions and translated into law-like concepts was a product of the "adequacy to meaning"[9] of such concepts, which, precisely "because of [their] degree of conceptual consistency [would] probably never assume [an] absolutely ideal pure form in reality" (Weber 2019, 97). So the imaginative rational constructs of sociological knowledge were achieved by virtue of a necessarily unbreachable "distance from reality" (2019, 97). They were neither natural laws nor normative epistemological categories. In none of those ways were such concepts representations of the patterns that governed the flux of human life, but only meaningful approximations.

Christaller's gloss on Weber's ideas was quick but accurate. "We must," he wrote, "get used to seeing in such deductive considerations systems of questions with which one approaches reality, and not representations of reality itself" (1968 [1933], 16n3).[10] Economic geography had to begin not with "a description of reality," but instead with a deductive theory that was "valid completely independently of what we may view as concrete reality, but only by virtue of its logic and 'adequacy to meaning'" (Christaller 1966, 4, translation emended; 1968 [1933], 16, quotation marks in the original). Like Weber's "ideal types," Christaller's "ordering principles" did not seek to represent reality, but merely attempted to *make sense* of it. In other words, they were hypotheses about the correspondence between space and political economy, based on standard economic assumptions.

For Hilberseimer, too, regularities in the "distribution of land and goods" (1949, 25) established causal relationships between the "economic structure" and the "settlement structure" (1944, 34), which could be traced through historical time. In comparison with the "theoretical scheme," reality presented a "complex appearance" (Christaller 1966, 112), full of "deviations" (Hilberseimer 1944, 22; Christaller 1966, 112) caused by a multitude of heterogeneous "influences" (1944, 22): "social, spiritual, and economic forces" for Hilberseimer (1944, 19); for Christaller, "geographical [...], historical, political, ethnic, and personal factors" (1966, 112). Like Christaller, Hilberseimer would sometimes graphically demonstrate the necessary distance between a schematic proposal and its potential built form by means of a topological distortion. For example, the diagram from *Entfaltung einer Planungsidee* (see "Visuals", p. 299, fig. 46) is illustrating adaptation to the natural topography of site, but neither is it a site plan, nor does Hilberseimer have a concrete site in mind. The schema communicates adaptation to "deviations" as a basic principle, rather than any concrete case. In *Großstadtarchitektur*, the architect described his Hochhausstadt drawings as "experiments in theoretical demonstration" intended to "develop, in the abstract, the fundamental principles of urban planning," thus helping the metropolis "discover the law-like tendency [*Gesetzmäßigkeit*] proper to it" (Hilberseimer 1927b, 51, 45; Hilberseimer 2012, 112, 90, translation emended). He would often repeat the assertion from the

1920s forward. In *The New City* (1944, 128), he declared his proposals to be "abstractions," which "must remain in the realm of theory, [because] absolute cities do not exist." And looking back on his life's work in the 1960s, he called it a "principle-based theory" (Hilberseimer ca. 1963, 74). "[R]eality," he wrote, "will always tend to modify our abstract ideas. City planning is not an abstract task" (ca. 1963, 28).

In the early decades of the twentieth century, both Hilberseimer and Christaller belonged to an intellectual milieu preoccupied with the relationship between knowledge and reality, which circumscribed the potential of conceptual solutions to societal problems. Its leading lights were the social scientists of the Verein für Sozialpolitik (Association for Social Policy), founded in 1871, whose members included Christaller's economics mentor Alfred Weber and his brother Max, Werner Sombart, Georg Simmel, and others. The association had close ties to the Deutscher Werkbund, established in 1907 to promote the quality of German industrial products, a group that numbered in its membership practically all the prominent architects and planners of the time. Frederic Schwartz has demonstrated that the animating debates of the Werkbund circle before World War I shared an assumption, rooted in Romantic idealism, that the apparent plurality of societal phenomena concealed a movement of unifying "formal laws" of Spirit or Will (Schwartz 1997). Werkbund designers sought to arrest the proliferation of eclectic styles in consumer goods on the speculative market through *Typisierung*, the use of models or types as bases for standardization. The "abstract regularity" [*Gesetzmäßigkeit*] of such models, according to Wilhelm Worringer (1908), would serve as a spiritual-aesthetic counter to the anomic fragmentation and alienating abstraction of modern life (Schwartz 1997, 67, translation emended). The rift between subject and object brought about by the wrong "capitalist" kind of mechanized reproduction would be healed through the right "spiritual" kind of reproduction.

We commonly accept that the culture of modern architecture in the 1920s was shaped by the terms of those prewar debates, and it can certainly be said that Hilberseimer's search for ordering principles was in part rooted in the representational dialectics of *Typisierung*.[11] However, the interwar period also brought with it new concerns. Writing in 1939, architect and Werkbund founding member Fritz Schumacher recast the organization's prewar goal of total design that proceeded "from the sofa cushion to city planning" in a new retrospective light. The "struggle for our own artistic expression" in the time of "eclectic perplexity" at the start of the century, he wrote, focused at first on the individual object of use, moving from that to the interior, then the building, and finally, "the street, the square, the settlement" (Schumacher 1951, 8–9). But "today's generation," he concluded, had reversed that teleology in its new call: "to arrive at the sofa cushion, in God's name, begin with city planning!" This more "conscious grasp of the importance of city planning" (1951, 9) had displaced the earlier concern with the object of production.

As the new paradigm in which design problems were cast, planning addressed itself to different kinds of mass phenomena. The severing of intimate links between product and producer, subject and object, in the mass production of artifacts was no longer at issue. Rather, urban concentration, the rapid growth in the "accumulation of people," was now diagnosed to be the paramount social problem caused by industrial production. The urban masses had diverse needs, such as those for "work, recreation, education, and housing," which called for different "organizational facilities." The new design tasks thus had to do with organizing those "elements of daily necessity" in urban space (Schumacher 1951, 9). Likewise, for example, in the writings of the architect and planner Martin Mächler, which had an important influence on Hilberseimer, the metropolis was an "organism" consisting of different "elements." The planner sought to discover the "ordering principle" [*Ordnungsprinzip*] that organized relationships among those parts (Mächler 1921, 185). The city, echoed Hilberseimer, was "an all-encompassing economic system, […] a collective organism" (Hilberseimer 2012, 84, translation emended). The region, likewise, had to be conceived as "an organic entity, an organism in which the whole [was] related to the parts, as the parts [were] related to the whole" (Hilberseimer 1949, 89).

The conceptualization of the city as organism was commonplace in the interwar discourse of planning, and it shifted attention away from the subject-object dialectic with which the Werkbund had attempted to subdue the proliferation of eclectic differences in mass production under one denominator.[12] In the organism, uniformity was impossible because the whole was subdivided from the start. Urban mass phenomena confronted the planner with problems of organized complexity, in confrontation with which the proper method was not representation but distribution, the ordering of parts within a whole. "Settling," wrote Mächler (1921, 183), "means grouping within a community formation according to [diverse] economic, social, hygienic, technical, and aesthetic points of view." "The essential task of city planning," echoed Hilberseimer (1944, 56), was "the proper placing and the organic ordering of the various elements of the city."

For Schumacher (1951, 9), planning was a problem of "social architecture," rather than "representational architecture." This meant, concretely, that the distributive tasks of planning called for the application of social scientific techniques. But the "sociological condition with which the planner must reckon," Schumacher explained elsewhere, did not "reveal itself in an immediately comprehensible form" to the eyes (Schumacher 1931, 3). While the ultimate ends of the planner's work were made evident in the urban fabric, the mass phenomena his work addressed were rather statistical entities such as population, trade, and traffic figures. The relationship between numbers and physical spaces was difficult to grasp. Statistical diagrams "ma[de] visible the currents of force and the functions of the invisible inner organs" of the city, thus making them more accessible to comprehension (Schumacher 1931, 4). Hilberseimer explained his diagrammatic drawings similarly. "Diagrams," he wrote, "have a clarifying character; they express underlying ideas abstractly. [T]hey are easy to comprehend, and they always show most directly the relation of the various parts of the city" (Hilberseimer n.d., 27).

Statistical graphics were ubiquitous in planning in the early decades of the twentieth century. I have begun to argue elsewhere that they were an important visual and conceptual source for the schematic diagrams created by some German planners to present their proposals (see Vallye 2020; and Kamleithner 2020, 63–114). The abstraction of the statistical diagram was not conceived to represent the essential properties of physical space but rather to demonstrate social relationships that, like population density, were both quantitative and distributive. When mapped out across physical territory, statistical diagrams (cartograms) were understood to operate by means of an elimination of specificity, a kind of smoothing that necessarily made them inadequate as representations of actual space. In the words of a statistician writing in 1911, while "the geographic map records all the individual settlements down to the hamlets and individual farms and makes the uninhabited areas appear as such; the statistical map, on the other hand, establishes the average population density per 1 square km […] and scatters the inhabitants over the entire area in question" (Klose 1911, 238). The cartogram dealt in statistical averages, not actual population numbers on the ground. Where the geographical map was an abstracted and codified representation of physical territory, the cartogram was a relational diagram valid only for the purpose of comparative analysis.

Schumacher (1931, 4) believed that statistics set the "basis for the type, scope, and timing of the problems to be dealt with," and were a comparative measure against which to check the design of urban plans. But between the plan, conceived as a distribution of social relationships across physical territory, and its execution in built form interceded a categorically different process. The plan, as Schumacher (1951, 2) defined it, was "the graphically formulated instruction for the basic outlines according to which people other than the author of the plan [were] to build something at a usually undetermined point in the future." Therefore, its design required an "anticipatory imagination," an ability to envision a range of potential outcomes of the plan's openings and constraints, the way it "h[eld] possibilities at decisive points, [which should not be] too narrow" (1951, 32). The schematic abstraction of the plan, like that of the statistical diagram, was not seen to represent either existing or future reality reduced to its essential features, but to convey the plan's status as a guideline or tool against which to measure a reality understood to be essentially irreducible. Social science prescribed an unbreachable distance between its theoretical projects of meaning-making and the empirical social world, understood to be thick with contingencies, irregularities, heterogeneities—the recalcitrant stuff of life. Planning, likewise, assumed that a critical distance would intervene between the design and its realization that left any prescriptive intention destabilized.

From the beginning, the question of expression or representation—the way in which a work mediates its world—has continued to fascinate Hilberseimer's reception. An architect who, at least in the first half of his life, thought deeply about art and aesthetics invites such inquiry. But, starting already in the later 1920s, Hilberseimer also viewed himself as a planner.[13] In the context of planning, conceived in those years to be an applied science in dialogue with related disciplines of social knowledge, the problem of mediation took on a different bent. No longer addressed to the task of conveying reality but rather the challenge of intervening within it, the distance imposed by theoretical knowledge was a deferral of agency. The agency of planning knowledge was deferred to an empirical social space foreclosed in advance to attempts at direct, or immediate, translation of expert visions, a space thick with resistances and frictions and thus not subject to unilateral solutions, because it was ultimately, to put it concretely, democratically governed. Hilberseimer's diagrammatic images should be placed within the range of visual tools developed in the context of such forms of social knowledge.

Notes

1   Unless otherwise noted, all translations are my own.

2   Hilberseimer not only read Wedepohl's review but was miffed enough to write a letter to the editor, primarily rebutting some unsubstantiated accusations of plagiarism. See *Der Städtebau* 1928.

3   For Pommer (1988, 17) the designs were stand-ins for "the horrors of modern housing and city planning." On the humanist critique of Hilberseimer, see Fabricius 2013. See also Hays 1992.

4   Christaller 1968 (1933); Christaller 1966.

5   See Alfred Weber 1922. On diagrammatic modeling in Weber and Christaller, see, for example, Chao 2018.

6   Translation emended. In Christaller 1968 (1933): "die Natur sei viel zu mannigfaltig, als daß sie sich in ein auf Grund von konstruierten Figuren gewonnenes Schema einordnen ließe" (12); in Christaller 1966: "because nature is so diverse, one should refrain from trying to order it into a scheme easily constructed on the basis of statistical figures" (2).

7   Christaller cites Max Weber (1922). See Christaller 1968 (1933), 16n3; and 1966, 9n20 (translation incomplete).

8   Weber 2019, 92. On the Weberian methodology of "understanding," see for example, Fred R. Dallmayr and Thomas A. McCarthy, *Understanding and Social Inquiry* (Notre Dame: University of Notre Dame Press, 1977).

9   Tribe translates the concept as "meaningful adequacy," in Weber 2019, 97. Following earlier translations of Weber, Baskin suggests "sense of adequacy," "adequacy on the level of meaning," or "satisfying level of knowledge," in Christaller 1966, 4.

10 This passage is missing from Christaller 1966.

11 Richard Anderson has proposed that the overarching concern of *Großstadtarchitektur* was the search for formal principles as a counter to the social and aesthetic "chaos" defining the urban products of speculative capital. See Anderson 2012. Hilberseimer's youthful immersion in popular philosophies of Romantic anti-capitalism points to similar preoccupations. See also the chapter by Scott Colman in the present volume p. 194–207.

12 On the organismic metaphor in German city planning from the mid-1800s through the early decades of the twentieth century, see Kamleithner 2020, 141–44 and 277–79.

13 Wedepohl's critique was possibly so irksome, and eventually memorable, for Hilberseimer precisely because of its discursive positioning, published in a planning journal and holding the author to task for not being up-to-date on contemporary planning debates, mainly around decentralization.

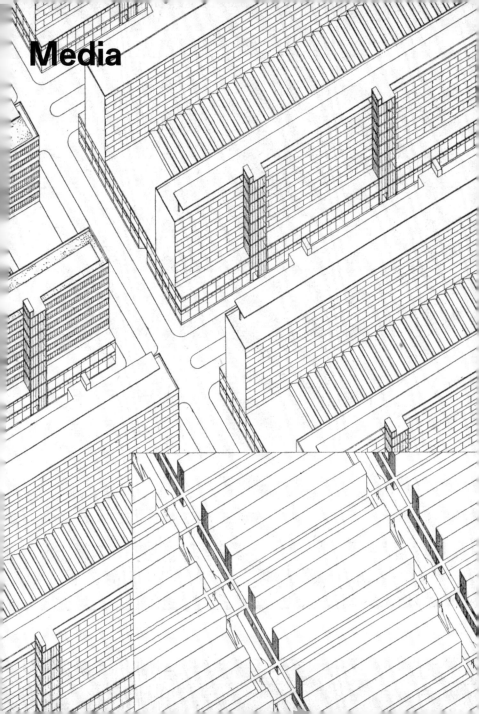

Media

Hilberseimer and Creative Indifference

Scott Colman

When Ludwig Hilberseimer's activity is categorically reduced to a particular discipline or the geographical and temporal fissures in his career are
emphasized, we fail to appreciate the breadth of his activity, his conception
of architecture, and his most important contribution to an understanding
of the city. Hilberseimer saw his activity—as an art critic, theorist, architect,
educator, designer, and planner—as cultural work, and the built environment, like all manifestations of culture, as the materialization of a spiritual
worldview. This is an understanding that our own era, in its preoccupation with method, history, specialization, and instrumentality, has almost
entirely forgotten, although very few have ever taken this profound idea
seriously. It was precisely a hegemonic, spiritless, myopically materialist *un-
culture* that Hilberseimer rejected, from the time of his very first published
writings until his laments about the course of contemporary architecture in
his later years.[1]

Although Hilberseimer was trained as an architect and was developing his
thinking on architecture and the city before World War I, architecture did
not become the predominant focus of his publications until 1922. His career
as a writer begins as a cultural critic. Hilberseimer formulates his commitment to cultural work through his involvement with the varying trajectories
of avant-garde artists and intellectuals orbiting the journal *Der Einzige* (The
Individual, The Only One, or The Singularity[2]) (fig. 1). The location for Hilberseimer's first published writings, *Der Einzige* was edited by the individ-
ualist-anarchist Anselm Ruest and the satirist Mynona, pseudonyms for the
philosophers Ernst Samuel (1878–1943) and Salomo Friedlaender (1871–1946),
the ideas of whom are now recognized as central to Expressionist and intrinsic to Dadaist thought in Berlin (see Taylor 1990; Bergius 1989; and Bergius
2000). Hilberseimer's theory of culture synthesizes Ruest and Friedlaender's
philosophy with the latest ideas in art history, recent avant-garde artistic

Figure 1: Cover of: *Der Einzige*. 1919, 1, 1 (January 19), 1919

practice, theories about the visual perception of art, and an appreciation for the artistic expression of non-European worldviews.

Hilberseimer's earliest writings on the city and systematically conceived urban designs are drafted in parallel with his early cultural criticism. In the first drafts of *Großstadtarchitektur* (*Metropolis-Architecture*), circa 1919, which Hilberseimer coauthored with the lawyer, art critic, collector, and fellow contributor to *Der Einzige*, Udo Rukser (1892–1971)—and then independently developed and published as a book (Hilberseimer 1927b)—Hilberseimer and Rukser argue "metropolis-architecture" is a new genre of art.[3] They understand the metropolis as a new medium in the same way Dadaist artists such as Raoul Hausmann, Hannah Höch, and Hans Richter, who were also under the influence of Friedlaender, saw new technologies, like the phonograph, the illustrated press, and film, as new means of art, and the architect Ludwig Mies van der Rohe—who would also become a member of the Friedlaender circle and was probably influenced by Hilberseimer's ideas—would soon explore the potentials of new construction technologies and building programs for a new kind of architecture.

The first issue of *Der Einzige*, edited by Ruest, and its literary supplement, edited by Mynona, appeared on Sunday, January 19, 1919. The Paris Peace Conference had begun the previous day and Berliners were going to the polls to elect representatives to a national assembly who would write the democratic constitution establishing the Weimar Republic. In his inaugural editorial, "Die letzte Revolution" (The Final Revolution), Ruest (1919b) rails against the reduction of humanity to the state, be it monarchic, communist, or democratic. He questions the wisdom of reflexively committing to a political order from which one could not choose to withdraw. And he implies the rush to democracy is yet another manifestation of the centuries-long, repeatedly tragic desire for German unity. The journal's epigraph and title were drawn from *Der Einzige und sein Eigentum* (*The Ego and His Own*), a book published by the anarchist philosopher Max Stirner in the ferment of the revolutions that engulfed Europe in 1848 (Stirner 1845). Ruest was devoted to Stirner's ideas. Friedlaender and many of the contributors to the journal were far less committed. Nevertheless, the frequent appeals to Stirner in *Der Einzige*, as well as to Friedrich Nietzsche, whose philosophy Ruest considered closely aligned with Stirner's thought, allowed Ruest to attract contributors who shared an abiding resistance to reification and the sense that modern skepticism had undermined the vitality and value of culture.

Such was the context for the thirty-three-year-old Hilberseimer's first published essay, "Schöpfung und Entwicklung" (Creation and Development), printed directly following Ruest's inaugural editorial. Constituting his foundational statement on art and culture, it's possible the five essays Hilberseimer published in *Der Einzige* were conceived together. The first three—"Schöpfung und Entwicklung," "Umwertung in der Kunst" (Revaluation in Art), and "Form und Individuum" (Form and Individual)—surely were, as they were published in consecutive issues over the span of just three weeks. "Der

Naturalismus und das Primitive in der Kunst" (Naturalism and the Primitive in Art) and "Kunst und Wissen" (Art and Knowledge) followed in March.[4] At the same time, Rukser, who wrote criticism of literature, music, and the visual arts in the first years after the war, published three essays (Rukser 1919a, 1919b, and 1919c) in the journal that also evidence a commitment to Ruest and Friedlaender's ideas.

Written in a context that he describes as the "collapse of the European world" and hopes is the dawn of international community, Hilberseimer's essays in *Der Einzige* assert the fundamental equality of global and historic cultures (Hilberseimer 1919c). Europeans had perpetuated an erroneous understanding of culture, Hilberseimer scolds. Valuing development, which they equate with technical advancement, they dismiss the artworks of non-European societies as "primitive." Yet, despite this desire for technological achievement, they hold up ancient Greece and Rome as the height of civilization and imitate the artworks of these historical cultures in a self-conscious effort to attain beauty. They forget that the art they celebrate had its origin in primal creativity. They make art into an analytical method by praising archaeological felicity and a technique by favoring naturalistic imitation. Europeans mistake the possession of knowledge and skill for culture because they confuse a capacity to record and manipulate the physical world for a unified spiritual understanding of nature and creation. "The essential is not shown in the extremely sophisticated formations of the so-called high cultures," Hilberseimer writes in the second of his *Der Einzige* essays; "it shows itself in the primitive formations that still arose in complete unselfconsciousness. Where there was nothing but idea and material. Still no models. And, therefore, still no inhibitions" (Hilberseimer 1919e, 4).[5]

Hilberseimer argues that art is the material expression of a spiritual idea, for a people, for humanity, and for eternity. All art, despite its great diversity, is born of a universal capacity for creativity, even as the works of different times and places are each independent and original. Creativity is not born of detached reflection on reality but from the compulsion to invest it with meaning. Art expresses understanding in the face of chaotic existence, embodying, in this way, the organizing metaphysics of a people. Creative form is the expression of an idea, a statement of self-conception, and therefore a means of self-realization. All cultures rise and decline in a struggle between will and material. Their summits—the high points of style—are constituted by the greatest correspondence between meaning and form; but their decay, the waning of culture, comes as form, the virtuosity to produce it is used unconditionally, and the significance of culture is questioned, even lost. Architecture, as an abstract art and the product of society as a whole, is the clearest indication of a society's metaphysical strength or weakness.

The cultures Europeans call "primitive" were commonly societies with a unified worldview like those that once existed in Europe but were gradually undermined by the skepticism that, seeded in ancient Greece, took root in the Renaissance. The secularization that came with the growth of humanist doubt progressively liberated creation from the bonds of the church but drove a wedge between the conception of the arts and the inquisition of the sciences. Creativity was no longer whole—analytical and synthetic faculties were separated—nor guided by a common metaphysics. Moreover, in the interests of the church and the state, the Renaissance fascination with Antiquity and the self-conscious idealism of Enlightenment Romanticism were used to fetter humanist liberties with a classicizing and naturalistic ideology. Art and science were bound into the service of material despotism. The circulating forms of aesthetic and empirical knowledge were drained of spiritual significance as the indigenous value of culture and the liberal coinages of humanism were replaced by the paper promises of a stultifying capitalist civilization.

Hilberseimer cast his broad-ranging and synthetic worldview against the myopic and analytic intellectualism of modern European civilization in which accidental impressions rather than essential expressions were the expected product of art and science. The disciplined analysis and imitation of historical and natural fragments, rather than a synthetic conception of the whole, had become celebrated intellectual activity. Creativity—which gives validity to work—was questioned if it departed from expectations and accepted knowledge. Distributed through the mechanisms of state education, learning had become standardized, formulaic, and rote, producing not a vital community but a deadened mass indignantly convinced of its superiority. Rather than cultivate imagination and curiosity, modern civilization rewards commodified beauty and specialized training; it replaces collective feeling with the stability of convention, the comfort of expectations, and the luxury of convenience. Civilization takes its own laws and its own representations as natural, forgets that art and science are symbolizations, and blinds itself in superficial devotion to an assumed reality.

When a vital culture looks to the constitution of reality to create lawful works of art and science, Hilberseimer believes it adapts its imagination and curiosity to the world, humanizing what can never be fully grasped by investing material reality with transcendental import. Creativity, the primal capacity for expression, is always innately present, to be exercised at any moment. The great surveys of non-European culture that emerged in the late nineteenth and early twentieth centuries did not just bring to view the insights of societies hitherto overlooked or unseen by Europeans, they contributed to the revival of the creative intuition that could give rise to a post-European future. Hilberseimer sought the recreation of community and the reaffirmation of creativity. Freed of the stultifying worldview of modern European civilization, Hilberseimer believed a renewed spiritual investment in the material world would inaugurate a new kind of culture, a new aesthetics, and a new rationality: a spiritual materialism that would "absorb and annihilate capitalism" (Hilberseimer 1919d, 5) and invest modern knowledge and technical capacity with creative significance.

Through the content of his editorials and the publication of Hilberseimer's essays on art directly following his own more philosophical statements, Ruest enjoined Hilberseimer's effort to liberate creation from the restraints of modern materialism with his own program of individualist anarchism. Hilberseimer's idea of a renewed spiritual materialism was at the core of Ruest's philosophy. In *Max Stirner: Leben, Weltanschauung, Vermächtnis* (Max Stirner: Life, Worldview, Legacy), Ruest (1906) presents Stirner's call for self-realization as the crucial inflection point in nineteenth-century German thought between a naturalistic and materialist rejection of idealism and Nietzsche's affirmative assertion of human will as a vitalist form of practical reason.

Friedlaender's philosophy, consistent with this commitment to self-realization and spiritual materialism, beginning with his interpretation and critical development of Nietzsche's philosophy, and reaffirmed by his conversion to the neo-Kantian theories of Ernst Marcus in 1918, elaborates the means by which this cultural work could be undertaken (see Friedlaender 1911; Friedlaender 1919). Friedlaender elaborates the conjunction of material and spirit as what he calls, following Nietzsche, an "artistic science" ("künstlerischen Wissenschaft," Friedlaender 1911, 28)—a praxis Friedlaender describes in the title of his 1918 book as "creative indifference" (fig. 2). By *indifference*, Friedlaender means not only what the word usually conveys in English ("no particular interest"; "neither good nor bad") but also, following Romantic philosophy, "nondifference" (that is, in-difference), "identity," or "oneness" (Stevenson and Waite 2011, 723; Fortey et al. 2006, 268). He uses the term to emphasize the singularity of existence (the generative substance) that lies behind all differences, including our own vital indifference from—our oneness with—the universe (see Schelling 2006 [1834], esp. 44, 68, and 168–69n95). Insofar as we are indifferent from nature, Friedlaender argues, short-circuiting Kantian skepticism, we have a vital and immediate relationship to the cosmos. If we can overcome our *Bildung*, the learned formalizations that prejudice our worldview by imprinting themselves upon us and structuring us from within, we can become in-different: both integrally singular and open to—which is to say undivided from—the world. Free of established preconceptions, we possess the sovereign capacity to creatively form and reform, constitute and reconstitute ourselves in correspondence with experience. By cultivating our aesthetic capacity (our powers of sensorial observation and discrimination), our power of reason (our capacity to organize sensations into a logical worldview), and our artistic means of material expression, Friedlaender argues we extend our comprehension of the universe and thus extend our imagination in creative correspondence with existence. Through the development of our spiritual insight into the universe—which is indistinguishable, in Friedlaender's philosophy, from both our aesthetic experience and scientific understanding of nature—we constructively cultivate our ability to willfully materialize our creative conceptions.

S.FRIEDLÆNDER
SCHÖPFERISCHE
INDIFFERENZ

Looking to the natural philosophy and aesthetic theory of Johann Wolfgang von Goethe, Friedlaender celebrates Goethe's patient consideration of phenomena, uncorrupted by theoretical preconceptions, and his assertion that the organic world (including human nature) continuously and vitally recreates itself through a process of polar division and synthesis (Friedlaender 1911, 125; see also 93, 131; and Friedlaender 1907). Based on Goethe's observations on the metamorphosis of organisms, Friedlaender advances a strategy of extreme polarization and equilibration, through which we empirically expand the limits of our aesthetic perception by organizing our sensory experience according to polar extremes. By rationalizing these polar extremes as equivalent opposites, we mathematically invest the chaos of nature with lawful coherence. Just as certain montages of Dada, such as Hannah Höch's *Schnitt mit dem Küchenmesser Dada durch die letzte Weimarer Bierbauch-Kulturepoche Deutschlands* (Cut with the Dada Kitchen Knife through the last Weimar Beer-Belly-Cultural Epoch of Germany, 1919), which includes references to Friedlaender (fig. 3), reorganize the visual experience of the city into polarized coordinates, Hilberseimer and Rukser apply the strategy of equilibrated

Figure 3: Hannah Höch, *Schnitt mit dem Küchen-messer durch die letzte Weimarer Bierbauchkul-turepoche Deutschlands* (Cut with the Dada Kitchen Knife through the last Weimar Beer-Belly-Cultural Epoch of Germany), collage, 1919

polarization to their consideration of metropolis-architecture. Hilberseimer and Rukser understand the typological functions of the metropolis as proportional expressions of elemental formal values—polar gradients of density, height, complexity, compactness, openness, transparency, color, brightness, saliency, scale, rhythm, meter, pattern—that are conditioned by the given socioeconomic, technological, and environmental context. As his oeuvre evolves, Hilberseimer expands these elemental dimensions of metropolis-architecture, calibrating his creations in greater extent and increasing refinement with nature and human nature, which comes to include not only the technological, sociological, psychological, and economic conditions of society but also, in a work such as his 1951 Plan of Chicago (see "Visuals", p. 308, fig. 59), perhaps his most comprehensive urban design, the regional landscape, the extant pattern of settlement, and inherited architectural fabric. As is clear from his own reflections, Hilberseimer's European and American periods do not represent distinct approaches but the progressive expansion and intensification of his creative indifference (Hilberseimer 1963).

Hilberseimer believed, following Friedlaender's philosophy, that *Stadtbaukunst* [city building art], like all artistic work, is born of a synoptic and synthetic conception that demands the greatest possible breadth of (artistic) vision and the deepest (scientific) insight into the present material and spiritual conditions of existence. "So long as the religiosity of the creator accords with that of their era, there can be no talk of dependence," he writes in "Form and Individual." "Through the harmony of the metaphysical every inhibition is eliminated as the works of all genuine primitives show. Dualism only occurs, then, when the creative succumbs to skepticism, when their world image sustains a rupture" (Hilberseimer 1919b, 7). Focusing solely on specific aspects or problems of settlement, be they architectural, economic, technological, geographic, climatological, or some such other would forsake the singularity of existence and betray the spiritual—at once artistic, scientific, and philosophical—ambition of investing our vital being with a coherent, integral worldview.

Like both Ruest and Friedlaender, Hilberseimer understood this spiritual activity as a willful act of reason—intentional, sober, and objective. Unlike Ruest, however, Hilberseimer shared the younger generation's sense of imminent sociopolitical change. Rather than waiting for the cultural process of individual self-realization to unfold—and thus accept that contemporary society should be regulated by an inherited, grotesquely materialist, bourgeois-capitalist culture in the interim—Hilberseimer sought to actively and constructively rebalance the extant values of metropolis-architecture for an egalitarian society. He and Rukser, like the other Dadaist artists under the influence of Friedlaender, sought to invest the mechanical with the metaphysical. Hilberseimer and Rukser theorize an urban environment with an integral yet expressive order. In contrast to the chaotic appearance and polluted atmosphere of the extant metropolis, Hilberseimer produces architectural and urban designs with an immediately graspable—which is to say, primitive—visual saliency (see "Visuals", p. 279, fig. 11).

Hilberseimer and Rukser shared with other associates of the *Der Einzige* circle, such as Hausmann, a commitment to a socialist interpretation of history and the principle of self-realization. As the title of the journal made clear, its contributors believed individual self-realization was the basis of all knowledge and culture. Nothing resonated more with this group than the critique of German liberalism: the promise of freedom had been so corrupted over the course of the nineteenth century it had ultimately led millions to their deaths. Liberalism had become a form of illiberalism as the aristocracy and a compliant bourgeoisie shaped all aspects of society in their interests (Taylor 1990, 6–7). Stirner's philosophy had attacked this pseudo-liberalism, seeking to overcome the impediments he felt European societies had placed in the way of self-realization. Ruest's book on Stirner—following the resurrection of Stirner's thought by the Scottish-German anarchist John Henry Mackay (1898) and the explosion of interest in Nietzsche in the 1890s—contributed to the intermingling of Stirner and Nietzsche's philosophy in a climate in which progressive German intellectuals were increasingly expressing muted dissatisfaction with Wilhelmine society. Ruest's involvement in the prewar literary avant-garde (with Kurt Hiller, Ruest assisted Franz Pfemfert in establishing the literary and political journal *Die Aktion* in 1911) contributed to the prominence of Stirner's ideas among German Expressionists. *Der Einzige*, which took up the graphic format of *Die Aktion*, began where the prewar avant-garde left off (Geerken 1980, 1:344; Exner, 177–78). It attacks—as do the Berlin Dadaists elsewhere and Hilberseimer in his early writings—the militarism, authoritarianism, nationalism, materialism, cronyism, historicism, positivism, and paternalism of Wilhelmine society. Following Nietzsche, the journal, and especially Hilberseimer, advocates for vitalist (aesthetic) expression to combat the naturalistic determinism and bourgeois cultural and sociopolitical norms that the editors felt were pervasive in German society. But intervening events had radically changed the meaning and reception of Expressionist politics. What had been a bold albeit necessarily measured, rebellion against an oppressive regime found itself confronted with an apparently open prospect, even as the vision of communism and the felt imperative to determine the contours of a future, more democratic, society were compelling action. Within the limited scope of Stirner's or Nietzsche's interpretations, one could shift emphasis from critique to prescription. But the vocation of interpreting nineteenth-century philosophy and prevailing practices of cultural critique, no matter how reactionary that thought might have been, were rendered solipsistic by recent events. Sociopolitical flux invested intellectual and artistic activity with a newfound urgency. The evident necessity for collective action forced many Expressionists, hitherto engaged in cultural commentary or a circumscribed aesthetic rebellion, to reconsider their political postures. The reconciliation of theory and practice, of the individual and the collective, of culture and politics, and of the intellectual and society were no longer theoretical ambitions but pressing problems.[6]

Even though it persisted for a number of years, *Der Einzige* stumbled within months of its founding, partly from the financial pressures of postwar inflation, but also because of growing discord between the editors and conflicts between Ruest and his contributors (Geerken 1980, 1:345; Exner 1996, 182).[7] It is probably no accident that when Hausmann, who also wrote for *Der Einzige*, fell out with Ruest, after Ruest overzealously edited Hausmann's work to make it appear more supportive of his own strictly individualist political position, Hilberseimer and Rukser also ceased writing for the journal (see Hausmann 1919). Although Ruest believed communism was an impediment to self-realization, Hilberseimer and Rukser, like Hausmann (Panarchos 1919), saw the communist equalization of society as a necessary step toward anarchist socialism.[8] By expressing the indifferent, common denominators of existence, communism had the potential to unify society, establishing mutual self-realization and individual diversity as a common law in the same way that the organs of a body differentiate themselves in reciprocity with the life of the organism as a whole. In their drafts for *Großstadtarchitektur* (see "Visuals", p. 281, fig. 15) at this time, Hilberseimer and Rukser identify and rationalize the common denominators of metropolis-architecture as the basic elements through which individual buildings would realize their own integrity in mutual relationship with the city as a whole, thus creating the kind of spiritual community that Friedlaender in his 1913 essay, "Das Individuum und die soziale Frage" (The Individual and the Social Question), called a "differentiated individual" (Friedlaender 1913).

Just as Friedlaender, following Goethe, understood natural philosophy as an animating spiritual activity that through the expansion of our aesthetic capacities allows us to invest phenomenal appearance with vital coherence, Hilberseimer understood cultural work as an artistic science. By indifferently observing given existence, such as the phenomena of the capitalist metropolis, and creatively transforming it—overcoming extant urban chaos by investing the metropolis with lawful integrity—the cosmos, including the metropolis and its architecture, gains spiritual significance. Hilberseimer understood the potential realization of such a spiritual materialism—the imaginative (re)calibration of human nature with nature as a whole—as the dawn of a new, potentially international, culture and community, correspondent with the world-integrating scale of modern technics and society, equivalent to the coherent worldviews of historical and existing non-European cultures. The communal individualism of a creatively indifferent metropolis-architecture would realize the liberal promise hitherto undermined by the decadent and possessive, naturalistic and materialistic, colonizing worldview of modern European civilization.[9]

Notes

1 See Hilberseimer 1964. On Hilberseimer's "cultural work" in the United States, see Colman 2006; and Colman 2014.

2 On *Der Einzige* see Pârvulescu 2006 and Pârvulescu 2018. Seeing a parallel between Ruest's and Friedlaender's ideas and poststructuralist philosophy, Pârvulescu translates the title of the journal as *The Singularity*.

3 Ludwig Hilberseimer and Udo Rukser's undated typescripts with handwritten notes and emendations are in the Karl Ludwig Hilberseimer Papers, Ryerson and Burnham Art and Architecture Archives, series 8, box 1.

4 Unless stated otherwise, the following summary of Hilberseimer's ideas is based on Hilberseimer 1919a, 1919b, 1919c, 1919d, and 1919e. All translations are the author's unless otherwise noted.

5 Although the concept of the "primitive" had an emancipatory sense after Jean-Jacques Rousseau, the idea gained currency with the racist worldview of colonization. While the adoption of the notion by progressive artists in the late nineteenth and early twentieth centuries was usually part of an effort to invert and undermine presumptions of European superiority, their effort perpetuated, albeit in a negative sense, an echo of the insidious charge of the term. By 1919 "the primitive" in avant-garde German art discourse signified creative artistic volition unrestricted by accreted formal prejudices, be that the non-European artworks that had influenced the last decades of avant-garde production, the art of children, or the artworks of what were taken to be originating periods of European history. For example, in *Kunstgeschichtliche Grundbegriffe* (*Principles of Art History*, 1915), the art historian Heinrich Wölfflin (1864–1945) refers to the Quattrocento as the "primitive" Italian renaissance, preceding its maturation into the "High Renaissance" at the turn of the fifteenth century. Wölfflin 1950, 234, also 151 and 185.

6 For a thorough explication of Expressionist politics and its embrace of Nietzsche's ideas, see Taylor 1990.

7 The twenty-eighth issue was published on November 1, 1919. Friedlaender left the journal by the end of the first year. Only eleven issues were published in the following six years.

8 For Ruest's concerns about communism, see Ruest's reply to Arthur Goldstein, "*Der* 'Einzige' *und Sozialismus*" published in Ruest 1919a; and Ruest 1919c.

9 This essay restates ideas in my forthcoming book, *Ludwig Hilberseimer: Reanimating the Metropolis* (London: Bloomsbury Visual Arts).

Elementary-Magical: Hilberseimer as Media Theorist

Lutz Robbers

> We are conditioned by conditions we condition. We, the created creators, shape tools that shape us. We live by our crafts and conditions. It is hard to look them in the face.

John Durham Peters (2015, 51)

Media Horror

Hilberseimer's urban visions trigger the feeling of horror. Over and over again, architectural critics have passed a clear and often violent judgment on the "horrors of modern housing and city planning" his images arouse, calling him the "gravedigger" of modern architecture (Pommer 1988, 17). Still today, the "eerie, uniform blocks" (Curtis 1996, 251) of his Hochhausstadt prompt visceral reactions that easily exceed the ordinary degree of scholarly passion. Usually, the sensation of horror, as the most mundane horror movies demonstrate, is generated by the shocking encounter with familiar things, creatures, spaces and visions that suddenly become unfamiliar: subjectless gazes, inert objects becoming animated, undead beings unexpectedly gaining agency and turning against their "masters," the uncanny lurking behind homely surfaces (Carroll 1987; Vidler 1992). In the case of Hilberseimer's abject cityscapes, it is rather the encounter with a *horror vacui*, with empty forms and spaces devoid of symbolic inscriptions, historical signification, and human presence that sends the shivers down the critic's spine. In the case of Hilberseimer, the urban uncanny takes the form of elementary abstraction (see "Visuals", p. 278–79, fig. 9–11).

Well-meaning scholarship's most common explanation is that Hilberseimer's metropolitan horror exposes what we usually sublimate as reified visions of urban utopia, namely the city as "economic form of capitalist imperialism"

(Hilberseimer 2012, 86). The viewer/inhabitant shudders because he or she recognizes the monstrous countenance of capitalism's ghosts. Just like horror films that provoke salutary encounters are repressed (the body, the other, history, the lifeworld), Hilberseimer's abstractions are experienced as "the most extreme economy of form, the most extreme primitiveness" (Hilberseimer 1914) that function as an antidote to the chaos of the capitalist metropolis.

Yet equating abstraction with the utmost reduction of form and renunciation of signification might miss the point Hilberseimer tried to make when drawing up his antihumanist *Großstadtarchitektur* visions during the 1920s. Both the images' original intentions, the discursive environment within which they evolved, and their persistent critical agency for questions of capitalist urban development need to be further explored. The argument I want to develop here is that Hilberseimer's images are intentionally ghastly because they fundamentally question regimes of representation and, as a corollary, conceptions of modern subjectivity as centered and empowered and of objects as what Bruno Latour calls "immutable mobiles" (Latour 1990, 26–35): entities that are readable, combinable, scalable, measurable, and moveable in space.

I want to suggest that by interrogating the status of his imagery from a media theoretical perspective, new avenues of thinking open up. By investigating his close association with various avant-garde currents converging in Berlin between the late 1910s and early 1920s, by charting his position amid networks of Dadaists, Constructivists, Neoplasticists, and Expressionists who in different ways actively incorporated new media technologies in their artistic works and theoretical reflections, I propose to approach Hilberseimer's written work, his drawings, and his photomontages not as representations but as media: less in the sense of highly persuasive vehicles for communicating information and more as apparatuses that determine the situation, "mediators" (Martin 2014) that govern what can be said, known, experienced, and, ultimately, designed.

A media philosophical perspective might help resolve the often-cited "peculiar conflict" (Davidovici 2017; Kilian 2002) that seems to pervade the work of Hilberseimer between, on the one hand, his preoccupation with speculative aesthetics culminating in his *Großstadtarchitektur* and, on the other hand, his penchant for objective urban planning solutions exemplified by *The New City* (1944). What the downright rejection of Hilberseimer (horror) has in common with the interpretation of his work as divided is that both approach his images as conventional representations of objects in urban spaces, adhering to specific conventions of architectural imagery. Both assume that these images can be read, drawn, scaled, communicated, and projected in order to be built. While Manfredo Tafuri advanced the discussion by crediting Hilberseimer for not approaching abstraction as a "purist" enterprise and for avoiding the "crisis of the object" by shifting the debate to questions of "organization" (Tafuri 1998, 22), he falls short of entering the media theoretical debates Hilberseimer actively engaged in.

Rather than abandoning the question of the object altogether, I propose to shift the attention to what Keller Easterling calls, the "medium of activities and latent potentials that those objects generate" (Easterling 2021, x). My argument here is that Hilberseimer displays an acute awareness of media theoretical questions that allows him to formulate a critique of capitalist urban development while avoiding the pitfalls of transcendental subjectivity, reifying objectivity and technocratic determinism. That way, he shifts the focus of designers from the creation of objects or the application of organizational models to "the interplay between things—active forms that enact change in urban spaces, larger territories, and even planetary atmospheres" (Easterling 2021, xi).

The argument developed here hence operates on two levels: first, by presenting historical evidence of his active engagement with discourses and practices of new image technologies, I want to show that Hilberseimer's horror evinces the premeditated encounter with the city as media. Second, his eerie visions touch upon modernism's awkward relation with the image. Following Jacques Rancière's interpretation of modernism as a "project of liberation from the image" (Rancière 2003, 29), which tried to eliminate images' mediating agency from its practices, I wish to show that Hilberseimer aspires—especially through his collaboration with artists working with the new medium of film—the opposite, namely an affirmation of their agency, responding to the desire for a "radical transformation of reality, of life into image [*Verbildlichung*]" (Hilberseimer 1922a, 741).

The evolution of Hilberseimer's thinking is closely intertwined with that of Ludwig Mies van der Rohe. They probably met in 1919 in connection with the exhibition *Unknown Architects* organized by the Arbeitsrat für Kunst, where the "architectural clarity" of both of their rejected submissions appeared to contradict, as Hilberseimer notes, the "romantic nature of the exhibition" (Hilberseimer 1967b, 30). From that moment on, their careers developed in parallel. As members of Novembergruppe, Werkbund and Zehnerring and as teachers at the Bauhaus and later at IIT, they consolidated their institutional influence. Perhaps more significant for understanding their shared understanding concerning architecture's relationship with technology and media was their affiliation with the so-called *G* group. The short-lived journal *G – Material zur elementaren Gestaltung* (1923–26) became the crystallization point around which a diverse group of Constructivists like Hans Richter and El Lissitzky, Dadaists such as Raoul Hausmann, Neo-Plasticists like Theo van Doesburg, as well as critics like Adolf Behne and an architect like Mies assembled (Richter 1967, 69; Graeff 1962). What held them together was the common denominator *elementare Gestaltung* (elementary form-creation), a vague terminology implying an enigmatic blend of Nietzschean and Bergsonian motives, neo-Kantian thought and technology-affirming materialism—all combined with an unambiguous affirmation of new technologies and media practices (Elder 2007).

In the past, architectural scholars have suggested an imbalanced relationship between Mies and Hilberseimer. While Mies has been given the role of the sophisticated modernist genius, Hilberseimer had to content himself with that of the one-dimensional and dogmatic constructivist. Yet, especially considering Hilberseimer's prolific activities as a writer from 1919 onward for journals such as *Sozialistische Monatshefte*, *Der Einzige*, or *Das Kunstblatt*, their relationship appears rather complementary: Hilberseimer plays the part of the articulate and erudite commentator of Mies's architecture—rectifying more than once potentially false readings of Mies's designs. Hilberseimer's informed insights in arts, technology, and politics helped contribute to the discursive basis needed for Mies's groundbreaking architectural idiom in the early 1920s.

For example, it was Hilberseimer who came to the rescue when Mies's design for the Alexanderplatz competition in 1928 was rejected by the jury for violating the competition brief. In contrast to the brief requiring all entries to conform to the demands of car traffic's movement and density, Mies proposed a rhythmic composition of seemingly autonomous solids. Hilberseimer, who had been intimately familiar with Mies's design as the isometric drawing of the Alexanderplatz project done by Hilberseimer attests (raising questions about Mies's sole authorship), fervently defends Mies's design of altogether eleven office buildings because the latter acted "according to architectural principles alone," demonstratively refusing to subordinate architecture to the primacy of purely functional infrastructure demands. His project shields architecture from being "raped by the traffic" (Hilberseimer 1929c, 39–40)—a conviction reminiscent of the unpublished notes from 1926, in which Mies rejects all functionalist precepts directed at the metropolis and the "brutal violence" with which traffic has affected the "organisms of our cities" (cited in Neumeyer 1986, 315).

A second parallel can be found in the particular ways both present their architectural imagery. In 1928, for example, both produce similar photomontages for projects located in Berlin. Both use aerial photographs of the city's dense urban fabric onto which charcoal or ink drawings are mounted, Mies for his Alexanderplatz design (fig. 1) and Hilberseimer for the Friedrichstadt project (see "Visuals", p. 282, fig. 17). Not only do they opt for and master the same montage techniques, they also disrupt the depicted space of architectural representation in a similar way: Mies upsets the perspectival space of both photograph and drawing with, in the bottom left corner, what seems like a clumsily pasted cutout of a typical Berlin city block. Due to the sharp and straight-lined division between the blackened fabric of the historical city and the radiant vacuity of Alexanderplatz, one gets the impression that Mies forgot to crop the insert properly (what he did in the other sections of the image where drawing and photograph meet). The clumsily pasted piece of urban fabric depicts the existing dense courtyard structures between Landsberger

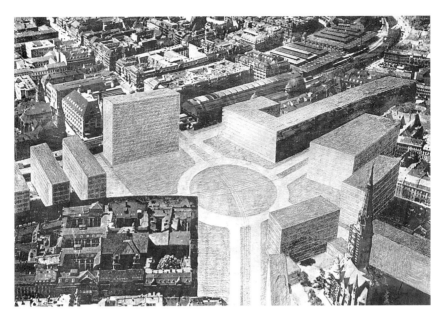

Figure 1: Ludwig Mies van der Rohe, Urban Design Proposal for Alexanderplatz, Berlin-Mitte, aerial perspective, 1929

Straße and Alexanderstraße, which Mies leaves untouched, except for the blunt cropping of the building front on Landsberger Straße facing north—a design decision that further emphasizes Mies's deliberate disregard of the historical context.

Hilberseimer makes a similar insert. In the right bottom corner of the isometric drawing of his Friedrichstraße project, we can discern a smaller drawing of his 1924 Hochhausstadt project. In a play of scale, the insert mimics the larger drawing, mirroring its representational regime (isometry) and point of view (oblique and aerial) and suggesting a causal lineage traversing time. At the same time, the autoreferential frame within the frame ironically works against the very idea of the frame. In numerous of his drawings—for example, his *Settlement Units Density Studies* (1943) with a field of L-shaped low-rise houses or his proposal for a uniform series of high-rise apartment blocks in Berlin-Haselhorst (1928)—Hilberseimer presents infinite series of objects intersecting with and spilling over the frame's delimitation. The viewer becomes conscious of the picture's material condition—like the frame—that determines what a picture shows, what kind of space it produces, and which role the spectator can play.

A mis-en-abime of representations is set in motion whose aim seems less the correct notation of actual projects and more a destabilization of visual regimes in place. As Hilberseimer repeatedly points out, these projects are "purely theoretical schema without any intention of realization" (Hilberseimer 2012, 125). The task of all art was no longer, as Hilberseimer already points in "Wille zur Architektur" (1923) "to make reproductions [*Abbilder*] but to produce entities [*Gebilde*]" (Hilberseimer 1923, 133)—implying a semantic shift with the word *Bild* (image), which reenacts the conceptual shift from what an image shows to what it does.

With Hilberseimer, as with Mies, we do not always see what we get. As Michael K. Hays put it, Hilberseimer's drawings function like a mask, "a tissue of representation that reveals only their most salient contours." And underneath the mask, one does not discover some kind of origin, essence or authorship but "metaphors for the city's own productive and functional procedures, mediating those procedures through the conventions of architectural form" (Hays 1992, 180). The forms and images we see do not operate as *Abbilder* of a real that exists or a future real to be built. Rather, the images precede the situation they claim to represent.

Motion Art

An exploration of Hilberseimer's entanglement with media discourses during the early 1920s, in particular those concerned with the exploration of the new medium film, begins with the article he publishes in 1921 entitled "Bewegungskunst" (Hilberseimer 1921b). It was part of a whole series of articles on the same subject that appeared in different journals all written by those who two years later will constitute the core of the *G* group: Theo van Doesburg, Raoul Hausmann, and Hans Richter publish in *De Stijl* (Doesburg 1921,

71–75; Hausmann 1921; Richter 1921), Adolf Behne in *Die Freiheit* and in *Sozia-listische Monatshefte* (Behne 1921a; 1921b), Viking Eggeling in *MA* (Eggeling 1921). In what seems like a concerted effort, the emergence of abstract film is propagated as evidence for a completely new art form. In all these articles, the notion of *Bewegungskunst* is framed in similar ways: they share the idea that motion art is present in all the arts and, in a teleological logic, inevitably culminates in the fundamentally new medium film, and in particular in the abstract film experiments conducted by Eggeling and Richter. Faced with this novel experience of motion art, a fundamentally new understanding and perception of space is theorized.

The different articles on *Bewegungskunst* convey the idea that filmmakers operate like architects—and vice versa, that film should serve as the model for architects to follow. Eggeling's abstract film experiments are framed as blueprints for an expanded idea of architecture, its conception of space as well as its practices of representation. Van Doesburg, who most likely saw sequences of Eggeling's unfinished and lost *Horizontal-Vertikal Orchester* during his brief visit to Berlin between late 1920 and early 1921, points to the affinities with the conception of *De Stijl*. He stresses the films' "beeldende bepaaldheid"—a Dutch term which can be best translated as a "visual certainty" or "visual concreteness" inciting both the construction of concrete objects and the creation of immaterial images (Doesburg 1921). Behne praises Eggeling's experiments as a step forward toward an art form that no longer records "movements in the sense of changes of place, that take place in a natural space," but instead depicts "pure, disinterested laws of movement in an ideal space" (Behne 1921b, 1117).

The term *Bewegungskunst* itself had already been introduced in 1920 by the critic Hans Liebmann in a response to the comments Peter Behrens made on the phenomenon of cinema. While Behrens reluctantly accepts the new "technical invention" cinema, hoping to lift it to the "higher value" of painting (Behrens 1920, 8), Liebmann, by contrast, stresses film's fundamental novelty producing a completely new art form he calls "Bewegungskunst." It is film that renders tangible what before was unthinkable and unknowable. Through the film lens, the mass public sees "sequences of motion that

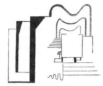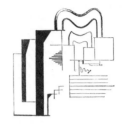

Figure 2: Viking Eggeling, *Drei Momente des Horizontal-Vertikalorchesters* 8
Three moments of the horizontal-vertical orchestra) and Hans Richter, *Drei
Momente der Komposition „Schwer-Leicht" (Präludium)* (Three moments of
the composition „Heavy-Light" (Prelude)), published in: *De Stijl*, 7, 1921: 85

from now on are unambiguously determined in an optical way" (Liebmann
1920, 5). Rhythmic movement alone becomes the material of expression for
the practioner of motion art who "senses in appearances, senses pictorially"
(Liebmann 1920, 6).

Hilberseimer's interest in motion art was certainly due to his acquaintance
with Hans Richter, whom he met already in 1912. The pioneering work with
abstract film started around 1920 by Richter and Eggeling can be seen as a cul-
mination of prior experiments with artistic forms that are animate and time-
based, notably their sequential scroll drawings of evolutive forms (fig. 2) that
grew out of their involvement with Zurich Dadaists like Hugo Ball, Tristan
Tzara, and Richard Huelsenbeck and their interest in the contrapuntal musical composition of Ferruccio Busoni as well as Rudolf von Laban's dance notation system (Wollen 1997, 150–53). Through the medium of cinematography,
the actual experience of animate form becomes possible. "Eidodynamics," as
Eggeling calls it—a term he takes from Bergson, denoting "a stable view taken
auf die instability of things" (Bergson 1998, 315)—served as a model for a new
"universal language."

Form Follows Film

In his own contribution to the promotion of *Bewegungskunst,* Hilberseimer reflects on movement in art as a means for attaining elementary forms through abstraction. He introduces his argument by way of reference to the sculptor Alexander Archipenko, whose sculpture he interprets as relational and paving "the way to a dynamic architecture" (Hilberseimer 1921a, 466). Like his colleagues, Hilberseimer concludes that the various experiments with motion art eventually lead to Eggeling and Richter, whose abstract film experiments confirm his own criticism of representation: "The abstract forms, like music, avoid all analogies or memories of natural objects, find tension and resolution in themselves. Because all material comparisons and memories become obsolete, they are elementary-magical" (Hilberseimer 1921b, 467).

The central importance of a self-referential original language Hilberseimer detects in Eggeling and Richter's abstract films would later resurface in his definition of the *Großstadtarchitektur.* The basis for the experiments with abstract film was the idea of a prelinguistic "universal language" of primordial forms and rhythms providing the basis for *elementare Gestaltung.* It was through the new cinematographic technology that the possibility of designing with this new visual language emerged. The shaping and experiencing of "magic" form as a whole made of time or "blocs of time-space" (Deleuze 1982) allowed for an entirely new type of space to emerge that is rhythmic, intensive, affective, and temporal as opposed to a space that is metric, extensive, and measurable.

Echoing Hilberseimer's interpretation of motion art, Richter aptly summarizes his reconception of film in the first issue of *G.* He defines film as the organization of "forms" as a temporal whole: "The task of the whole is to shape the nature of the light [...]. The 'forms' we see in his films are "neither analogies nor symbols nor means to beauty" (Richter 1923). The meaning communicated through film happens no longer on the level of representation but on the level of the relations and contrasts of light. The aim is purely "to organize the film such that the individual parts stand in active tension to one another and to the whole, such that the whole remains intellectually [*geistig*] mobile within itself" (Richter 1923).

Film is presented as an exemplary medium for the design of things in duration or made of time—a model for architecture and urbanism to follow. Just like film was regarded as a completely new art, *Großstadtarchitektur* is, as Hilberseimer wrote four years later, "a new type of architecture with its own forms and laws" (Hilberseimer 2012, 264). Form becomes dissociated from the idea of solid and static objectivity's serving as inert vehicles of representation and signification. Instead, in a collapse of scales, parts exist only as relational agents for a whole. For Richter, the new common objective is the creation of a contained whole that organizes the single parts in tense constellations. This connection between parts and the whole, like the single film frame being indissociable from the *durée* of the cinematographic sequence, would later serve as a guiding principle for a serial urbanism that does not reproduce but evolves in duration (see "Visuals", p. 292, fig. 33). The linking of individual cell and the whole urban organism becomes "a determining factor of the city structure, which is the actual objective of architecture" (Hilberseimer 2012, 270).

"The true means of construction is light," Richter (2010) writes in the first issue of *G* with respect to his own abstract film experiments—a formulation mirrored and transposed to the field of architecture four years later by Hilberseimer in his *Großstadtarchitektur*, in which he argues that architectural design "lives as a result of light. The entire rhythm receives its vitality through it" (Hilberseimer 2012, 268–69). Like Eggeling and Richter, Hilberseimer blends his techno-affirmative materialism with vitalist ideas of a world of matter brought to life through the agency of light (Robbers 2017). Just as the rhythmic montage of rectangular forms and emerging shapes in Richter's *Rhythm* films and Eggeling's *Symphonie diagonale* (1924) are manifestations of a time-based, tactile visual language, architecture also operates as, Hilberseimer notes, a "bearer of rhythm" that depends "on the relationship of the form to light: they are based on the contrast of the lightness of the surface and the darkness of the recessions that penetrate it" (Hilberseimer 2012, 271), the idea that light could become an active agent for emanating images and constructing a time-based constructivist utopia of bodily presence.

In abstract film, Hilberseimer identifies the conceptual outlines of a language that refuses all processes of signification based on mimetic references in favor of a language of rhythmic intensities. Abstract film's pure light rhythms prompt the emergence of "a deeply meaningful organic language for all of humanity" that holds the "principles of constructions of our own nature" (Hilberseimer 1921b, 467). Eggeling and Richter's films are "elementary-magical" because they allow us access to a prelinguistic, rhythmic *Ur*-language, to a noncontingent substratum of being, "a language which resonates in an elementary way since the beginning of our existence, whose rhythm we continuously inhabit" (Hilberseimer 1921b, 468).

Emanations

The idea that images do not represent the objective world but rather precede it, creating a new conception of space, was central in the thinking of other artists Hilberseimer was acquainted with during this period. One of them, the artist Otto Freundlich, a friend and fellow member of the Novembergruppe and associated with the *G* group, provides Hilberseimer the idea of "a new language, a new identity of word and image," as well as a "new visibility [*Sichtbarkeit*], a new spiritual reality that emanates pictorially [*bildhaft*] towards matter" (Hilberseimer 1921c, 466). Hilberseimer cites Freundlich's article "Der Raum" (1919) at length, in which he imagines tactile exploration of "in-between spaces," spaces that function as "media [*Mittler*] between all those damned and banned by boundaries" (Freundlich 1982, 106). Once the subject decides to rid itself of the constraints of "scientific vision" and to "move inquiringly into the void," he or she will experience "iron, stone, and all solid things coming alive" (1982, 106). Anticipating the conviction among the *G* group that light should be considered a building material, Freundlich poses the question: "Doesn't light belong to space? Is there a space other than dynamic space?" (1982, 106)

Some of Hilberseimer's ideas appear to be taken directly from Freundlich, who in turn—like other members of *G* such as Raoul Hausmann, Eggeling, and

Behne—refers to the obscure theories of the Neo-Kantian philosopher Ernst Marcus. Marcus had developed the esoteric concept of "eccentric sensation" based on the idea that the human senses expand beyond the limits of the body (Harrasser 2016). Marcus reverses the idealist model of perception: it is not the seeing subject that perceives and actualizes dead matter. Quasi-empathically the subject penetrates every object and, vice versa, every object sends off, as Hausmann puts it, "relationally rich emanations" (Hausmann 1921, 137). For Behne, it is Marcus who shows that the human spirit is not "a stiff machine of reception." The "retina of our bodily eye," rather than inscribing visual phenomena, emanates sensations toward the "firmament"—leading Behne to the conclusion that one should no longer produce "retina architecture" (*Netzhaut-Architektur*) but "cosmic architecture" instead (Behne 1998, 50).

Hilberseimer concludes his article with a work assignment for Eggeling and Richter. He acknowledges that their work demonstrates that we need to master this new art form. Now it is a "life necessity" to invent, an "optical piano" for reconnecting mankind with, as Hilberseimer calls it, this original rhythm—an unconcealed reference to Thomas Wilfred and other pioneers of "color music" experiments such as Claude Bragdon, Wallace Rimington, or Alexander Scriabin, who orchestrated projections of abstract moving shapes analogous to musical scores and who were repeatedly cited by critics and artists such as Hilberseimer, Hausmann, and Moholy-Nagy as exemplary manifestations of a new space (Hausmann 1921, 141; Moholy-Nagy 1976, 18).

In Hilberseimer's later writings on film, he connects the lesson of *Bewegungskunst* with cinema as mass entertainment. Especially in the work of Charlie Chaplin, he discerns film's "intrinsic nature" and "fundamental elements" (Hilberseimer 1922a, 743). Chaplin "consciously exploited film's potential" by enacting through his body the discrepancies between the organic and the mechanical world. His humor remains devoid of all outside reference, "absolute gesture per se [*vollkommene Geste an sich*]" (1922a, 743). In other words, Chaplin, like film—and by extension architecture and urbanism—does not reproduce the real by positioning the spectator inside a story or space but rather presents the multiple unstable dispositions of the body's interplay with the animated objective world.

In the last issue of *G* in 1926, Hilberseimer directly reacts to the current debates on the censorship of *Battleship Potemkin* (1925). Accompanying the text with various stills from Sergei Eisenstein's masterpiece, he underlines film's intrinsic political charge for the "propagation of a new social order" (Hilberseimer 1926b, 136). Hilberseimer even dreams up the future of film as an "eccentric" medium, which, "through wireless transmission" and across all borders, becomes "immediately visible" to everyone. He hence repeats *G*'s technology-affirmative agenda proposed by Hans Richter, who proclaimed that the material presented in the pages of *G*—whether film, architecture, urbanism, art, fashion, and so on—is made for a new man "already equipped with all the modern apparatuses of instinct, reception, and transmission, which assure his connection with life" (Richter 1924, 3).

Hilberseimer was at the forefront of architects and planners who designed media. During the early 1920s, he sketches the outlines of a concept of architecture and urbanism as media that operate, to quote John Durham Peters, "vessels and environments, containers of possibility that anchor our existence and make what we are doing possible" (Peters 2015, 2). Those who react to the horror of Hilberseimer's images with the anxiety of loss might lose the connection with these environments. Those who look the horror straight in the face might perceive them as elementary-magical and hence gain new room for play. Mies anticipates precisely this idea of media when, in his introduction to *The New City* (1944), he argues that Hilberseimer's vision is not a final representation of an urban world to come but that the underlying order "acts as a medium in which [the diverse factors of the city] can grow and unfold" (Hilberseimer 1944, xv).

Structure as Infrastructure:
The Interrelation of Fiber and Construction

Sandra Neugärtner

"The underlying problems of the new architecture are not stylistic but structural," Ludwig Hilberseimer (1928, 5) claims in *Internationale neue Baukunst*. As in another volume from the same year, *Beton als Gestalter*, co-authored with Julius Vischer, Hilberseimer deals with the revolution in building materials through the rise of concrete and iron. In both publications, he contrasts his earlier paradigm, which was subordinate to elementary design. Hilberseimer advocates the model of the ready-to-assemble reinforced concrete framework that, for instance, Le Corbusier used for the construction of single-family houses in Paris (Hilberseimer and Vischer 1928, 9). By employing prefabricated concrete components and aligning post spacing and heights with the standardized construction elements, the new reinforced concrete buildings can be erected within months—a design that reflects streamlining efforts. Not the design, but "the nature of the design process defines the character of the new architecture," Hilberseimer (1928, 5) maintains. His interest in architecture is thus made manifest not simply by way of the choice of material but also by how his writings prompt their organization. He states that "material and construction are the material means of [the building's] architecture. In addition, manufacturing technology and operations management, environmental and sociological aspects exercise a significant influence" (1928, 5).

Asking how—rather than just what—to plan, Hilberseimer (1963, 7) affirmed in retrospect that he had wanted to solve various problems in order to achieve a harmonious relationship between people, nature, and technology. As with Stephen Collier (2011), whose interest is not in infrastructure per se but rather in what it tells us about material systems, administrative techniques, and practices of government, the aim of my essay is to steer the analysis upstream, that is, away from infrastructure's social effects and toward practices of conceptualization that precede the construction of the systems themselves and which are built into them.[1] At issue are the conditions implicit in Hilberseimer's question of how to plan. To this end, I will concentrate on the years of Hilberseimer's involvement at the Bauhaus—a phase in which his conception of planning under the special conditions of the school developed substantially. After giving a guest lecture in the winter semester of 1928, he taught regularly from 1929 at the Bauhaus building department newly founded by Hannes Meyer. In Dessau and from 1932 in Berlin, a number of urban planning studies were carried out with the participation of his students, which formed the basis for his planning ideas.[2]

I assume that the administrative techniques and principles at the Bauhaus encompassed the way in which planning processes were directed and controlled and how they could unfold at the same time.[3] These integration processes affected the entire Bauhaus production, and I argue that they were particularly salient in textile production, as textiles manifest the peculiar and fraught experience of planning and working amid large-scale technical systems and, in this respect, epitomized crucial processes of transformation. Today, as in the past, scholars have recognized the capacity by which textiles and their production function as a theoretical engine for the modernist project at large. Smith encapsulates that the history of textiles provides us with a very clear example of what Marx called "formal subsumption," whereby an earlier technique is taken up by and routed through the mode and means of capitalism (2015, 82). In this way, textiles have acquired a paradigmatic importance for the development of modern art scholarship (Frank and Watson 2015, Buchmann and Frank 2015). As Christine Checinska and Grant Watson highlighted, textiles have the ability to act as a catalyst for new ways of thinking (2016, 288). I invoke textiles as a subject of negotiation here because I assume textiles touch on a number of aspects to gain insights into the constellation under which Hilberseimer developed his ideas of how to plan. Not least, the newly established building department benefited from the experience that the weaving workshop had with industry as one of the most economically successful workshops for a long time, namely in outsourcing and industry cooperation. By mobilizing not only the analogy but also the distinction between textiles and architecture, I wish to address the planning of infrastructure that organized Western European modernism.

In parallel with concrete and steel, the new building materials at the beginning of the twentieth century, new materials were also introduced in textiles. This implied that textile production was extended to include another stage, namely, the finishing of the fabric. Although Anni Albers asserts in her seminal book *On Weaving* that "every fabric is mainly the result of two elements: the character of the fibers used in the thread construction, that is, the building material, and the construction, or weave, itself," she also notes that "the dominant conditioning factors are, perhaps no longer, the character of the raw material and that of the weave." While she mentions rayon, nylon, cellophane, vinyon, aralac, and fiberglass as materials for new yarns, she suggests focusing on the "finishing of the fabric, which is becoming increasingly important today" (1965, 59). Even though the chapter is titled "Interrelationship of Fiber and Construction," Albers concludes that this interrelationship has almost lost its meaning within textile production; whether materials can be water-repellent, wrinkle-resistant, flame-retardant, moth-resistant, fluorescent or shrinkage-controlled is a result of the finishing treatments, not of the weave.

The fact, often criticized by Albers, that "the engineer-work of fabric construction has barely been considered" (1946, 26) also applies to textile production at the Bauhaus. Although there was guidance and a sound training program under the initial leadership of textile expert Helene Börner, fabric construction was not particularly sophisticated in the early years, as Börner's traditional or even Art Nouveau approach to textile production did not fit with modern form theory and was rejected by students (Droste 1998, 12).[4] Börner's successor, Gunta Stölzl, was in turn no expert, but had acquired at best a makeshift basic knowledge of fabric construction in a two-month course in Krefeld in 1924 (Elste n.d.). When the school was moved to Dessau, the degradation of textile construction further manifested itself in conjunction with the involvement of industry. The workshop became a production facility due to increasing orders, and even began to hire workers for contract work. After Walter Gropius complained that individual pieces were still being produced that could easily have been woven by the meter, it became imperative to develop patterns and find manufacturers who would take over machine production (Stölzl 1987, 126). It was no longer enough to discover personal inclinations playfully by chance and to let individual pieces grow organically on the loom. Rather, weavers in Dessau proceeded methodically to solve a variety of design problems almost as if they worked in a laboratory. Advances were made not only in the development of synthetic fibers such as artificial silk and cellophane, but also in the production of new fabrics, like an iron yarn (Eisengarn) fabric. This was, however, not the result of any particular construction, but of the combination of new materials. Finishing processes gained in importance. In textile industry facilities in Sorau, Lower Lusatia, and in Krefeld, students—among them Lena Meyer-Bergner and Lis Beyer-Volger—acquired special knowledge of textile dyeing, which they brought to the Bauhaus dye works.[5] The weaving workshop reached a stage that was in line with the Bauhaus's steady evolution toward designing prototypes, but even exceeded this progression. Unlike the other traditional workshops, such as the metal workshop, the weaving workshop almost stopped producing one-offs. As Margaretha Reichardt's photomontage reveals, education was forced along the assembly line *(Erziehung am Fließband)*, while how to weave *(Wie weben?)* remained a question (fig. 1). The practice in the weaving workshop demonstrates that the approach to design ignored construction practices, but was oriented toward intangible conditions that served the economic structure. Knowledge of fabric calculation and logistics of textile production were now essential. Planning had become the determining factor in the design process.

At this time, between 1928 and 1929, a fundamental change in faculty took place at the Bauhaus. Marcel Breuer, László Moholy-Nagy, and Oskar Schlemmer resigned, while new appointments included Walter Peterhans and Ludwig Hilberseimer. While the theater department was closed, a photography workshop was established. The greatest innovation was the founding of the building department. Upon taking office in 1928, Meyer had immediately deemphasized the unity of art and technology, upholding only the latter. Meyer appears to have introduced what the Swiss historian Sigfried Giedion defines as a consequence of the rise of new materials in the early twentieth century:

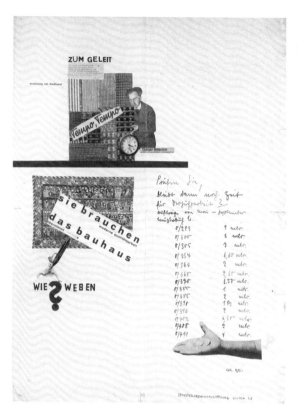

Figure 1: Margaretha Reichardt, *Sie brauchen das Bauhaus* (You Need the Bauhaus), 1928

Art had been liberated of its fundamental functions; the potentials ascribed to art—of redefining common ground and bringing critical voices into the political sphere—could now be ascribed to infrastructures (1995, 87; see also Benjamin 1999). The provision of infrastructures is intimately caught up with the sense of shaping modern society. Infrastructures are "instigating waves of societal progress," write Graham and Marvin (1996, 42). It was the new infrastructural materials and productive powers that broke through the architecture, transcended it and, in Brian Larkin's words, were "offering revelation into the state of things and shaping the emergence of modern subjects" (2013, 338). In architecture, as in textiles, we are dealing with a shift through the detachment of the functional from the formal, an observation that is also central to Hilberseimer's theory:

> The invalidation of the architecture of the past century is essentially rooted in the fact that, as a result of the inherently correct separation of the fields of work of the engineer and the architect, both disciplines began to coexist rather than collaborate; the sense of connection between material, construction, and form was entirely lost (Hilberseimer and Vischer 1928, 17).

It seems that within the new approach, material-dependent construction has lost its authority. The formalist approach that Moholy-Nagy had represented and taught, for example in his treatise *From Material to Architecture*, was no longer valid. Meyer's denial of architecture as an artistic discipline meant a sharp rejection of the traditional creative process conducted with artistic methods. "As drywall, the new house is an industrial product, and as such it is the work of specialists," Meyer defines. "The architect *was* an artist and *becomes* a specialist in the organization" (1928, 13). As a reflexive response to the rationalization processes running at full speed in industry and the first attempts at an industrialization of construction, the design methodology in Meyer's new building department followed tendencies accentuated by rationalism, while it simultaenously corresponded to complex sociologically oriented analyses. The new maxim of architecture was "to collectively […] meet all the necessities of life; its realizations governed by the path of least resistance and economics" (1927, 14). It was associated with a high level of planning and organizational effort. This logic corresponded to the requirements of the developing productive forces and higher degree of the division of labor.

Within the building department, the concept of scientifically based architectural analysis and rational planning became particularly fruitful in the architecture theory (Baulehre, see Winkler 1989, 82). This study section was led by Hilberseimer starting in 1929.[6] Apprentices who had completed the preliminary course and the building workshops attended this section from the fourth to the sixth semester to be trained in the "scientific way of thinking about building: building means designing life processes" (Bauhaus Dessau 1929). After the architecture theory, students were eligible to work for three more semesters in the architecture office, the last section within the apprenticeship in the building department. The architecture theory was therefore the central section for students of the department.

The traffic study by Konrad Püschel is a typical example of the pictorial-statistical and diagrammatic representations that were created in Hilberseimer's lessons (fig. 2). Instead of form experiments with the material, students systematically investigated a whole range of phenomena related to architectural or urban planning and carried out studies on solar orientation (*Durchsonnung*) and ideal building density (*Bebauungsdichte*). Observations, surveys, evaluations, calculations, and statistics were intended to enable students to engage in analytical thinking. The working methodology was no longer directed toward objects or prototypes but rather toward the diagram and the elaborated plan. Albers echoes this shift from the three-dimensional to the two-dimensional in textile production. In her words, "the process of forming has been broken by divorcing the planning from the making. […] The spontaneous shaping of a material has been lost and the blueprint has taken over" (Albers 1946, 23).

In textiles, the change was particularly evident in the new focus on functional fabrics. In 1931 Gunta Stölzl noted: "From now on two fields of pedagogy that were initially interwoven parted ways sharply and irrevocably: Development into utility fabrics for interiors (types for industry) and speculative experimentation with material, form, and color in gobelin and carpet" (Stölzl 1931, 2). The development of standard types for industry implied the utilization of pattern drafts (*Patronenzeichnungen*). While in Weimar, there had already been textile designs on paper, pattern drafts were a completely new dimension of planning in Dessau. Although commonly taught in German textile schools, this kind of technical drawing on preprinted pattern paper had been unavailable to the Bauhaus weavers in the early years (Wortmann Weltge 1993, 22). For the schematic representation of the textile pattern on the paper, which is divided into squares, the pattern of the fabric is broken down into individual dots of color on the paper, forming a grid.

The reintroduction of the pattern draft involved replacing the linear structure of weaving with the flattened, abstracted grid of planning. This shift

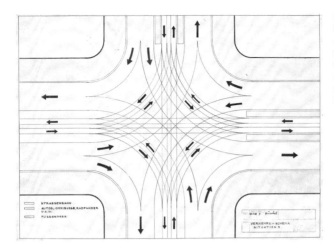

Figure 2: Konrad Püschel, traffic study for the general development plan Dessau, from the architecture theory lessons (basics of urban planning) of Ludwig Hilberseimer at Bauhaus Dessau, 1928

from the linear model to the grid is probably the most obvious corresponding link between the changes that took place in weaving and in architecture. As outlined by Rike Frank, the peculiarity of weaving technology not only consists in the woven structure resulting from "the rhythm of crossing threads," but with regard to the procedure, also in the weft-by-weft sequencing, that is "the processing of information organized in lines" (2015, 23). Hilberseimer's specification of traditional brick wall construction seems to map remarkably well onto Frank's depiction of linearity in weaving. He details a structure raised stone upon stone, that is, line by line. It appears that first wall construction was replaced with scaffolding. "Later, reinforced concrete construction extended these elements through the load-bearing slab and more recently by the load-bearing surface, from which it basically started" (Hilberseimer and Vischer 1928, 7). This implies a change in the construction method but also in its function. Whereas in brick wall construction the wall itself has a load-bearing function, "[the scaffolding] concentrates the load-bearing function by means of supports at relatively few points" (8). In other words, the load-bearing structure changed completely and its design was no longer based on the linear structure of the wall. This trend is in accord with the flattened plan, the grid, which can dispense with the vertical because

Figure 3: Unidentified city and land-use studies, noted on
the back: "Den Haag/Berlage/See Stübben p. 569"

it can designate the supports as dots and no longer has to take into account the
structural linearity of the material. Like the plan or grid in architecture, the
pattern design, or grid, in weaving dissolves the spatially and temporally linear sequence. Art historian Rosalind E. Krauss (1999, 9) succinctly describes
the peculiar ontology possessed by the grid:

> Flattened, geometricized, ordered, it is antinatural, antimimetic, antireal.
> It is what art looks like when it turns its back on nature. In the flatness that
> results from its coordinates, the grid is the means of crowding out the di-
> mensions of the real and replacing them with the lateral spread of a sin-
> gle surface.

As a juxtaposition of a figure-ground plan and a photomontage of crochet work
from Hilberseimer's estate suggests (probably taken from an as yet unidentified publication), Hilberseimer explored the formal analogies of the textile
to the city plan in terms of the grid—not in the textiles' linear construction in
weaving but rather as an ornamental category (fig. 3).
Following Krauss's account, for Hannah Higgins the modernist grid is an emblem of industry. It reflects standardization, mass production, and the new,
seamless mechanisms of transportation (2009, 6). In correspondence to this,

the pattern draft is an invention of industrialization and was introduced into textile production as early as the beginning of the nineteenth century as it is effectively a program for the Jacquard machine to run. It is one of the first applications of punch card technology, whereby a programmed-automated process replaced a manual one. Obviously, the most economical pattern draft in terms of planning (not in terms of production, which is automatic) results in a fabric whose structure is monotonous and does not contain many structural variations, that is, when the rapport—the smallest repeating unit—can be represented by a small number of rectangles. Such units can then be extended to infinity with relative ease.

Franco Panzini, referring to seriality, pointed out that weaving at the Bauhaus participated in the new direction of building in industrial forms, of which Dessau Törten is considered a prime example. According to Panzini, in Hilberseimer's planning of the plots for terraced houses in Törten, as in the production of the Bauhaus textile workshop, the search for a solution to the functional, economic and technical problems came to one and the same result: reduction to the essential (1985, 37). The grid demonstrates the process.

The common consideration of grids in weaving and architecture is suggested by the striking visual similarity of the results of planning in both fields, which

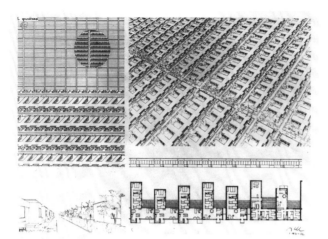

Figure 5: Pius Pahl, floor plan studies, left: floor plan in axonometric view, right: perspective view, from the architecture theory lessons of Ludwig Hilberseimer, 1931–32

found expression in the term *Teppichstadt* (carpet city). On the one hand, we have the close-up of an upholstery fabric (fig. 4); on the other, a layout for a housing development by Pius Pahl, created in Hilberseimer's course (fig. 5). The visual resemblances become even more apparent when the representation is not in perspective, but in axonometry, which was very common at the Bauhaus at the time. The reason Hilberseimer's popular axonometric draft showing high-rise buildings, published in *Das Kunstblatt 13* and on the cover of the design magazine *bauhaus* in 1929, could reinforce the impression of the analogy to the uniform, functional fabric is that axonometry is closer to the grid than perspective (see "Visuals", p. 283, fig. 18). While perspective is primarily concerned with depicting space, as Krauss asserts (1999, 52), the grid and axonometry are engaged with adequate lateral dimensions.

In Hilberseimer's design, as in Pahl's, the trimming at the four edges of the image causes us to perceive it as a detail of a larger whole and to know how the pattern continues beyond the limiting frame. In weaving, this principle corresponds not only to the law of the rapport 121 but also to the newly introduced yard goods, which, unlike the carpet, do not have a border. The principle is also reflected in the production of patterns, glued to cardboard, which could be passed as a sample card to the industry as a representative cutout of the yard goods to be manufactured. In weaving, as in architecture, this ultimately reflects the idea of creating standard types that can be infinitely reproduced and quantitatively scaled.

What finally makes the juxtaposition of functional fabric and city plan so significant is the fact that the two ultimately diverge and that the reason for this is already inherent in Hilberseimer's thinking before the Bauhaus. In *Großstadtbauten* (1925), in which Hilberseimer addressed the issue of the metropolis, he affirmed that the architecture of the city depends on the solution of two questions: the design of the elementary cell and the entire urban whole. And it is precisely this double solution, formally and structurally linked to the grid, that, according to Italian Marxist architect and critic Manfredo Tafuri, would highlight the very social dimension of Hilberseimer's organizational model for the city within the ceaseless evolution of capitalism. By calling this double solution the clearest analysis of the capitalist metropolis, Tafuri stands out in opposition to most later interpreters of Hilberseimer's architecture, who consider him the most important representative of a rationalist architecture and even value him as a reference point for an anonymous architecture (Aureli 2013, 345–46). What Hilberseimer prominently stated in *Großtadtbauten*, that "architecture is always related to the totality of the accompanying sociological, economic, and psychological circumstances" (1925, 2), came to fruition within the course of the Baulehre, where analyses and studies (as described, on solar orientation and ideal building density) were advanced and the concept of mixed development *(Mischbebauung)* was developed, which ultimately concerns the interrelationships of cell and whole and were recognizable by their expression of the grid. Thus, in architecture and in weaving at the Bauhaus, we see two diverging tendencies in terms of the diversity of the grid. The textile grid of the carpeting allows increasingly less differentiation, which is unequally related to capitalist and social dimensions.

Hilberseimer's concepts, which he developed as his experience in planning work at the Bauhaus progressed, demonstrate a remarkable turning away from the monotonous grid, which is further supported by the fact that he increasingly rarely used axonometry as a method of representation. The best example of his departure from the uniform, undifferentiated carpet-like structure is—next to the mixed development—the settlement unit. Both concepts are among Hilberseimer's greatest achievements at the Bauhaus (Oswalt 2019b, 155).[7] The planning of Dessau Törten exemplifies how the question of how to plan was pursued in the Baulehre. In study groups, students worked together to find solutions on an analytical basis. When a study group with Ernst Göhl and Hubert Hoffmann proposed the new steel lamella and timber skeleton construction method within the second construction phase of Törten, there was no element that was justified solely on the basis of formal-aesthetic considerations. The approach to textiles was precisely the opposite, as Bauhaus-trained textile designer Otti Berger (1931–32, n.p.) asserted firmly with disillusionment:

> For three years the watchword of the Bauhaus workshop has been "Function"! "Structure." Not textile pictures, but textiles, through structure? Today even more of a watchword, practically a construct of threads, a new formal element, but not textile. Its fulfillment is ornamentation. To cover up the hated word, people just say structure. Its right to exist lies only in the fact that the uneven surface is more susceptible to dirt and one can easily pull out the individual threads or catch them.

Berger's assertion that the meaning of the structure of the fabric is misunderstood and even misused as ornament takes up a conflict that is rooted in an architectural debate on the fundamental distinction between structural core form and decorative art form in the second half of the nineteenth century; a conflict that initially found a concise expression in Karl Bötticher's *Tektonik* (1852). Bötticher developed the concepts of structural "core" and "ornamental shell," to distinguish sculptural architectural elements from linear, two-dimensional ornaments, which he interpreted as decorations and as secondary to structure.

Gottfried Semper turned to this subject and established against classical exegesis and the hegemonic discourse of his time in the textile an ideal connection between structural core and shell. He formulated that architecture originally derived from textile structures. According to Semper, the earliest material technology was that of woven fibers, and from it the linear patterns that it generated subsequently migrated to other media. In this way, textile art moved to the center of scholarly reflection. As outlined by Georg Vasold (2015, 167), it not only accompanied the development of modern art history but also had a decisive influence on it. Alois Riegl, who belonged to a second generation of textile theorists in the late nineteenth century, significantly opposed Semper's theory of technical determinism. He held that each culture has a unique will to create ornamental design *(Kunstwollen)*, apart from materialist motivations. While Semper argued that art originated as the product of material and technique rather than from a creative drive, Riegl's studies on textiles exemplify how formalistic and sociohistorical perspectives intersect in materials, techniques, and processes (Buchmann and Frank, 2015b, 7–8). The conflict, which Berger concisely delineated, reveals the discrepancy between the two standpoints—the defense of the structural identity against the idea of an autonomy of form and its embedding in applied industrial procedures. Weaving and thread construction, which Berger may have equated with engineering work, were no longer an integral part of textile production. As Smith (2014, 129) emphasizes with reference to Anja Baumhoff, the socialistic utopia had a price, namely that it subordinated weavers to the ideology of architecture. Architecture was the model, and the fabric had to serve this model, while—under the related infrastructural conditions determining the design process—textile production was deprived of constructing. In other words, planning based on everything other than the structural core, that is, on economics and decorative value, for example, became the decisive factor in textile production. But this loss does not belong to architecture per se, for it has an equally persistent history within weaving's own medium. As studies in the field of gender have already emphasized, the historically evolved status of architecture and textiles persisted at the Bauhaus and was decisive for how infrastructural possibilities determined planning capacities in each case.

Notes

1 Scholars in science and technology studies mostly analyze infrastructures as material forms that mediate exchange over space, bringing different people and objects into interaction and forming the base on which to operate modern economic and social systems. These scholars hold that infrastructures function as systems, and that as systems, they both enable and constrain us. See Graham and Marvin 2001; Lefebvre 1991; and Larkin 2013; Star and Ruhleben 1996 reveals how choices and politics embedded in systems become articulated components.

2 In the preface of *Entfaltung einer Planungsidee* (1963), he thanks the students of the Bauhaus in Dessau for their help in developing his general planning idea.

3 My thinking here is indebted to Michel Foucault, who coined the term *governmentality* for a concept that combines techniques of mastering others and techniques of the self. Governmentality can offer a perspective on how students behaved in a more or less open field of possibilities. See Foucault 1983, 224; and Foucault 1997, 225.

4 The weaving workshop, founded as a "women's class," emerged from Börner's textile workshop, which the Bauhaus had taken over in 1919 in the course of its foundation. Initially students produced tapestries, garments, toys, and blankets as individual pieces, often from old fabrics and industrial waste. As weaving came to the fore, the constructions remained primitive—merely alternating between the basic three types (plain, twill, and satin weave) or combinations of them. Variations mainly resulted from color and change of material, while on the side of construction, mostly plain weave was applied. Very few students had any previous professional craft training.

5 For a compelling study of knowledge transfer from Krefeld to the Bauhaus, and of other networks, see Blümm Lange 2019.

6 Hilberseimer had been teaching in this section since 1928. His field of activity also included construction design and, in part, tasks of the Bauatelier.

7 For the concept of combining high-rise and low-rise buildings, which was advanced in a joint planning effort of Hilberseimer, Meyer and students, who created a scheme of a "mixed development" of multi-story buildings and single-family houses in Dessau-Törten, see Andreas Buss's essay in the present volume.

Writing Architecture: On the Genesis of Ludwig Hilberseimer's *The New City*

Florian Strob

When the architect, art critic, and urban planner Ludwig Hilberseimer moved to Chicago in 1938, he didn't speak any English. You would think that you cannot rob an architect of his tools for expressing his ideas when you take away his ability to make himself understood in writing. Yet, this is what happened in Hilberseimer's case, author of several hundred articles and essays and five German language books at the time (see Kilian 2002, 154–64). He arrived in Chicago with a manuscript entitled "Gesellschaft und Städtebau," largely written in Nazi Germany over six years, and he would spend the following six years translating, rewriting, and revising this text into English until he arrived at *The New City: Principles of Planning* in 1944 (see "Visuals", p. 297, fig. 43). Hilberseimer's first book in English appeared at a crucial point in time toward the end of World War II. It summarizes various urban theories from different sources of the past decades without really minding ideological boundaries or prejudices. And yet, it is also at the beginning of a new postwar period of reconstruction and modernist building programs around the world, proposing Hilberseimer's solution for the city. Therefore, one could argue that it sits at a center of the modern discourse—a discourse about which Adrian Forty in his book *Words and Buildings: A Vocabulary of Modern Architecture* wrote: "Modernist architecture, as well as being a new style of building, was also a new way of talking about architecture, instantly recognizable by a distinctive vocabulary. Wherever two or more of the words 'form,' space, design order or structure are found in company, one can be sure that one is in the world of modernist discourse" (Forty 2000, 19). Forty, however, also reminds us that "one of the most distinctive features of modernism has been its suspicion of language" (2000, 19). In fact, language itself became a prominent metaphor in architectural writing; the metaphor of language is, for example, to be found at important moments in Hilberseimer's texts (see Hilberseimer 1927b, 26).

Although I won't be looking at the vocabulary of Hilberseimer's *The New City*, this excursion at the beginning allows me to stress the importance of texts and writing in modernist architecture. Because of the skepticism of language, it was maybe inevitable to make use of words to do architecture. "I have no need whatsoever to draw my designs. Good architecture, how something is to be built, can be written. One can write the Parthenon," Adolf Loos remarked in 1924 (Forty 2000, 29). And Walter Gropius, one of the modernist architects who might have published and talked more than he built once said: "Das Wort, der kritische Kampf ist die Fräse, mit der man den geistigen Boden vorerst beackert." (The word, the critical struggle is the tiller with which you plow the soil of the mind for the time being) (Nerdinger 2019, 9).

Today, in times of a global climate crisis, we are confronted with the built legacy of modernism. We live in it and with it, only to find us struggling to adapt it, to reuse and recycle it. Demolishing old and building new structures seems increasingly untenable. Late modernity, as described by the sociologist Andreas Reckwitz (2019), is a period in which stories of progress have come to an end; it marks the "end of illusions" and has made way for ambivalence. We might be well advised to reconsider the writings of modern architects to understand the illusions inherent in modern architecture. By opening up the often dogmatic or at least apodictic texts, one could discover alternatives, a messy multiplicity of unrealized possible futures within modernism. Something could open up like the communal park in the middle of Hilberseimer's settlement units (see "Visuals", p. 299, fig. 46–47).

In the following, I will attempt to open up *The New City* by Ludwig Hilberseimer, a book that reads very much like a final word, a definitive text. I will take a closer look at Hilberseimer's archive and discover the messy, disquieting and exciting, complicated and rich, seemingly endless writing process that lay as a tool or as an infrastructure, if you will, underneath his achievements. Twelve years of writing, translating, and rewriting that didn't end at the publication of the book in 1944, as Plácido González Martínez has shown in his monograph *In the Light of Hilberseimer*, but continued, also physically, by dissecting the typescript and collaging it together again, with his following books (González Martínez 2016, 76–82).

Archival Afterlives

Entering the archive requires preliminary remarks of caution. Beatriz Colomina, in her seminal book *Privacy and Publicity: Modern Architecture as Mass Media*, states: "The archive is private, history is public [...]. 'Out' of the archive history is produced, but when writing history the utmost care is traditionally placed on producing a seamless account of the archive, even though all archives are fractured and partial. The messy space of the archive is thus sealed off by history. History then is a facade" (Colomina 1994, 9).

Walter Gropius or Le Corbusier, for example, were concerned with their afterlives in a way that Hilberseimer never was, and they consciously worked against the partial nature of the archive by collecting and institutionalizing a lot of material. To quote Colomina once more (1994, 9): "Modernity [...] coincides with the publicity of the private." Hilberseimer, contrary to the examples of Gropius and Le Corbusier and the modern trend, kept the private private and bequeathed his belongings largely to his former student, colleague, and friend George Danforth, who eventually gave the materials mostly to the Art Institute of Chicago.[1]

This serves as an explanation for what is to be found in Hilberseimer's archive. It generally portrays his writing process, as a tool or infrastructure. The social aspect justifies such characterization. Just as a piece of infrastructure is only upheld through its use and users, Hilberseimer deployed his teaching as well as his professional and personal network to write his texts. For example, his 1927 book *Großstadtarchitektur* was written in collaboration with Udo Rukser, as stated in the imprint, and at the end of *The New City*, he thanks his students at the Bauhaus and at the IIT.[2]

It is striking to see that he emigrated with most of the typescripts and manuscripts of his writings, from his earliest publications onward and often in several versions. His teaching is also relatively well documented in the archive, his personal life and even his work as an architect much less so. It becomes clear that he indeed must have considered his previous writings a tool for producing the next piece and his writing process as ongoing.

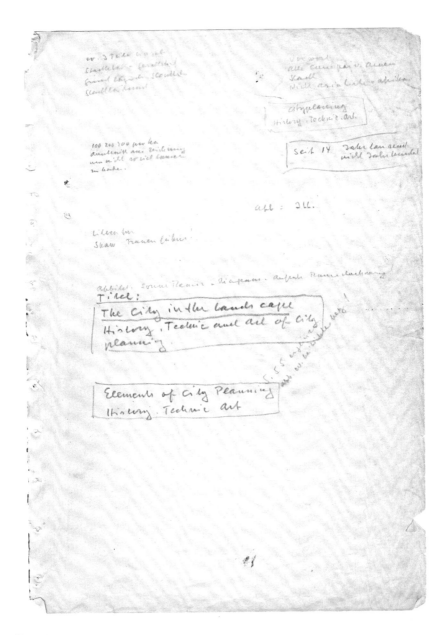

Figure 1: Ludwig Hilberseimer, first page of the manuscript "Gesellschaft und Städtebau," n.d.

This is especially true, it seems, for the genesis of *The New City*, as preserved in the archive. There are four different German versions of the typescript with manuscript annotations. What we might consider the last version of the German-language manuscript *Gesellschaft und Städtebau* gives on its cover different possibilities for an English title: "The City in the Landscape: History, Technic and Art of City Planning" or "Elements of City Planning: History, Technic, Art" (AIC, Hilberseimer, Series 8/1, Box.FF 1.10) (fig. 1). There is an uncertainty here, a multiplicity of options and versions, possible futures. When we look at the advertisement for the finished, translated book, we see that the title of the book in English was even then not a sure thing: "The New City: Elements of Planning." Today we know it as "Principles of Planning." This subtitle of course makes a difference, if only because it sets the tone, a definitive one. Yet, definitive, the archive shows, is hardly anything about *The New City*. It evolved, was altered through translation and for a different cultural context, published and finally rewritten by its author as *The Nature of Cities*.

Apart from the German typescript versions, one should also mention several articles and speeches in German and English written between his time at the Bauhaus and 1944, often in manuscript and typescript versions, that were crucial for the writing process behind what became *The New City*. Of particular importance here are his studies on the influence of sunlight on room layouts and urban planning. These studies, including collected articles by others and student works from his classes, fill several files in the archive.[3]

"City planning is a social task" (Hilberseimer 1944, 17). This is the paradigmatic beginning of *The New City*. Book-making as well as writing are social tasks in their own rights, as seen by the long and complex work on *The New City*. Former students, colleagues, and friends were involved, surviving correspondence speaks of this, and it won't be possible to comment on all of these here. However, there is one correspondence, letters signed by a Siegfried Risch, that is unusual. Hilberseimer, at least one could conclude from his archive, did not keep most letters—even the correspondence with famous contemporaries seems to be incomplete or missing. The letters by Siegfried Risch, on the contrary, were largely kept. Risch translated "Gesellschaft und Städtebau" together with Hilberseimer, without a mention of this fact in the

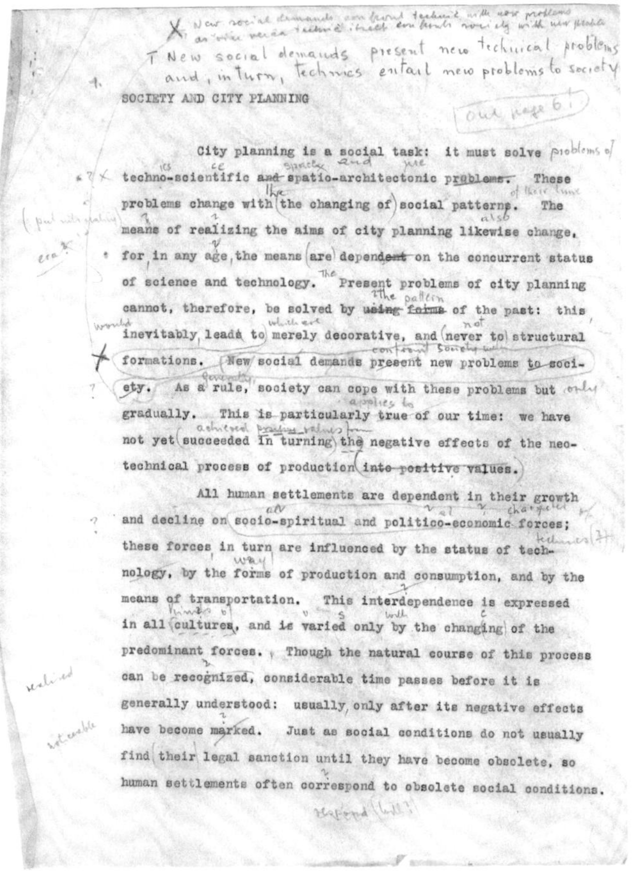
New social demands present new technical problems and, in turn, technics entail new problems to society

SOCIETY AND CITY PLANNING

City planning is a social task: it must solve techno-scientific and spatio-architectonic problems. These problems change with the changing of social patterns. The means of realizing the aims of city planning likewise change, for, in any age, the means are dependent on the concurrent status of science and technology. Present problems of city planning cannot, therefore, be solved by using forms of the past: this inevitably leads to merely decorative, and never to structural formations. New social demands present new problems to society. As a rule, society can cope with these problems but gradually. This is particularly true of our time: we have not yet succeeded in turning the negative effects of the neo-technical process of production into positive values.

All human settlements are dependent in their growth and decline on socio-spiritual and politico-economic forces; these forces in turn are influenced by the status of technology, by the forms of production and consumption, and by the means of transportation. This interdependence is expressed in all cultures, and is varied only by the changing of the predominant forces. Though the natural course of this process can be recognized, considerable time passes before it is generally understood: usually, only after its negative effects have become marked. Just as social conditions do not usually find their legal sanction until they have become obsolete, so human settlements often correspond to obsolete social conditions.

Figure 2: Ludwig Hilberseimer, First page of translation for *The New City* with manuscript changes, n.d.

published book. The letters by Risch document their long and difficult working process (see AIC, Hilberseimer, Series 2/1) (fig. 2).

Architect of Letters

There are 18 letters by Risch in the Hilberseimer archive in Chicago (dating from 1939 to 1941 and also 1946).[4] It is unknown so far how Hilberseimer and

Risch met or got in contact. The first surviving letter in the archive dates from November 4, 1939:

> Dear Mr. Hilberseimer, There was no doubt in my mind that you were going to doubt the humming bird story. I tried, therefore, to take a picture of him at the time but, unfortunately, he was very shy and I did not succeed.

Risch continues his letter by talking about books by Balzac and mentioning a poem by the nineteenth-century German poet Lenau, "Die Drei Indianer," before he writes about Hilberseimer's English and their translation work:

> Your English, incidentally, is very good. I hope you will continue writing in English. Why don't you send me regular exercises [...] which I can correct, grade and return? Thank you for the check. To show you that I have not been idle I am sending you the first part of your manuscript, about 85% finished. It requires various corrections, the footnotes are not carefully typed etc., but I want you to look it over and tell me what in your estimation could be expressed better etc. Just write the page, number and line, I have kept a copy. Next week I shall send the chapter "Despotic cities." I shall also return your book *Trotzdem* by Loos.
>
> I shall change page 76 as you have asked me to do. Here is the text of your pencil notes on page 93.

Risch closes with a quote by the American novelist Sinclair Lewis.

Already in this first letter, there is an awareness of the architect as writer; Adolf Loos had published his collected writings (1900–1930) in 1931, a book important enough to Hilberseimer that he took it with him into exile. Risch's letter establishes a multilingual space between nineteenth-century French and German references and the American present as lived by Risch or Hilberseimer and depicted by Lewis. It is in this globalized space of exile that Risch and Hilberseimer worked jointly on what would become *The New City*. From the letters between them, we learn that Hilberseimer also visited Risch several times on the East Coast (in 1939, 1940, and probably 1941) to work on the translation and take English lessons. Risch refers to Hilberseimer's need for quiet, green streets and nature, his "dislike of the city" (July 11, 1940) even. In the course of their work, Risch moved out of the city into a house with a garden and a view of a tree from his desk (November 6, 1940). Like birds, in particular humming-birds (November 4, 1939, and November 6, 1940), this tree and looking at trees or tree-lined streets are recurring themes in their correspondence—as are the problems of translating Hilberseimer's German text into English.

In his letter from January 18, 1940, Risch states, about half a year after having started his work on the translation: "Though it was not easy translating your book, I enjoyed doing it." Eight months later, after Hilberseimer's second visit to the East Coast and much deeper into the translation work, Risch, in a letter from September 28, 1940, talks about the problems he is facing:

> Dear Mr. Hilberseimer: I received your letter of September 22nd. You are right, the second part is better than the first (meaning, of course, the translation) for several reasons: When you were here, and I wanted to use different constructions to express in English what you had writ-ten, I could ask you, and your answer was either an emphatic "no," or an agreeing "yes." The translation is therefore freer, and yet accurate. Sec-ondly, it is not only your "Unmenschlichkeit" which had an excellent effect upon me, but you were also an inspiration because of your uncom-promising attitude which made me say: I'll show him that I can find the best expression. Even if we were quarreling, and I take most of the blame for it, there was often something resembling rhythm in work present at 250 Ashmont Street.

Yet another half a year later the quarrels between author and translator had gotten worse. Both men were unsatisfied with the result of their work, both had asked others to review the translation. On February 28, 1941, Risch wrote:

> I also believe that the translation could be loosened up, so to speak, by con-nective phrases, but I can hear you now—that is only decoration, you say, lesen Sie was Schopenhauer zu sagen hat ueber diese Sache, lesen Sie "Ue-ber Schriftstellerei und Stil." The German assertiveness is you, I am quite sure; Mies van der Rohe would say "er ist etwas doktrinaer."

Here it is again, the self-awareness of Hilberseimer as a writer. Risch closes by giving a hint about the nature of their interactions, Hilberseimer being the teacher, Risch the student:

I am enclosing an article which I have just finished. I don't think there is one original thought in it—I am repeating all that you have taught me—but I can say that I understand all that I have written, that is part of me now, and not just something which I am repeating automatically. Risch

Hilberseimer's dissatisfaction with the translation, or by then, the American version of his German manuscript grew in the following months. A letter by Risch, dated May 12, 1941, makes clear references to this dissatisfaction. It is worth citing the letter here at some length, as it concludes the collaboration:

Dear Mr. Hilberseimer:
I wanted to let some time pass before answering your letter of two months ago in detail. I wanted to let some time pass, so that I could be sure that it would not be written in the same manner as yours was,—rather ironical, I thought, and even acid.
These, then, are the facts: The translation is uneven, and incorrect; it is too much influenced from the German diction. [...]
You say that the translation has to be overhauled, that great parts have to be translated again, and then that the whole thing has to be rewritten again. Now I should like to raise these questions: How uneven is the translation, how incorrect is it, how much is influenced from the German?
I have spoken about this unhappy affair with a publisher, and it is his belief that even if the unevenness of the translation is remedied, even if its incorrectness has been remedied, even if the influence from the German diction has been modulated, you still would find yourself in the same position (after it has been translated again) where you are now, namely, that the manuscript would still have to be rewritten again if he were to publish it. As it is now, it would be best suited for architectural journals etc., he said.

Risch continues with harsh criticism on Hilberseimer's style of writing:

> [T]he city planning and housing which are so directly a part of human living have become lifeless, suggestive of written history, rather than of the spirit and muscles of the people who have built and are building the cities you write about. Do the faults of the translation, then, lie only with the translation, or has perhaps the original something to do with it too?

It seems, from all we know and all that can be found in Hilberseimer's archive, that author and translator saw each other nonetheless in the summer of 1941. They might have revisited the translation again. Not following his threat of having *The New City* retranslated by someone else, the book as we know it today represents most likely the joint translation efforts of Hilberseimer and Risch. It was an unusual and difficult working setup, only made likely by war and exile: the widely published author forced into a foreign language he didn't speak and a translator who had emigrated from Berlin before the Nazis came to power and worked as a bank clerk after World War II. From his last surviving letter to Hilberseimer, dated December 19, 1946, we know that Risch worked on translating German poetry together with the poet Howard Blake; he sent their translation of a poem by Friedrich Hölderlin in this last letter to Hilberseimer, but he appears to have never published any translation under his own name. Rather than retranslating *The New City*, Hilberseimer kept on rewriting and adding to the book after its publication in 1944, and subsequently published *The New Regional Pattern* (1949) and *The Nature of Cities* (1955).

The title of the third book in this series of publications, *The Nature of Cities*, is reminiscent of the discussions of nature in the letters by Risch. Nature and the importance of trees for life in general and urban planning in particular are an underlying thread of the writing and translation process of *The New City*. There is a hidden ecological backstory to be found in the archive. For the translation typescripts, Risch repurposed paper with lists of broad-leaved trees, the origin of which are unknown; behind many pages of the translation lie trees. It is thus probably not surprising that Hilberseimer initially intended to superimpose a photograph of a maple tree with a city plan for the book cover of *The New City* (figs. 3 and 4).[5]

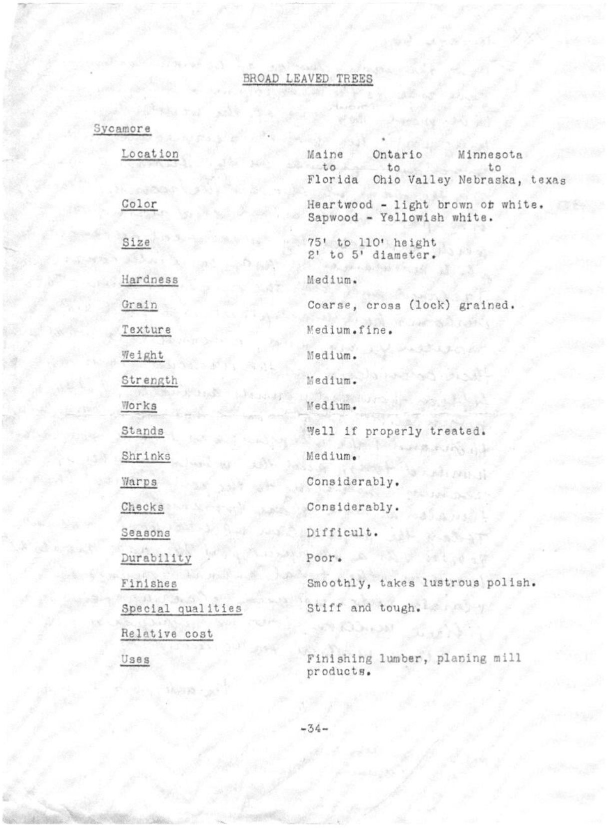

Figure 3: List of broad leaved trees on the back of a typescript of the translation for *The New City*, n.d.

BROAD LEAVED TREES

Sycamore

Location	Maine Ontario Minnesota to to to Florida Ohio Valley Nebraska, texas
Color	Heartwood - light brown or white. Sapwood - Yellowish white.
Size	75' to 110' height 2' to 5' diameter.
Hardness	Medium.
Grain	Coarse, cross (lock) grained.
Texture	Medium.fine.
Weight	Medium.
Strength	Medium.
Works	Medium.
Stands	Well if properly treated.
Shrinks	Medium.
Warps	Considerably.
Checks	Considerably.
Seasons	Difficult.
Durability	Poor.
Finishes	Smoothly, takes lustrous polish.
Special qualities	Stiff and tough.
Relative cost	
Uses	Finishing lumber, planing mill products.

-34-

Bauhaus in Translation

In his struggle to translate *The New City* with the help of an unexperienced translator, Hilberseimer turned to several old connections for support. During his stay with Risch on the East Coast, Hilberseimer sent a letter to the former Bauhaus student Howard Dearstyne dated August 23, 1940; it also gives a good impression of his proficiency in English (see AIC, Hilberseimer, Series 2/1):

73 & 74. CITY STREETS: Past, present and future.

99

Figure 4: p. 99 from:
Hilberseimer, Ludwig. 1944.
*The New City: Principles
of Planning.* Chicago:
Theobald.

Dear Mr Dearstyne,

I have a bad conscience for not answering your letter. But it was impossible for me to get a clear view about what I am able to do. I am nearly six weeks in Dorchester—near Boston—not to take English lessons, as I wanted, but to help to translate my book. It is nearly finished, but it was a hard write and I have had not much of my vacation. You will be wondering why I could be of any assistance. You are right. I don't know was it right but I know much better what is wrong. Therefore I could help something.

Already in the middle of translating the book, Hilberseimer sent Dearstyne, on November 20, 1940, "the part of my book which deals with the art

248

of city-planning." He asked his former student for advice on translating certain passages, including a drawing in his letter to make himself better understood (figs. 5 and 6):

At the piazza S Marco in Venice the tower "überschneidet" the buildings behind it. Which word can be used to express it? May be it can only expressed through a Umschreibung a expression in other words. But with which words? I have written about the function of this tower and I ask you whether it is possible for you to translate.

In his letters, such as the one dating March 5, 1941, Dearstyne comforts Hilberseimer by establishing a relationship that is based on continuity, rather than the experience of exile:

Lieber Herr Hilberseimer, You See above the power of habit; I fully intended to write you in English, but in spite of myself I started out with the customary German salutation. [...] Macht der Gewohnheit.

Despite the translation problems, Dearstyne praises Hilberseimer's text, not least because he knew its contents well from his years at the Bauhaus, and knew how to speak to the author:

So, I came only last night to a careful reading of your "Elements of City Planning." It's excellent; I think it's the clearest and most reasonable thing I have yet read on the subject. And furthermore the English is unassailable (I have no improvements to suggest this time!)

Dearstyne goes on to compare Hilberseimer's "important work" with that of Le Corbusier ("more practical and carefully thought-out") and Frank Lloyd Wright, which he calls "chaotic and over-aesthetic in its approach." Dearstyne was well aware of the context and importance Hilberseimer claimed for his work, which Dearstyne refers to as "ideas of more far-reaching significance" than the solution of practical everyday problems of the profession.
However, as if Dearstyne foresaw the future resistance with which Hilberseimer's ideas would be met in the urban development in the United States, he added to his praise a friendly warning:

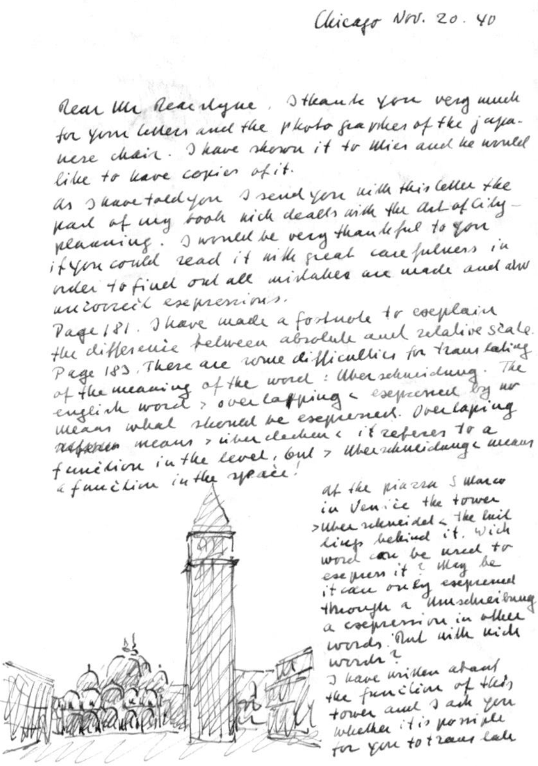

Figure 5: Ludwig Hilbers-
eimer, Letter to Dearstyne,
20th Nov 1940 (page 1 of 2)

You, of course, are under no illusion as to the obstacles standing in the way of the realization of a scheme so revolutionary as yours. It would be wishful thinking to hope to see a city built in our time on the basis of the idea that you propose. I'm sure you don't expect it. It would require a political and social revolution [...] and still more than that—a new regime with the foresight and intelligence to recognize the need of a radically new approach to city-planning.

Hilberseimer was not only confronted with the inadequacy of the translation and Dearstyne's friendly warning but also with no publishing company willing to take on his book project in the middle of World War II—until finally

Figure 6: p. 181 from:
Hilberseimer, Ludwig. 1944.
*The New City: Principles of
Planning.* Chicago: Theo-
bald.

129. PIAZZA ST. MARK, Venice.

130. PIAZZA ST. MARK, Venice.

181

the gallerist Paul Theobald stepped up. Hilberseimer needed all the support he could get. The three paratexts of the published volume are to be
read as an answer to the unstable process of creating and the uncertainty
of reception.

The first paratext, a poem about cities by Walt Whitman, would have been
chosen to suggest the legitimacy of speaking in the American context. The
other two paratexts both refer back to the Bauhaus; the foreword by Ludwig
Mies van der Rohe to testify to the author's authority in the realm of architecture and cities, and a note by the author at the end of the volume to create a
worthy pedigree and mention his hard work:

I began to write this book after teaching City Planning a number of years at the Bauhaus in Dessau. When the Nazis came into power I was forbidden to teach. There was then scarcely a chance to publish the book. Yet two parts of it, "Penetration of Sunlight into the Room" and "Penetration of Sunrays and Density of Population," were published in the *Moderne Bauformen* in 1935 and 1936. (Hilberseimer 1944, 192)

Concerning the bibliographical background, Hilbserseimer is not quite right, because he incorporated the articles from *Moderne Bauformen* in the typescript of "Gesellschaft und Städtebau" and extended and changed them. He could have not published the book we know today as *The New City* in Nazi Germany, as we have to consider the work done after his emigration to the United States; it is very much Bauhaus in translation. This is all the more apparent if we compare the German manuscript with the American book: the list of illustrations in the latter reads decisively more international. German references in text and illustrations have been cut. Hilberseimer's plans for Dessau from 1933, for example, were published with no mention of Germany or the exact place; it was but a "European industrial city" (Hilberseimer 1944, 134–35; see "Visuals", p. 288–89, fig. 26–27).

Ever-evolving Contradictions

Hilberseimer did not consider his work a purely scientific piece of writing, hence we can explain the missing bibliography, quotes, and so forth. *The New City* has been anthologized as a handbook, a manual of urban planning (see Davidovici 2017). The genesis depicted above, as well as the finished book, suggest otherwise. It is in the best sense of the word an unsecured hybrid in the midst and at a crucial point in a very long writing process. It is equidistant to science, the realm of art and architecture, history or philosophy, as hinted at by Mies van der Rohe in his introduction: "City planning is, in essence, a work of order; and order means—according to St. Augustine—'The disposition of equal and unequal things, attributing to each its place'" (Hilberseimer 1944, xv).

Stressing the process of writing, we are reminded of the similarity in Hilberseimer's thinking about the city and his proposed settlement units. At the end of part II of *The New City*, he writes about theory and reality: "The proposed combinations of settlement units to form cities constitute neither definite plans, nor suggestions for standardization. They are abstractions. Absolute cities do not exist. Cities are individuals" (Hilberseimer 1944, 128). Just as life is not static, the city isn't. Hilberseimer's settlement unit and its city landscapes are conceived of as an ever-evolving, inherently unfinished environment with an ambition on a planetary scale.

One could discern a certain likeness between these ever-evolving city landscapes and the writing process described above. Accepting the closeness of urban planner and architect as evidenced by Hilberseimer's own biography, we might find affirmation for the likeness between the settlement unit and the writing process behind *The New City* in Andre Tavares's study on *The Anatomy of the Architectural Book*:

> "[A]rchitects who make books often think of them as spatially equivalent to buildings. In buildings as in books, architects set up sequences and logical paths that generate meaning for those using them and thus both formats offer similar strategies by which to physically grasp spatial experiences, from page to page as from room to room" (Tavares 2016, 9).

Compared with Hilberseimer's few built projects, there is an uncounted number of unbuilt projects accompanying his publications. The lingering potentiality of his typological and generic solutions for the city seems to stem from an understanding of no authorship or shared authorship (the future architect finding specific formulations for Hilberseimer's generic solutions). The assertiveness of Hilberseimer's style of writing, somewhat remedied in the subtitle of *The New City* as "Principles of Planning," contradicts the potentiality of his city solutions, but only at a first glance. We need to look again; we need to see the process behind the finished books.

Uncompromising, hermetic, totalizing—these were some of the words used to describe Hilberseimer, his plans, and drawings in the last couple of decades. I would add a layer to this picture, or open up the facade of that history. There might be more contradictions in his work than we think, and it is precisely those contradictions and openings where we can enter today. The writing process acts as a counterweight to the published texts, just like Hilberseimer's replanning of cities to the chaos of existing modern urban environments. The methods of (re)writing and (re)planning were related (González Martínez 2016, 76). Modernity in the case of Hilberseimer is an ongoing, potentially never-ending process, reuse and adaptation that are so relevant today already inherent from the start. Openness is, after all, a central notion for Hilberseimer:

> Since the Gothic period, our spatial concepts have been moving steadily in the direction of greater freedom. We have become more and more concerned with widening and opening the city and merging it with open space. Today our spatial feeling tends to openness; so does our city structure. Different forces tend to dissipate the confinement of the city, to liberate the house, and with it, man; and to link man to nature once again. (Hilberseimer 1944, 190)

The writing process, as described and analyzed above, stresses the ecological and social aspects in Hilberseimer's modern planning theories. It draws the attention away from the modern facades, be they praised for their beauty in the case of Mies van der Rohe or condemned for their sternness in case of Hilberseimer's Hochhausstadt, and pulls it to the messy multiplicity of unrealized possible futures within modernism.

In 1988 The Art Institute of Chicago published the volume *In the Shadow of Mies* with famous as well as previously unpublished works by Hilberseimer. On pages 136 and 137, included in a portfolio of his works and projects, we find the design for a house in Sharon, Massachusetts (see "Visuals", p. 296, fig. 41–42). It was, as far as we know, Hilberseimer's last design for a single-family house; the client was Siegfried Risch, his translator, whom he visited at the East Coast several times. In an interview conducted by Betty J. Blum in 1987 as part of the Chicago Architects Oral History Project, Alfred Caldwell (former IIT student, colleague and collaborator of Hilberseimer) told the story of how he remembered the genesis of these drawings for Siegfried Risch:

> "When Hilbs first came to this country he went to New England in the summer time. I think he went to New England to improve his diction. He was a very methodical man. He became acquainted with this man who wanted a house. Hilbs came back and asked me, 'Would you do this house? The money is not important. It's not very much, the man doesn't have much.' I said, 'How much will you have?' He said, 'One hundred dollars.' I said, 'I'll make a plan for that.' Hilbs said, 'I'll make a sketch of how it should be and then you make the working drawings.' I did. […] Hilbs laid out the plan. Hilbs was a wonderful house planner. He knew exactly how every part of the house should be. He was wonderful. The plan of that house was very nice. It's a little wood house" (Blum/Caldwell 1987, 119).

There is no evidence for the house having ever been built.[6] Looking at the floorplan, you would have entered the house, turned ninety degrees to the left, and looked along a bookcase and a fireplace into the living room and out again through a big window into the leafy surroundings of New England.

Notes

1   Compare Pommer 1988, 114–17. The finding aid
    for the Hilberseimer Papers can also be retrieved
    online: https://www.artic.edu/artworks/243871/
    karl-ludwig-hilberseimer-papers. Some documents
    can be found in the holdings of the Bauhaus-Archiv/
    Museum für Gestaltung, Berlin, as well as in the
    archive of the Akademie der Künste, Berlin. Some
    books from Hilberseimer's private library are to
    be found in the Graham Resource Center at IIT,
    Chicago.

2   One of the typescripts of *Großstadtarchitektur*
    (1927) was even signed by both as coauthors. Com-
    pare Ludwig Karl Hilberseimer (1885–1967) Pa-
    pers at the Ryerson and Burnham Libraries, The Art
    Institute of Chicago (hereafter AIC, Hilberseimer),
    Series 8/1, Box.FF 1.1.

3   Compare AIC, Hilberseimer Papers, Series 4/3,
    Box.FF 4.26 to 4.30.

4   There are two draft letters by Hilberseimer on the
    back of Risch's letters.

5   Compare the letters in Theobald Papers to *Life* mag-
    azine. Theobald Papers, at the Ryerson and Burnham
    Libraries, The Art Institute of Chicago, The New City
    Production Information. 1992.3, Folder 2.22.

6   The Risch House seems to refer back to Hilbers-
    eimer's extandable house of 1932 (see "Visuals",
    p. 292, fig. 33).

The (Almost) Invisible Man: Ludwig Hilberseimer and Germany after World War II

Andreas Schätzke

I

The New City, the first book he published after immigrating to the United States, was part of Ludwig Hilberseimer's efforts to establish himself professionally in a new, though by then not entirely new, environment. He had already been a professor at the Illinois Institute of Technology (IIT) in Chicago for six years when the book appeared in 1944 after much preparation. Everything about it was obviously chosen with care: the book opens with an excerpt from the collection *Leaves of Grass* by the thoroughly American poet Walt Whitman; Ludwig Mies van der Rohe, Hilberseimer's internationally renowned colleague who also emigrated from Germany, contributed the introduction; and the author draws many of his historical and contemporary examples of urban planning from the US context (Hilberseimer 1944). An exhibition entitled *The City: Organism and Artifact*, which Hilberseimer was able to set up in the fall of 1944 at the Art Institute of Chicago to accompany a series of lectures, contributed to the promotion of the publication and its author (see Colman 2014). And even if there is no direct connection, it seems significant that Hilberseimer became a US citizen the same year his book was published.

In addition to clear nods to his American audience, *The New City* contains many references to the author's country of origin—both explicit and implicit. In his epilogue, he mentions his classes at the Bauhaus and his articles, declared as preliminary studies, that appeared in the journal *Moderne Bauformen* in the mid-1930s (Hilberseimer 1935; Hilberseimer 1936). In the treatise itself, numerous examples of older and more recent urban planning also refer to Hilberseimer's homeland. Most of them are named, but some without precise designation, such as his own proposed replanning for Dessau, which is mentioned only as a "European industrial city" (Hilberseimer 1944, 132–36).

Of course, his network of professional and private connections to Germany went far beyond the book published during the war. These connections were important for Hilberseimer's—comparatively minor—reception in postwar Germany, but they were not the only ones that mattered.

Hilberseimer was one of more than 300,000 people who left Germany in the 1930s as a result of National Socialism. In his country of exile, he not only had to learn a new language, which was difficult enough. He was in the comparatively comfortable position of having a professorship waiting for him in the United States, but all in all, emigration also meant an almost completely new beginning for him. When he took his position at the Armour Institute (later IIT) in the fall of 1938, Hilberseimer, unlike Mies van der Rohe, was, as George Danforth recalled, "an unknown person" to the students (Danforth 1988, 8).

II

After the National Socialists came to power in 1933, numerous members of the Bauhaus emigrated from Germany. Several hundred architects also left the country; most of them had no direct or indirect relationship to the Bauhaus. Some were prominent representatives of modernism, but the majority were lesser-known architects who were committed to very different positions. Looking at the overlap between these two groups of emigrants—Bauhaus members and architects—we can see the three most important teachers of architecture at the Bauhaus left Germany during the years of National Socialist rule, but under very different circumstances. All three found refuge in the US. Walter Gropius, who first settled in London in 1934, was able to take a position at Harvard University in 1937. Hilberseimer and Mies van der Rohe left Germany late, in 1938, to take up professorships in Chicago. (Hannes Meyer went to the Soviet Union in 1930 after his dismissal as director of the Bauhaus; later he moved to Mexico via his home country, Switzerland. Meyer was thus not an émigré from Germany, where he had lived for only a little over three years.)

Like Gropius and Mies van der Rohe, Hilberseimer did not return to Germany except for visits. This was also true for most of the other emigrated architects. Postwar German society had an extremely ambivalent relationship with its former fellow citizens who had left the country during National Socialism. In both West and East Germany, this tense relationship with the emigrants can also be observed in the profession of architecture. Many German architects, especially the younger ones, felt they had been cut off from decisive international developments during the previous twelve years. As early as the 1940s, therefore, exhibitions and publications—some of them initiated by the occupying powers—that informed about current building in the US, France, Great Britain, Scandinavia, or Switzerland, attracted considerable attention, even beyond the professional community. Especially in the West German professional press, emigrants after 1945 were often presented in a seemingly neutral way as German architects "abroad" or even as "architects of foreign countries." They were both guarantors of being able to tie in with modernism, which had been largely ostracized after 1933, but they were also the target of fierce criticism directed against the avant-garde. Emigrants attracted attention as sought-after experts whose loss to the German architectural scene was regretted. At the same time, they were seen as potential competitors in the reconstruction process whose advice and interventions had to be fended off.

Gropius came to Berlin in the summer of 1947. He traveled as a so-called visiting expert on behalf of the American government. He was to advise the military governor Lucius D. Clay on reconstruction issues, hold talks with German experts, and give lectures as part of the US information program. In his weeks of travel, Gropius toured a number of other heavily damaged cities in the western occupation zones, including Frankfurt, Hannover, Stuttgart, and Munich. In addition to receiving widespread approval in the press and from colleagues, he also occasionally experienced significant criticism. Mies van der Rohe, who had not yet returned to Germany, was also receiving renewed attention from the professional public at this time (see Schätzke 2000).

A few years later, in the summer of 1951, the Kestner-Gesellschaft art association in Hannover held an exhibition dedicated to the life's work of Gropius and Mies van der Rohe on the occasion of *Constructa*, the first major building exhibition to be held in Germany after the war (see Kestner-Gesellschaft 1951). In addition to this and other retrospectives and tributes to some well-known emigrants, specific projects became possible over time. Gropius, with The Architects Collaborative, was given the opportunity, among other things, to design an apartment building in the Hansaviertel neighborhood for the 1957 *Interbau* exhibition in West Berlin. In the early 1960s, the West Berlin Senate and some specialist journalists endeavored to give Mies van der Rohe an opportunity to realize a project in the city. As a result of this initiative, a museum based on Mies's design was built at the arising Kulturforum opposite Hans Scharoun's concert hall of the Philharmonic Orchestra. Mies's building opened in 1968 as the Neue Nationalgalerie. In the Federal Republic, there had already been interest in Mies van der Rohe designing representative buildings before that. However, his design for the National Theater in Mannheim from 1952/1953, as well as his later plans for the Krupp company in Essen and the Museum Georg Schäfer in Schweinfurt, were not realized for various reasons (see Schätzke 2000, 18–19).

Compared to Gropius and Mies van der Rohe, the attention paid to Hilberseimer in postwar Germany was negligible. Among professionals, Hilberseimer was of course as well known as the other two, especially to his older colleagues. They remembered the avant-gardist and theorist of the 1920s and his equally provocative and suggestive schemes, for example of a Hochhausstadt (High-Rise City). As a member of the Arbeitsrat für Kunst, the Novembergruppe, the Deutscher Werkbund, Der Ring, the Bund Deutscher Architekten, and other associations and groups, Hilberseimer had created a broad network for himself during the years of the Weimar Republic. He was remembered as the prolific publicist for the *Sozialistische Monatshefte*, *Das Kunstblatt*, and *Die Form*, the journal of the Deutscher Werkbund, as a Bauhaus teacher and perhaps also as an architect who had realized primarily residential buildings in Berlin. But all this was a long time ago—twenty to thirty years—and Hilberseimer did not appear as someone who could be of immediate interest in the postwar reconstruction. He was basically not a practicing architect, but primarily a theorist and teacher who continued to publish mainly on the subject of urban planning.

Nevertheless, a few articles by and about Hilberseimer can be found in the professional press. As early as 1947, the Berlin-based journal *Der Bauhelfer* printed excerpts from the book *The New City* in German translation (Hilberseimer 1947) (fig. 1). Architect Wils Ebert had written an introduction to the text, not always entirely accurate in the details, in which he praises Hilberseimer's work of the 1920s and 1930s as an essential contribution to establishing urban planning as an "exact science." Ebert had studied at the Bauhaus with Mies van der Rohe and Hilberseimer, among others, and received his diploma in 1933. He had then briefly worked in Gropius's office in Berlin. When Hilberseimer emigrated in 1938, Ebert took over his Berlin apartment; the two remained in correspondence thereafter (see Günther 1993, 20 and 128). Hilberseimer's text had been translated into German by the architect Hilda Harte, who had also worked in Gropius's office in the early 1930s.

In *Der Bauhelfer*, excerpts from "Elements of City Planning," the second part of *The New City*, were printed. However, it is obvious that it was not the book that served as the basis for the translation, but rather an article that Hilberseimer had published in December 1940 as a kind of preprint in the journal *Armour Engineer and Alumnus* (Hilberseimer 1940a). The German text corresponds exactly to the version published there; it was only slightly shortened at the end and supplemented by the German original of a study by the Berlin architect Peter Friedrich from 1931 quoted by Hilberseimer in his article. In addition, a large number of the illustrations of the 1940 essay were adopted.

Ebert was particularly interested in Hilberseimer's remarks on the relationship between the workplace and the home, which he regarded as a contribution to basic research on this question. Ebert, however, considered other factors, such as the importance of wind for industrial and residential locations, to be somewhat overrated. Obviously, the principle of separation of functions continued to be of central interest to Ebert, who had attended the fourth CIAM meeting in 1933 as a German delegate. Since 1945, German planners had already been concerned with the idea of the *Stadtlandschaft* in connection with

DER BAUHELFER

ZEITSCHRIFT FÜR DAS GESAMTE BAUWESEN

NUMMER **19** 1947
1. OKTOBER - HEFT

VERLAG UND REDAKTION BERLIN N 65 · CHAUSSEESTRASSE 72 · FERNSPRECHER 461615

TELEGRAMMADRESSE BAUHELFER BERLIN · CHEFREDAKTEUR: KARL STEGEMANN

PROFESSOR LUDWIG HILBERSEIMER

Elemente der Stadtplanung

Architekt Hilberseimer wurde 1936 durch Professor Mies van der Rohe als Lehrer für Städtebau nach Chicago/USA an das Amor-Institut berufen. Bevor er in der gleichen Aufgabe am Bauhaus Dessau von 1928—1933 lehrte, war er bereits durch seine städtebaulichen Veröffentlichungen bekannt geworden. Seine publizistische Tätigkeit begann mit gesellschaftskritischen Betrachtungen der verschiedenen Gestaltungsrichtungen der bildenden Kunst nach dem ersten Weltkrieg und Analysen von Bauwerken nach Zweck, Form und Konstruktion. Diese Arbeiten setzte er mit Forschungen und Darstellungen der den Wohnungsbau, insbesondere die Grundrisse beeinflussenden Faktoren: Bevölkerungsstruktur, Besonnung und Konstruktion über Zusammenhänge zwischen Hausgrundriß und Stadtplan fort. Hilberseimer leistete damit wesentliche Beiträge für die Überleitung des Städtebaues aus seiner ästhetischen Sphäre zur exakten Wissenschaft. Seine Aufsätze in den „Sozialistischen Monatsheften", ähnlich Hugo Häring und Dr. Alexander Schwab, über die Gestaltung der Stadt als energiepolitisches Problem im Sinne der Arbeiten von Martin Mächler, gehören wie die Städtebauausstellung in Gothenburg 1923 zu den Grundlagen des modernen Städtebaues.
Neben seiner Tätigkeit als Lehrer am Bauhaus und Vorstandsmitglied des Werkbundes arbeitete er in der Folge weiter an den Problemen durch Forschungen über Besonnung und Siedlungsdichte, Beanspruchung des Stadtraumes durch Flachbau, leistungsfähige Erdgeschoßgrundrisse usf. Seinem in Deutschland vorbereiteten und in USA erschienenen Buch „The New City", Arch, L. Hilberseimer, Paul Theobald Verlag, Chicago 1938, wurde die folgende Arbeit „Die Elemente der Stadtplanung" als ein weiterer Beitrag zur Grundlagenforschung der Ordnungsfaktoren zwischen Arbeits- und Wohnstätte entnommen (Übersetzung von Dipl.-Ing. Hilda Harte). Die Bedeutung des Windes und sein Einfluß hinsichtlich der Industrie erscheinen hierbei etwas überwertet. Wenn auch in der Vergangenheit die Mängel der Planung rücksichtslos auf Kosten der Gesundheit und der Wohnruhe dem einzelnen Bewohner aufgebürdet wurden, so zeichnen sich doch durch die Entwicklung der technischen Mittel und wirtschaftlichen Notwendigkeiten Lösungen ab, die die Schutzzone zwar nicht aufheben, aber zumindest eine starke Reduzierung des Abstandes und damit eine größere Planungsfreiheit erlauben.
*Baurat Sierks, im Abschnitt Verkehrsgestaltung erwähnt, ist als Opfer der vergangenen politischen Epoche gefallen. Der im Wortlaut wiedergegebene Abschnitt aus der Arbeit „Lineares Flußsystem" (1931) von Peter Friedrich wurde zum besseren Verständnis — als Zitat gekennzeichnet — aus dem Original ergänzt.   Architekt Wils **E b e r t***

Drei Hauptfaktoren haben im letzten Jahrhundert zu dem schnellen Wachstum der Städte geführt und die gegenwärtige Übervölkerung hervorgebracht: die Freiheit der Einwanderung, die Entwicklung der Industrie und die wachsenden Erleichterungen der Nachrichtenübermittlung. Aber weder ein regulierendes Prinzip noch ein gleichwertiges Ordnungsprinzip, um diese Entwicklung zu kontrollieren, konnte geformt werden. Die Folge war, daß ursprünglich konstruktive Kräfte bald zu destruktiven Kräften wurden.

Die meisten unserer Städte sind aus dem Zentralsystem gewachsen, das sich ursprünglich aus den Bedingungen entwickelte, die für eine Stadt der Fußgänger natürlich waren. Das Kultur-, Verwaltungs- und Geschäftszentrum lag immer im Herzen solcher Städte, leicht von der Peripherie zu erreichen. Mittel der Verkehrsverbindung für eine zu regulierende Überfüllung waren unnötig. So verhielt es sich bei Städten vom sogenannten organischen Typ, wie Nördlingen, und auch bei solchen, die geometrisch in ihrer Anlage waren, wie Priene; es gab immer die charakteristische Bewegung zum Zentrum.

Als die Städte wuchsen, manchmal zu ungeheurem Ausmaß, führten sie die Entwicklung des Systems der Zentralisation fort. Während dieses System für kleine Städte vollkommen genügte, hat es sich für die großen Städte unseres Zeitalters als unzureichend erwiesen. Die Übervölkerung brachte Probleme mit sich, die Städte nicht lösten. Der unaufhörlichen Nachfrage nach Wohnungen wurde durch eine Brut von ungesunden Mietwohnungen ohne genügend Licht und Luft begegnet. Große Fabriken, die ohne Rücksicht auf benachbarte Wohngebiete gebaut wurden, belästigten diese bald mit ihrem Rauch und ihren Ausdünstungen. Dies vergrößerte außerordentlich die schon unzureichenden sanitären Bedingungen. Der unaufhörlich anwachsende Stadtverkehr, der notwendig zum Transport der Bevölkerung war, ließ bald die Unzulänglichkeit der existierenden Stadtanordnung offenbar werden. Alle Verkehrsmittel führten zu einem einzigen Punkt, dem Stadtzentrum. Das Zusammenfließen aller Verkehrsgassen zum Herzen der Stadt rief dort ein unheilvolles Blockieren des Verkehrs hervor, während zur selben Zeit die Vororte der Stadt unter

3

Figure 1: First page of: Hilberseimer, Ludwig. 1947. „Elemente der Stadtplanung." In: *Der Bauhelfer* 2, 19: 3–8.

reconstruction. Not only Scharoun, under whose direction the Kollektivplan for Berlin had been developed in the first postwar months with a radical restructuring and a separation of urban functions, but also individual collaborators on this plan including Ebert as well as Peter Friedrich and Reinhold Lingner, published articles on such concepts.

Also in 1947, the Hamburg-based journal *Baurundschau* published a detailed and richly illustrated review of *The New City*. The article is a predominantly approving appraisal of Hilberseimer's book. However, the reviewer, whose name is not mentioned, notes that *The New City* does not offer a closed and realistic system of urban planning and that some points are not convincing and too theoretical (Baurundschau 1947).

III

The end of the National Socialist dictatorship and the war meant a deep break for Germany, despite many continuities that were to become apparent sooner or later. In the discussions between architects, urban planners, and publicists, a wide variety of attitudes could be discerned, but at first glance, modernism was in the foreground. By appealing to this supposedly unencumbered tradition, they sought to regain some of the credit that had been squandered. In 1947 the architect and journalist Alfons Leitl programmatically illustrated the first issue of his new journal *Baukunst und Werkform* not with works by foreign architects or German emigrants but with photographs of industrial buildings that Rudolf Lodders, Egon Eiermann, and others had erected during the National Socialist era in the spirit of modernism. In addition, *Baukunst und Werkform*, which in the 1950s was one of the most important professional publications in West Germany, occasionally gave emigrants a voice. Among them were Fritz Jaenecke in Sweden, Max Cetto in Mexico, and Mies van der Rohe, Konrad Wachsmann, and Martin Wagner in the United States. As early as 1949, the third issue of the journal was largely devoted to Mies van der Rohe (Baukunst und Werkform 1947–49).

At the end of 1956, the editor-in-chief of *Baukunst und Werkform*, Ulrich Conrads, asked Hilberseimer for a contribution. It was about projects that Hilberseimer believed could be of particular interest to urban planners in West Germany.[1] Despite the short notice of the request, the article entitled "Großstädtische Planungsaufgaben" appeared as planned in January 1957. Hilberseimer begins with simple, basic considerations about the separation of urban functions and the optimal nature of residential areas, work areas, and traffic routes. He then points out that these principles could be applied not only to newly founded cities but also to existing ones and that well-functioning entities could be created by replanning them. Hilberseimer then presents a planning project of his own, the phased reshaping of Chicago's South Side. He also describes the two projects he worked on with Mies van der Rohe, Lafayette Park in Detroit and Hyde Park in Chicago (Hilberseimer 1957b).

The essay was supplemented by an introductory contribution written by the young Munich architect Peter C. von Seidlein. Von Seidlein had studied at IIT in 1951/1952 with Mies van der Rohe and Hilberseimer. He attests to an extraordinary consistency in Hilberseimer's thinking over the decades and points out that his plans have so far remained largely theoretical. Most of it, he says, will remain theory, but it is never the less important because it enables an aspirational orientation to the future of the city (Von Seidlein 1957, 12).

Around the same time, Hilberseimer took advantage of an invitation from Germany to participate in a large-scale handbook on medicine and urban planning to again discuss specific plans, namely his projects for the transformation of large cities such as Chicago and Detroit (Hilberseimer 1957a). Remarkably, Hilberseimer, whose work had a high degree of abstraction and in which the fundamental was more significant than the specific, almost always explained his views in terms of concrete projects related to individual locations.

Beyond these contributions, only two more articles by Hilberseimer appeared in German journals in the 1950s and 1960s (Hilberseimer 1952; Hilberseimer 1964). There were, however, some late honors. In 1963 he traveled to Germany to accept a visiting professorship at the Technical University of Berlin proposed by Fritz Eggeling, the director of the Institute of Urban Planning. Eggeling had met Hilberseimer the prior year during a trip to the US.[2] As early as 1957, the year in which the city of West Berlin had awarded Hilberseimer its Art Prize in the field of architecture at the suggestion of the Academy of Arts (the jury consisted of Heinrich Lauterbach, Ernst May, and Wils Ebert) and works by the prizewinner had been shown as part of the *Große Berliner Kunstausstellung*, Hans Scharoun, then director of the Institute of Urban Planning, had brought up the idea of a visiting professorship.[3] However, such a position in Germany did not come about until six years later.

There is a report on the courses that the seventy-seven-year-old Hilberseimer offered in Berlin during the summer semester of 1963 by Thomas Sieverts, who was on Eggeling's staff at the time. Sieverts was placed at Hilberseimer's side as an assistant, "which proved to be a difficult task. In Hilberseimer's course, seemingly very simple tasks were set involving grouping residential buildings together. The students tried to build their newly acquired insights into the social dimension and cultural meaning of housing into the design exercises. But by reducing the arguments to the three factors of sun, wind, and circulation, Hilberseimer pushed them toward objectively verifiable functionalistic solutions, which naturally rather resembled each other. Utilizing their newfound questions and knowledge from the social sciences and semiotics, the students tried to draw Hilberseimer into a discussion, but that venerable monument of modernity repelled to all arguments from his intellectual bastion made of functional axioms of natural or engineering sciences" (Sieverts 2000, 13).

During his 1963 stay in Germany, Hilberseimer also spent a week in Darmstadt, where he visited the newly founded Bauhaus Archive under the direction of Hans M. Wingler and participated in a colloquium at the Technical University. Shortly before, he had also been accepted as an associate member of the West Berlin Academy of Arts, along with Arthur Korn, another leftwing modernist of the Weimar period who had emigrated to Britain (see Bauwelt 1963). During Scharoun's presidency from 1955 to 1968, the Academy added almost all of the still-living former members of the well-known and influential group of modern architects Der Ring, founded in 1926, to its

Architecture Section; beginning in the 1950s, in addition to Hilberseimer and Korn, these included Otto Bartning, Richard Döcker, Gropius, Hugo Häring, Wassili Luckhardt, Ernst May, Mies van der Rohe, and Max Taut (see Geist/ Kürvers/Rausch 1993, 108). The Technical University of Berlin also took advantage of Hilberseimer's stay to award him an honorary doctorate (see Technische Universität Berlin 1963).

The visit in the summer of 1963 was Hilberseimer's only stay in Germany after his emigration. The fact that a book by Hilberseimer was published in Germany in the same year for the first time since 1931 is one of the late attempts at reparation (see "Visuals", p. 314, fig. 67). The literary genre of this volume, *Entfaltung einer Planungsidee*, cannot be clearly defined. The author himself calls it an "Essay" (Hilberseimer 1963, 5). Hilberseimer looks at his own development from the 1920s to the 1960s, self-critically revises his early proposals such as the Hochhausstadt, and traces the steps that led him to his then current views on architecture and urban design.

The book appeared in the newly founded Bauwelt Fundamente series published at Ullstein Verlag by Ulrich Conrads, by then editor-in-chief of the review *Bauwelt*. The paperback series was widely read in professional circles in West Germany, including architects, urban planners, historians, and students. The first volumes already indicated the program Conrads was pursuing. There are historical texts, mainly from the first half of the twentieth century, as well as essays on architectural history and theory, and contributions on current issues of architecture and urban planning. The first volume, an anthology of programs and manifestos, was edited by Conrads himself. It was followed by new editions of classic modernist texts by Le Corbusier, Bruno Taut, and Adolf Behne, as well as Jane Jacobs's *The Death and Life of Great American Cities*, which had been published in English in 1961.

It is obvious that Hilberseimer reemerged as a book author in Germany at the moment when, on the one hand, modernism was already being historicized and, on the other, harsh criticism of misguided and wrongly developed modern architecture and urban planning was beginning. By denouncing the fact that the diversity of the historical city—with its characteristic mixture of functions—was being destroyed, Jane Jacobs represented something like the counterposition to Hilberseimer's radical concepts of transformation and decentralization (Jacobs 1963).

IV

As a former Bauhaus member who had taught housing and urban planning in Dessau and Berlin from 1929 to 1933, Hilberseimer was only marginally noticed in the postwar period. However, members of Hilberseimer's close professional circles, particularly his former students and a few key researchers including Wingler, did make reference to the Bauhaus years of his biography. The Bauhaus itself attracted a great deal of attention in postwar Western Germany and was seen in a predominantly positive light, although harsh criticism was occasionally voiced as early as the 1950s. Gropius worked tirelessly as a propagandist on his own and the institution's behalf; the common Bauhaus image of the time was due in no small part to his influence. West Germany was very receptive to this image, because the Bauhaus seemed to be both a globally successful German product and politically unencumbered.

In the Federal Republic, in addition to the influential book *Das Bauhaus* by Wingler (1962), one of the early efforts to document the Bauhaus also on the basis of texts was a publication from 1964. The privately run Göppinger Galerie in Frankfurt prepared it on the occasion of its exhibition *Bauhaus: Idee–Form–Zweck–Zeit*. In contrast to Wingler's work, this was made up not predominantly of historical documents, but rather of the recently written recollections of former Bauhaus members (Neumann 1964).

The editor of the catalogue, Eckhard Neumann, had also asked Hilberseimer for a contribution, but he declined because of a lack of time, stating that he had not been in Chicago for some time.[4] He had probably only just returned from his trip to Europe. It is safe to assume that Hilberseimer, as a professional writer, would have been able to contribute a short text. Possibly he did not want to appear primarily as a representative of the historical Bauhaus but as an urban planner with still current relevance. In this respect, he resembled

LUDWIG HILBERSEIMER
Berliner Architektur
der 20er Jahre

Neue Bauhausbücher

Figure 2: Cover of: Hilberseimer, Ludwig. 1967. *Berliner Architektur der 20er Jahre.*
(Mainz: Kupferberg, design by Herbert Bayer).

Mies van der Rohe, who had been, after all, one of the three directors of the Bauhaus. Thus it came about that the 1964 publication contains contributions by Alfred Arndt, Herbert Bayer, Max Bill, Gustav Hassenpflug, Hubert Hoffmann, Fritz Hesse, Gerhard Marcks, Georg Muche, Alexander Schawinsky, Lou Scheper, Lothar Schreyer, Gunta Stölzl, and many others, but no text by Hilberseimer. Gropius, on the other hand, had contributed a foreword, among other things. A few years later, Neumann published his more comprehensive book *Bauhaus und Bauhäusler* (Neumann 1971) based on this work. Here, too, Hilberseimer is missing.[5] He was, however, represented in the large retrospective that was shown in Stuttgart in 1968 on the occasion of the fiftieth anniversary of the founding of the Bauhaus. In the case of Hilberseimer, who had died the year before, the focus was on his work in the US (see Herzogenrath 1968, 171–73).

In East Germany, on the other hand, there was almost no reception of Hilberseimer—considered a *Westemigrant*—during his lifetime, neither as a contributor to socialist journals, an avant-gardist of the prewar period and a Bauhaus member, nor as an urban planner and theorist of the present. In the GDR, the Bauhaus, like modernism as a whole, was branded "cosmopolitan" and "formalist" soon after the founding of the state in 1949, in the wake of the confrontation between political systems during the Cold War (see Thöner 2005). Even when the first initiatives to take a somewhat less ideologically restricted look at the Bauhaus were taken and politically permitted in a few publications and exhibitions in the 1960s, Hilberseimer remained almost unmentioned.

All in all, while it can be said that Hilberseimer did not completely disappear in postwar Germany, particularly in the West, at least in the 1940s and 1950s, if we compare him with Gropius and Mies van der Rohe, he remained almost invisible. In his afterword to Hilberseimer's last, posthumously published book (fig. 2), Wingler attempted to outline the status the author still enjoyed among German—especially West German—experts well into the 1960s: "Although there was an awareness of Hilberseimer's importance in professional circles, even among these, those who sought to define his accomplishments were generally at a loss. During a colloquium at the Technical University of Darmstadt, this was during the visit to Germany in 1963, Hilberseimer was asked by a student what he had accomplished, to which he responded with the absolute honesty that was a mark of his character: He had accomplished nothing" (Wingler 1967, 102). Hilberseimer's confession, which was certainly also due to the situation described by Wingler, is probably not to be understood as a final judgment. However, it characterizes his position in the architectural and urban planning discourses of the time quite accurately and allows an insight into the specific condition of an emigrant's life marked by upheavals and fractures.

Notes

1   Letter from Ulrich Conrads to Ludwig Hilberseimer,
    November 15, 1956, Ludwig Karl Hilberseimer
    Papers, Ryerson and Burnham Archives, The Art
    Institute of Chicago, Series 8: Literary works, 8/3:
    Manuscripts and articles, 2.32.
2   See the letter from Fritz Eggeling to Ludwig Hilber-
    seimer, June 1, 1962 (carbon copy), Technical Uni-
    versity of Berlin, University Archives, holding 206,
    no. 88, box 22.
3   See the letter from Hans Scharoun to Ludwig Hilber-
    seimer, May 21, 1957, and the letter from Hilber-
    seimer to Scharoun, May 27, 1957 (carbon copy),
    Ludwig Karl Hilberseimer Papers, Ryerson and
    Burnham Archives, The Art Institute of Chicago,
    Series 2: Correspondence, 3.2.
4   Letter from Ludwig Hilberseimer to the Göppinger
    Galerie, October 11, 1963, Bauhaus Dessau Foun-
    dation, Collection.
5   An English edition of the book with slightly fewer
    contributions had been published in New York in
    1970.

Visuals

The following is a visual tour through Ludwig Hilberseimer's career: from his first known publication of unbuilt projects in 1919 to his last books. This overview reflects the themes and angles of the essays collected in the previous chapters. While necessarily incomplete, it proposes an arc to Hilberseimer's career and intellectual development. Wherever possible, the reference to the first publication during Hilberseimer's lifetime is given. Posthumous first publications are not included.

Figure 1: Pitched-roof houses around a village square, c. 1905 (or 1919?), published in: Wagenführ, Max. 1919. "Architektonische Entwürfe von L. Hilberseimer." In: *Deutsche Kunst und Dekoration*, 6 (June), 208–216.

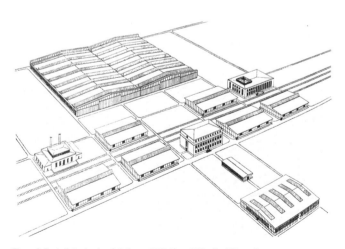

Figure 2: Test pilot school and station, c. 1916–18, published in: Hilberseimer, Ludwig. 1962. *Entfaltung einer Planungsidee*. Berlin/Frankfurt a.M./Vienna: Ullstein, 122.

Figure 3: Chicago Tribune project, 1922, published in: *G (Material zur elementaren Gestaltung)*, 2 (1923): 3; and on the cover of: Hilberseimer, Ludwig, *Großtadtbauten: Neue Architektur I*, Merz 18/19. Hannover: Aposs-Verlag.

Figure 4: Wohnstadt project, block view, 1923, published in: Hilberseimer, Ludwig. 1927. *Großstadtarchitektur*. Stuttgart: Verlag Julius, 33.

Figure 5: Wohnstadt project, commercial street view, 1923, published in: Hilberseimer, Ludwig. 1925. *Großstadtbauten: Neue Architektur I*, Merz 18/19. Hannover: Aposs-Verlag, 8; and: Hilberseimer, Ludwig. 1927. *Großstadt-architektur*. Stuttgart: Verlag Julius, 33.

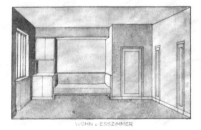

Figure 6: Interior views of kitchen, living room, and bedroom with built-in furniture, published in: Hilberseimer, Ludwig. 1925. *Großstadtbauten: Neue Architektur I*, Merz 18/19. Hannover: Aposs-Verlag, 16.

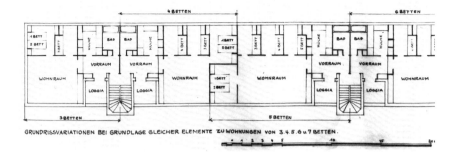

Figure 7: Floor plan variations based on the same elements for apartments of 3, 4, 5, 6 and 7 beds, 1925, published in: Hilberseimer, Ludwig. 1925. *Großstadtbauten: Neue Architektur I*, Merz 18/19. Hannover: Aposs-Verlag, 24.

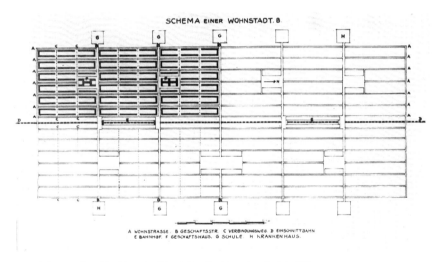

Figure 8: Scheme of a residential city, B, 1923, published in: Hilberseimer, Ludwig. 1925. *Großstadtbauten: Neue Architektur I*, Merz 18/19. Hannover: Aposs-Verlag, 25.

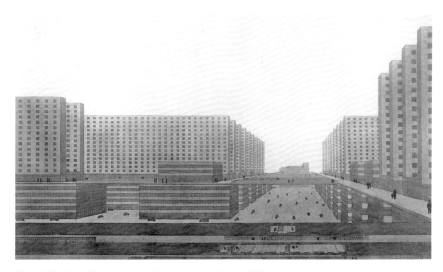

Figure 9: High-Rise City (Hochhausstadt) project, perspective view, 1924,
published in: Hilberseimer, Ludwig. 1925. *Großstadtbauten: Neue Architektur I*,
Merz 18/19. Hannover: Aposs-Verlag, 12; and: Hilberseimer, Ludwig. 1927.
Großstadtarchitektur. Stuttgart: Verlag Julius, 19.

Figure 10: High-Rise City (Hochhausstadt) project, north–south street view,
1924, published in: Hilberseimer, Ludwig. 1925. *Großstadtbauten: Neue Architektur I*, Merz 18/19. Hannover: Aposs-Verlag, 14; and: Hilberseimer, Ludwig.
1927. *Großstadtarchitektur*. Stuttgart: Verlag Julius, 18.

Figure 11: High-rise building, factory (Hochhaus, Fabrikanlage), 1924, published in: Hilberseimer, Ludwig. 1925. *Großstadtbauten: Neue Architektur I*, Merz 18/19. Hannover: Aposs-Verlag, 19.

Figure 12: Welfare city (Wohlfahrtsstadt), model photograph, 1927, authorship not yet definitively secured, photographer unknown.

Figure 13: Single-family residence, Weißenhof Estate, Stuttgart, Germany, 1927,
photographer unknown

Figure 14: Ludwig Hilberseimer, apartment building, Wohnanlage Süßer Grund,
Berlin-Adlershof, 1929–1930

LUDWIG HILBERSEIMER

BAUBÜCHER BAND 3

GROSS STADT

ARCHITEKTUR

JULIUS HOFFMANN
VERLAG / STUTTGART   MIT 229 ABBILDUNGEN / KART. M 9.50

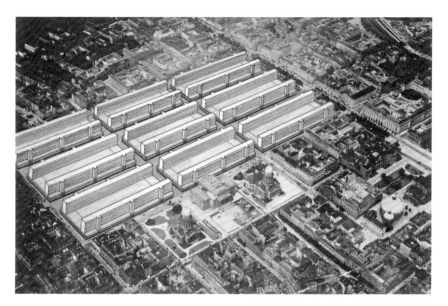

Figure 16: Proposal for office and commercial buildings, Berlin Friedrichstadt
District, photo-montage, c. 1930, published in: Hilberseimer, Ludwig. 1930.
"Vorschlag zur City-Bebauung." In: *Die Form: Zeitschrift für gestaltende
Arbeit* 5: 608–611, here 608.

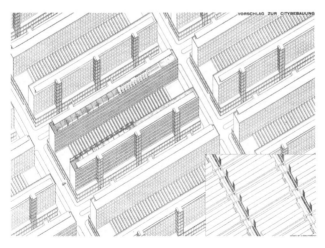

Figure 17: Proposal for office and commercial buildings, Berlin Friedrichstadt
District, isometric drawing, c. 1930, published in: Hilberseimer, Ludwig. 1930.
"Vorschlag zur City-Bebauung." In: *Die Form: Zeitschrift für gestaltende
Arbeit* 5: 608–611, here 609.

Figure 18: Proposal for office and commercial buildings, Berlin Friedrichstadt District, (City-Bebauung. Vorschlag), 1929, from: *Das Kunstblatt 13*. 1929 (March), 95. See figure 17, bottom right.

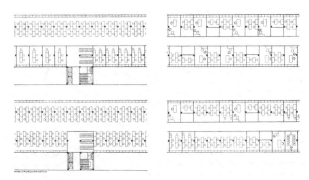

Figure 19: Proposal for office and commercial buildings, Berlin Friedrichstadt District, furnishing variants of an office building (Vorschlag zur City-Bebauung, Möblierungsvarianten eines Bürohauses), c. 1930, published in: Hilberseimer, Ludwig. 1930. "Vorschlag zur City-Bebauung." In: Die Form: Zeitschrift für gestaltende Arbeit 5: 608–611, here 609.

Figure 20: Ludwig Hilberseimer and Hugo Häring, 1:1 model of the kitchen type R1 at the exhibition *Die neue Küche* of Der Ring, 1929, photographer unknown.

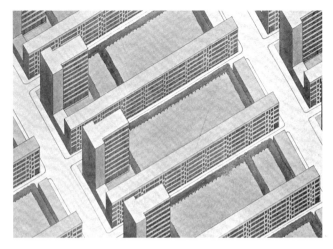

Figure 21: Gesamtüber-
sicht Kleinstwohnungen
(General overview micro
apartments), 1928, pub-
lished in: *bauhaus* 3, no. 2
(April–June 1929), cover
image.

ludwig hilberseimer:
wohnungen von 48, 58 und 70 qm mit 4, 6 bezw. 8 betten

Figure 22: Apartments of
48, 58 and 70 sqm with 4, 6
and 8 beds respectively,
published in: Hilberseimer,
Ludwig. 1929. "kleinstäd-
tische kleinwohnungen." In:
bauhaus, 2: 2.

ludwig hilberseimer:
wohnungen von 22,5 und 37 qm mit 1 bezw. 2 betten

Figure 23: Apartments of
22,5 and 37 sqm with 1 and
2 beds respectively, pub-
lished in: Hilberseimer,
Ludwig. 1929. "kleinstäd-
tische kleinwohnungen."
In: *bauhaus*, 2: 2.

180.-181. DIAGRAMS OF SUN PENETRATION ON DECEMER 21

180. EAST EXPOSURE *10 A.M.–12 Noon*

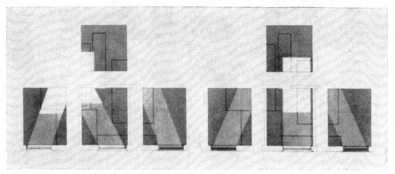

181. SOUTH EXPOSURE 10 *A.M.–12 Noon*
on December 21 with South Exposure the sun in a room is at a maximum.
with East Exposure at a minimum.

Figure 24: Diagrams of sun penetration on December 21, top: East exposure
10 am–12 noon, bottom: South exposure, 10 am - 12 noon on December 21 with
South Exposure the sun in a room is at a maximum, with East Exposure at a minimum; published in various publications by Ludwig Hilberseimer, e.g.: Hilberseimer,
Ludwig. 1944. *The New City: Principles of Planning*. Chicago: Theobald, 82.

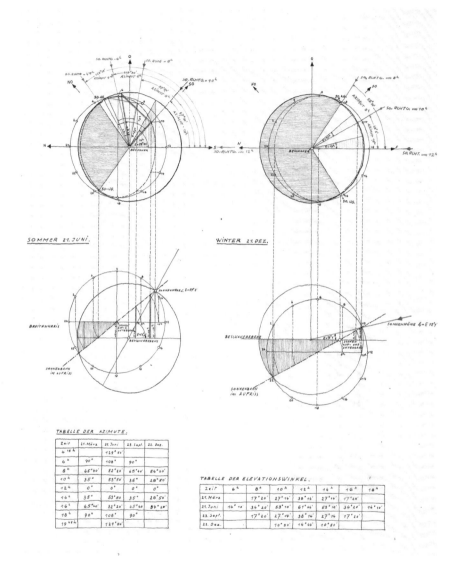

Figure 25: Reinhold Rossig (from the lessons of Ludwig Hilberseimer at Bauhaus
Dessau), sun exposure schemes, 1930.

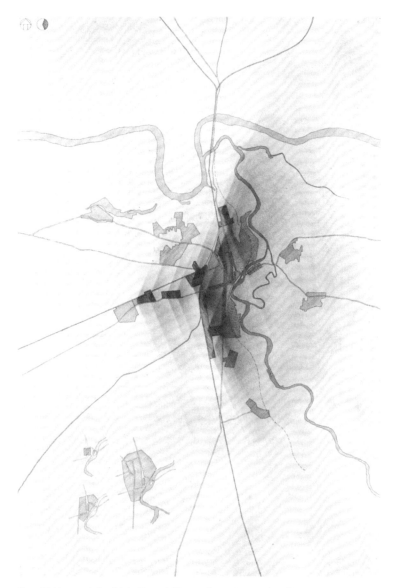

Figure 26: European industrial city [Dessau]. Diagram of present state and condition. In lower left corner, the historical development during six centuries—at 1200, 1400 and 1800 A.D., published in: Hilberseimer, Ludwig. 1944. *The New City: Principles of Planning*. Chicago: Theobald, 134.

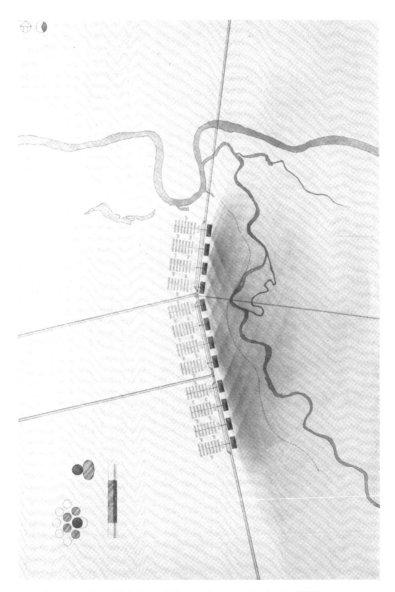

Figure 27: European industrial city [Dessau]. Diagram of its proposed replanning, 1933. In the lower left corner, three schemes; the upper showing present state; the left a replanning around the exiting industrial area; the right as a ribbon development, published in: Hilberseimer, Ludwig. 1944. *The New City: Principles of Planning*. Chicago: Theobald, 135.

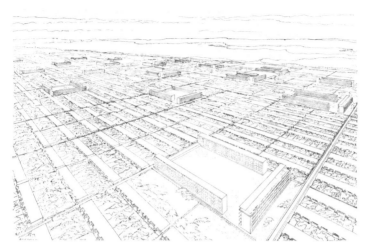

Figure 28: Mixed height development, row houses (ground-floor houses), storey houses, houses with balcony access, published in: Hilberseimer, Ludwig. 1932. "Flachbau und Flachbautypen." In: *Moderne Bauformen* 31: 471–478, here 473.

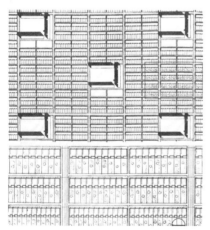

Figure 29: Mixed height development, row houses (ground-floor houses), storey houses and houses with balcony access, block access through walkways, published in: Hilberseimer, Ludwig. 1932. "Flachbau und Flachbautypen." In: *Moderne Bauformen* 31: 471–478, here 471.

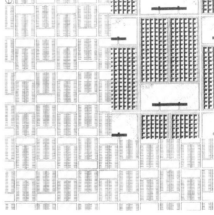

Figure 30: Mixed height development, detached L-shaped houses (ground-floor houses) and houses with balcony access, block access through walkways, published in: Hilberseimer, Ludwig. 1932. "Flachbau und Flachbautypen." In: *Moderne Bauformen* 31: 471–478, here 472.

Figure 31: Mixed height housing development (Mischbebauung), Berlin,
Germany, aerial perspective, c. 1930, published in: Hilberseimer, Ludwig. 1932.
"Flachbau und Flachbautypen." In: *Moderne Bauformen* 31: 471–478, here 473.

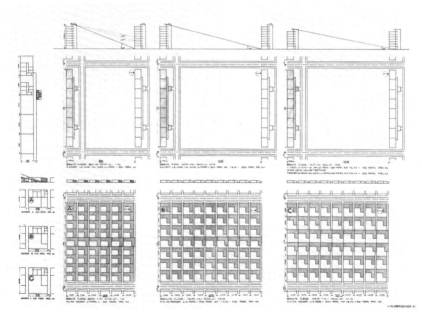

Figure 32: Study of the demands on urban space due to high-rise and low-rise
buildings, published in: Ludwig Hilberseimer, "Flachbau und Stadtraum." In:
Zentralblatt der Bauverwaltung vereinigt mit Zeitschrift für Bauwesen, 53–54,
1931, 774.

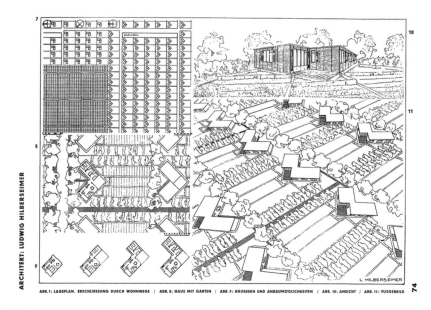

Figure 33: Design for the extendable house, top left: site plan, access through walkways, bottom left: house nucleus and extension possibilities, top right: exterior view, bottom right: aerial view, published in: Wagner, Martin, ed. 1932., *Das wachsende Haus.* Berlin: Deutsches Verlagshaus Bong & Co., 74.

Figure 34: View of the dining room of the extendable house, built at the exhibition Sonne, Luft und Haus für Alle, held in Berlin Charlottenburg in 1931, photographer unknown.

Figure 35: Residential street (Wohnstraße), perspective view, Berlin, n.d.
(ca. 1930s). See fig. 29 on p. 290.

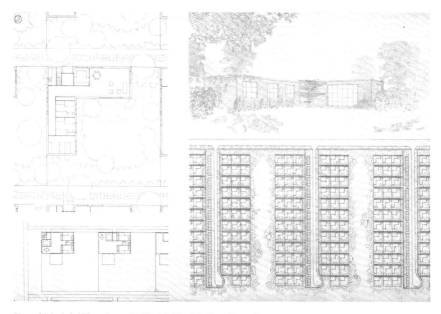

Figure 36: Ludwig Hilberseimer with Alfred Caldwell, L-shaped house in
settlement units, multiple views, (early 1940s).

Figure 37: Blumenthal House, exterior view, 1932, photographer unknown.

Figure 38: Blumenthal House, interior view, 1932, photographer unknown.

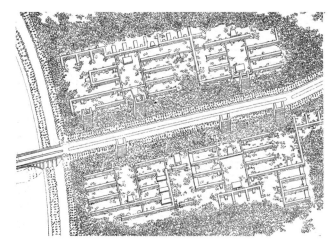

Figure 39: Isometric plan for the University of Berlin, 1937, published in: Hilberseimer, Ludwig. 1963. *Entfaltung einer Planungsidee*. Berlin/Frankfurt a. M./Vienna: Ullstein, 126.

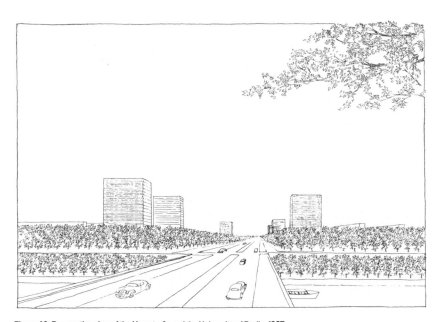

Figure 40: Perspective view of the Heerstraße and the University of Berlin, 1937, published in: Hilberseimer, Ludwig. 1963. *Entfaltung einer Planungsidee*. Berlin/Frankfurt a. M./Vienna: Ullstein, 126.

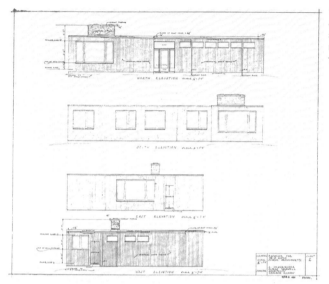

Figure 41: Ludwig Hilberseimer with Alfred Caldwell,
S. Risch House, Sharon,
Massachusetts, elevations,
1942.

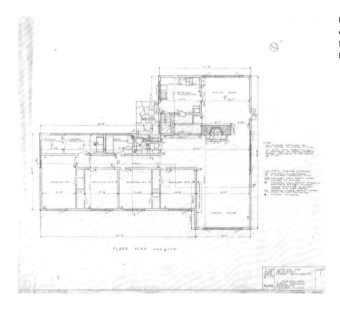

Figure 42: Ludwig Hilbers-
eimer with Alfred Caldwell,
S. Risch House, Sharon,
Massachusetts, plan, 1942.

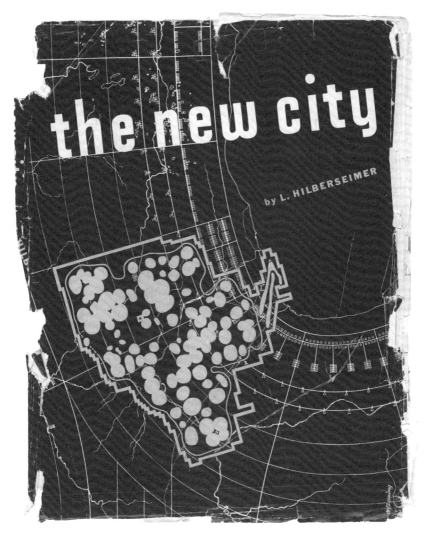

Figure 43: Cover of: Hilberseimer, Ludwig. 1944. *The New City: Principles of Planning*.
Chicago: Theobald, design by William Fleming.

Figure 44: Ludwig Hilberseimer with Alfred Caldwell, The city in the landscape, 1942, published in: Hilberseimer, Ludwig. 1944. *The New City: Principles of Planning*. Chicago: Theobald, 146.

Figure 45: View of a commercial area, 1944, published in: Hilberseimer, Ludwig. 1944. *The New City: Principles of Planning*. Chicago: Theobald, 92.

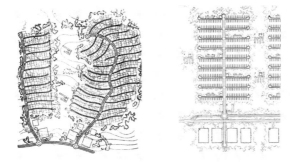

Figure 46: Settlement unit, adapted to the topography, published in: Hilberseimer, Ludwig. 1963. *Entfaltung einer Planungsidee*. Berlin/Frankfurt a. M./Vienna: Ullstein, 40.

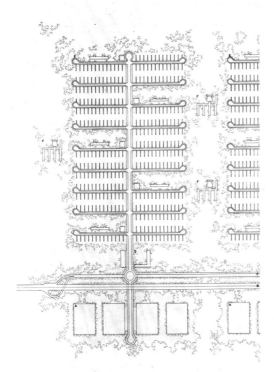

Figure 47: site plan of a typical settlement unit, c. 1940, published in: Hilberseimer, Ludwig. 1944. *The New City: Principles of Planning*. Chicago: Theobald, 106.

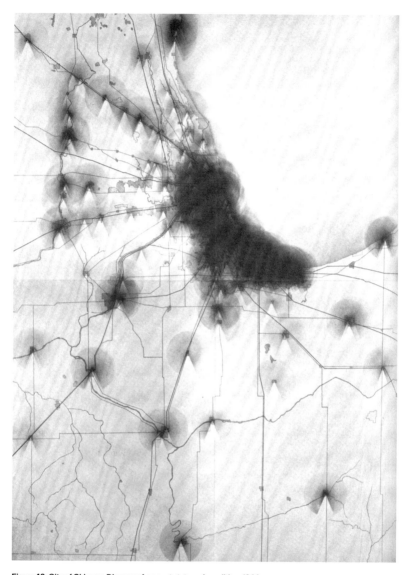

Figure 48: City of Chicago. Diagram of present state and condition, 1944,
published in: Hilberseimer, Ludwig. 1944. *The New City: Principles of Planning*.
Chicago: Theobald, 142.

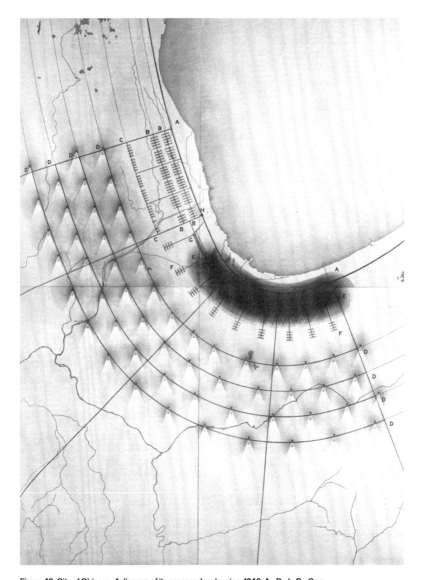

Figure 49: City of Chicago. A diagram of its proposed replanning, 1940. A—Park. B—Commercial area. C—Smokeless industry. D—Smoke-producing light industry. E—Heavy industry. F—Residential areas for heavy industry. G—Airport and central station. H—Harbor, freight yard and warehouses, published in: Hilberseimer, Ludwig. 1944. *The New City: Principles of Planning*. Chicago: Theobald, 143.

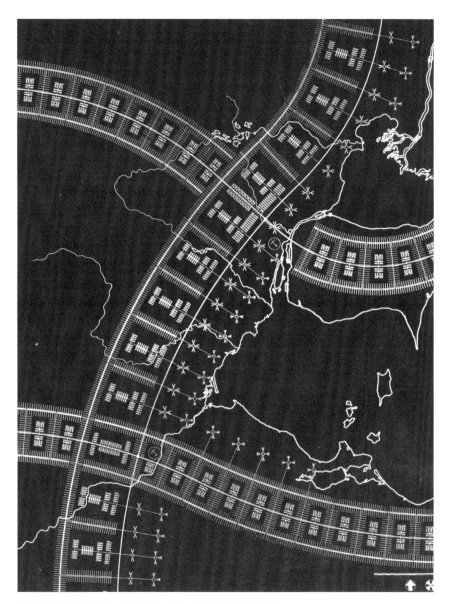

Figure 50: Detroit area, planning diagram, c. 1945, published in: Hilberseimer,
Ludwig. 1949. *The New Regional Pattern: Industries and Gardens, Workshops
and Farms.* Chicago: Theobald, 173.

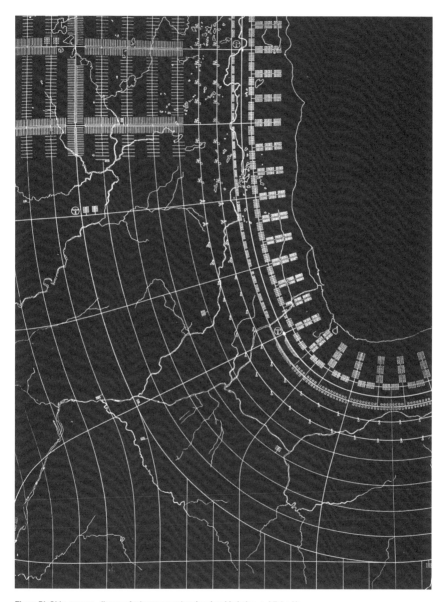

Figure 51: Chicago area, diagram for its proposed replanning. Variation, published in:
Hilberseimer, Ludwig. 1949. *The New Regional Pattern: Industries and Gardens,
Workshops and Farms*. Chicago: Theobald,, 161.

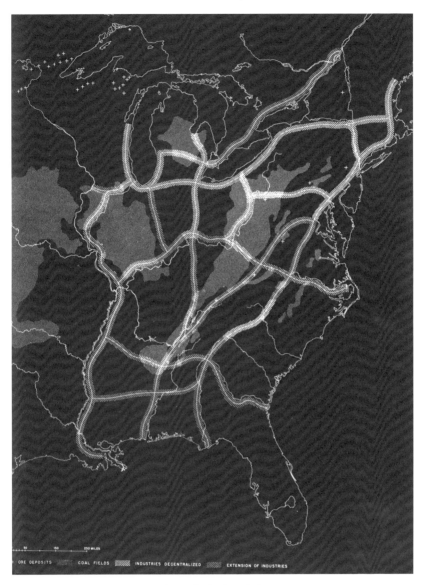

Figure 52: Eastern United States, industries decentralized and extended to
the South, regional planning scheme, published in: Hilberseimer, Ludwig. 1949.
The New Regional Pattern: Industries and Gardens, Workshops and Farms.
Chicago: Theobald, 169, also used as cover image for this publication.

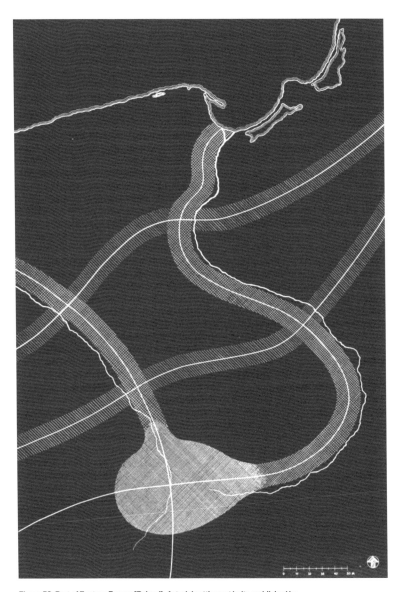

Figure 53: Part of Eastern Europe [Poland]. Arterial settlement belts, published in:
Hilberseimer, Ludwig. 1949. *The New Regional Pattern: Industries and Gardens,
Workshops and Farms*. Chicago: Theobald, 177.

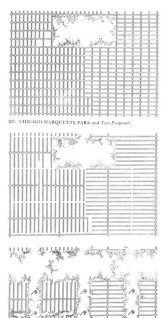

207. CHICAGO MARQUETTE PARK *and Two Proposals*

Figure 54: Chicago
Marquette Park and two
proposals, published in:
Hilberseimer, Ludwig. 1949.
The New Regional Pattern:
Industries and Gardens,
Workshops and Farms.
Chicago: Theobald, 227.

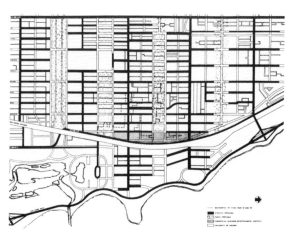

Figure 55: Hyde Park redevelopment street patterns,
c. 1956, published in: Hilberseimer, Ludwig. 1963.
Entfaltung einer Planungs-
idee. Berlin/Frankfurt a.M./
Vienna: Ullstein, 119.

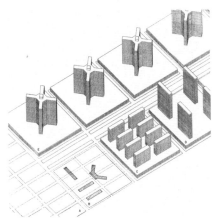

Figure 56: Chicago, commercial area replanned, published in: Hilberseimer, Ludwig. 1955. *The Nature of Cities: Origin, Growth, and Decline, Pattern and Form, Planning Problems.* Chicago: Theobald, 248.

Figure 58: Chicago, Near North & West Loop development, 1950s.

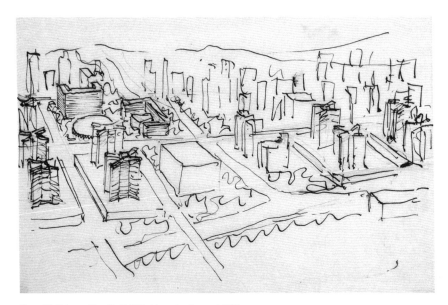

Figure 57: Chicago, Near North & West Loop development, 1950s.

Figure 59: Model photographs, illustrating the combined study of density and typological variation, for Ludwig Hilberseimer, et.al., "Plan of Chicago," June, 1951, photographer unknown, published in: Hilberseimer, Ludwig. 1955. *The Nature of Cities: Origin, Growth, and Decline, Pattern and Form, Planning Problems.* Chicago: Theobald, 212–213.

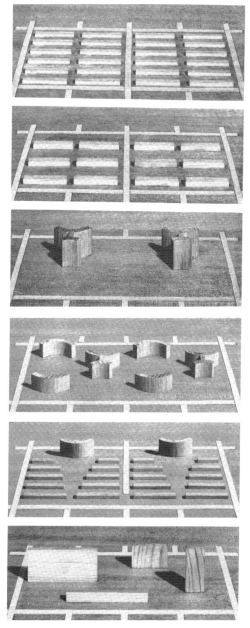

Figure 60: Proposed replanning for the south side of Chicago, model photograph, photographer unknown, published in: Hilberseimer, Ludwig. 1955. *The Nature of Cities: Origin, Growth, and Decline, Pattern and Form, Planning Problems*. Chicago: Theobald, 225.

Figure 61: Ludwig Hilberseimer, Ludwig Mies van der Rohe and Alfred Caldwell, Lafayette Park redevelopment area and new buildings, 1959, photo: Hubert Henry for Hedrich Blessing Photographers.

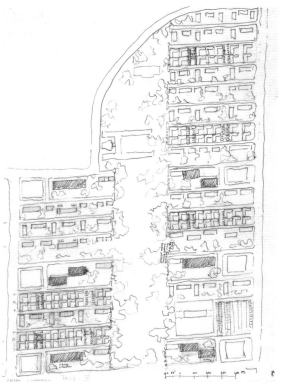

Figure 62: Ludwig Hilberseimer, Lafayette Park, preliminary site plan, 1956.

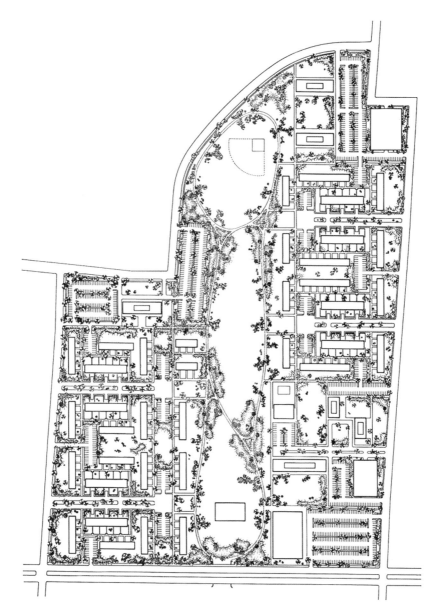

Figure 63: Ludwig Hilberseimer, Ludwig Mies van der Rohe and Alfred Caldwell, site plan,
Lafayette Park, 1956.

Figure 64: Population distribution in the Chicago region, 1950, published in:
Hilberseimer, Ludwig. 1963. *Entfaltung einer Planungsidee*. Berlin/Frankfurt a.M./
Vienna: Ullstein, 108.

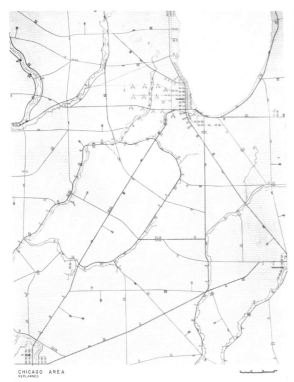

Figure 65: Regional plan of Chicago, published in: Hilberseimer, Ludwig. 1963. *Entfaltung einer Planungs-idee*. Berlin/Frankfurt a.M./Vienna: Ullstein, 112.

CHICAGO AREA
REPLANNED

Figure 66: New plan for the City of Chicago, c. 1963, published in: Hilberseimer, Ludwig. 1963. *Entfaltung einer Planungsidee*. Berlin/Frankfurt a.M./Vienna: Ullstein, 98–99.

Figure 67: Cover of: Hilberseimer, Ludwig. 1963. *Entfaltung einer Planungsidee*. Berlin/
Frankfurt a. M./Vienna: Ullstein, design by Helmut Lortz.

Bibliography

"1919–1931." 1931. In *Bauhaus. organ der kostufra. sprachrohr der studierenden*, no. 5 (June): n.p. [3–5].

Achilles, Rolf, Kevin Harrington, and Charlotte Myhrum, eds. 1986. *Mies van der Rohe: Architect as Educator*. Chicago: Illinois Institute of Technology.

Albers, Anni. 1946. "Constructing Textiles." In *Design* 47, no. 8 (April): 22–26.

Albers, Anni. 1974 (1965). *On Weaving*. London: Studio Vista.

Anderson, Richard. 2012. "Introduction: An End to Speculation." In Hilberseimer 2012, 15–81.

Anker, Peder. 2005. "The Bauhaus of Nature." In *Modernism/Modernity* 12, no. 2: 229–51.

Architektur Basel. 2018. "Aus Basel I: Herzog & de Meuron und die Arbeitersiedlungen im Hirzbrunnen." *Architektur Basel*, December 5, 2018. https://architekturbasel.ch/aus-basel-i-herzog-de-meuron-und-die-arbeitersiedlungen-im-hirzbrunnen/. Accessed December 31, 2021.

"Architektur, Soziologie oder Klassenkampf." 1930. In *Bauhaus. organ der kostufra. sprachrohr der studierenden*, no. 3 (September): n.p. [7–8].

Aureli, Pier Vittorio. 2011. "Architecture for Barbarians: Ludwig Hilberseimer and the Rise of the Generic City." In *AA Files* 63: 3–18.

Aureli, Pier Vittorio. 2012. "In Hilberseimer's Footsteps." In Hilberseimer 2012, 334–63.

Aureli, Pier Vittorio, and Martino Tattara. 2018. "Soft Cell: The Minimum Dwelling." In *The Architectural Review* (July): 106ff.

"Aus Boudoiren und Amtszimmern." 1930. In *Bauhaus. organ der kostufra. sprachrohr der studierenden*, no. 3 (September): n.p. [9–10].

Banfield, Edward C. 1961. *Political Influence: A New Theory of Urban Politics*. New York: The Free Press.

Barnes, Trevor J. 1998. "Envisioning Economic Geography: Three Men and Their Figures." In *Geographische Zeitschrift* 86, no. 2: 94–105.

Barnes, Trevor J., and Claudio Minca. 2013. "Nazi Spatial Theory: The Dark Geographies of Carl Schmitt and Walter Christaller." In *Annals of the Association of American Geographers* 103, no. 3 (May): 669–87.

Bassin, Mark. 1987. "Imperialism and the Nation State in Friedrich Ratzel's Political Geography." In *Progress in Human Geography* 11, no. 4 (September): 473–95.

Bauhaus-Archiv, ed. Bauhaus-Archiv, ed. 1986. *Der vorbildliche Architekt: Mies van der Rohes Architekturunterricht 1930–1958 am Bauhaus und in Chicago*. Mies van der Rohe Centennial Project. Berlin: Nicolaische Verlagsbuchhandlung Beuermann.

Bauhaus Dessau. 1929. "bauhaus – junge menschen kommt ans bauhaus!" Promotional brochure, Dessau.

Baukunst und Werkform. 1947–49. "Ludwig Mies van der Rohe." In *Baukunst und Werkform* 1, no. 3: 10–40.

Baurundschau. 1947. "L. Hilberseimer. The New City" [book review]. In *Baurundschau* 37, no. 15/16, illustrated supplement (August): 81–96.

Bauwelt. 1963. "Ludwig Hilberseimer in Deutschland." In *Bauwelt*, 54: 679.

Bax, Marty. 1991. *Bauhaus Lecture Notes, 1930–1933*. Translated by Kist Killian Communications, Michael O'Loughlin, Robert Odish. Amsterdam: Architectura & Natura Press.

Beck, Raimund. 1995. "Arbeitsräume für Angestellte." In Lauterbach 1995, 152–65.

Behne, Adolf. 1921a. "Bewegungskunst." In *Freiheit* 4, no. 452: 2.

Behne, Adolf. 1921b. "Der Film als Kunstwerk." In *Sozialistische Monatshefte* 27, no. 20 (December): 1116–18.

Behne, Adolf. 1998. *Die Wiederkehr der Kunst*. Berlin: Gebr. Mann.

Behrendt, Walter Curt. 1911. *Die Einheitliche Blockfront als Raumelement im Stadtbau; ein Beitrag zur Stadtbaukunst der Gegenwart* (Berlin: Bruno Cassirer, 1911).

Behrens, Peter. 1920. "Kino-Kultur." In *Das Werk - Mitteilungen des Deutschen Werkbundes*, no. 5: 8–9.

Benjamin, Walter. 1999. *The Arcades Project*. Translated by Howard Eiland and Kevin McLaughlin. Cambridge, MA: Harvard University Press.

Berger, Otti. 1931–32. "Stoffbesprechung." Manuscript used in her own teaching. Bauhaus-Archiv Berlin.

Bergius, Hanne. 1989. *Das Lachen Dadas: Die Berliner Dadaisten und ihre Aktionen*. Berlin: Anabas Verlag.

Bergius, Hanne. 2000. *Montage und Metamechanik: Dada Berlin – Artistik von Polaritäten*. Berlin: Gebr. Mann Verlag.

Bergson, Henri. 1998. *Creative Evolution*. Mineola: Dover.

Berliner Tageblatt. 1927. "Wie wird Berlin in hundert Jahren aussehen." In *Berliner Tageblatt*, January 1, 5. Supplement, clipping preserved in Ludwig Karl Hilberseimer Papers, Ryerson and Burnham Archives, The Art Institute of Chicago. Series 9/5, portfolio 7, folder 5.

Bernoulli, Hans. 1930. "Das Hirzbrunnenquartier in Basel." In *Das Werk* 17, no. 9: 265–82.

Bluestone, Daniel. 1998. "Chicago's Mecca Flat Blues." In *Journal of the Society of Architectural Historians* 57, no. 4 (December): 382–403.

Blümm, Anke, and Christiane Lange. 2019. *Bauhaus und Textilindustrie: Architektur, Design, Lehre, Gestaltung als Innovationsstrategie*. Munich: Prestel.

Blundell Jones, Peter. 1989. "AJ Review: Books – City Father." In *Architect's Journal* 190, no. 7 (August): 75.

Boesiger, Willy, and Oscar Stonorov, eds. 2013 (1930). *Le Corbusier and Pierre Jeanneret: Œuvre complète 1910–1929*. Basel: Birkhäuser.

Boesiger, Willy, and Oscar Stonorov, eds. 2013 (1935). *Le Corbusier and Pierre Jeanneret: Œuvre complète, 1929–1934*. Basel: Birkhäuser.

Boone, Véronique. 2017. "Le Corbusier et le cinéma: La communication d'une œuvre." 2 vols. PhD diss. Ecole d'architecture de Lille/Université libre de Bruxelles.

Bötticher, Karl. 1852. *Die Tektonik der Hellenen*. Potsdam: Riegel.

Bryan, Mary Lynn McCree, and Allen F. Davis, eds. 1990. *100 Years at Hull-House*. Bloomington: Indiana University Press.

Bücher, Karl. 1893. *Die Entstehung der Volkswirtschaft*. Tübingen: Verlag der H. Laupp'schen Buchhandlung.

Buchmann, Sabeth, and Rike Frank, eds. 2015a. *Textile Theorien der Moderne: Alois Riegl in der Kunstkritik*. Berlin: b_books, PoLYpeN.

Buchmann, Sabeth, and Rike Frank. 2015b. "Einleitung." In Buchmann and Frank 2015a, 7–17.

Bulmer, Martin. 1986. *The Chicago School of Sociology: Institutionalization, Diversity, and the Rise of Sociological Research*. Chicago: University of Chicago Press.

Canguilhem, Georges. 1965. *La connaissance de la vie*. 2nd ed. Paris: Vrin.

Canguilhem, Georges. 2001. "The Living and Its Milieu," translated by John Savage. In *Grey Room* 3 (Spring): 7–31 (original publication: Canguilhem, Georges.

1952. *La connaissance de la vie*. 1st ed. Paris: Hachette).

Carroll, Noël. 1987. "The Nature of Horror." In *The Journal of Aesthetics and Art Criticism* 46, no. 1: 51–59.

Chao, Hsiang-Ke. 2018. "Shaping Space through Diagrams: The Case of the History of Location Theory." In *Research in the History of Economic Thought and Methodology*, 36-B: 59–72.

Checinska, Christine, and Grant Watson. 2016. "Social Fabric: Textiles, Art, Society and Politics." In *The Handbook of Textile Culture*, edited by Janis Jefferies, Diana Wood Conroy, and Hazel Clark, 279–91. New York: Bloomsbury Academic.

Chicago Sun Times. 1955. "4 Glass-Steel Homes Planned Near Elmhurst." In *Chicago Sun Times*, May 22.

Christaller, Walter. 1940. "Die Kultur und Marktbereiche der zentralen Orte im Deutschen Ostraum und die Gliederung der Verwaltung." In *Raumforschung und Raumordnung* 4, 498–503.

Christaller, Walter. 1966. *Central Places in Southern Germany*, translated by Carlisle W. Baskin. New Jersey: Prentice-Hall, Inc.

Christaller, Walter. 1968 (1933). *Die zentralen Orte in Süddeutschland: Eine ökonomisch-geographische Untersuchung über die Gesetzmäßigkeit der Verbreitung und Entwicklung der Siedlungen mit städtischen Funktionen*. Darmstadt: Wissenschaftliche Buchgesellschaft.

Cohen, Adam. 2000. *American Pharaoh: Mayor Richard J. Daley: His Battle for Chicago and the Nation*. Boston: Little, Brown and Company.

Collier, Stephen J. 2011. *Post-Soviet Social: Neoliberalism, Social Modernity, Biopolitics*. Princeton: Princeton University Press.

Colman, Scott. 2006. "Organism and Artefact: The Ludwig Mies van der Rohe Circle and the Chicago School: Architecture, Planning and Sociology circa 1944." PhD diss. University of Sydney.

Colman, Scott. 2014. "Promoting the New City: Ludwig Hilberseimer at the Art Institute of Chicago, 1944." In *Exhibitions and the Development of Modern Planning Culture*, edited by Robert Freestone and Marco Amati, 111–29. Farnham: Ashgate.

Colman, Scott. 2021. "Ludwig Hilberseimer's Plan of Chicago." Unpublished conference paper for *Histories of Urban Design: Global Trajectories and Local Realities*. Eidgenössische Technische Hochschule, Zurich, November 15–17.

Colomina, Beatriz. 1994. *Privacy and Publicity: Modern Architecture as Mass Media*. Cambridge, MA: MIT Press.

Colquhoun, Alan. 1971. "The Superblock." In *Essays in Architectural Criticism: Modern Architecture and Historical Change*, 83–102. Cambridge, MA: MIT Press.

Constant, Caroline. 2004. "Hilberseimer and Caldwell: Merging Ideologies in the Lafayette Park Landscape." In *Hilberseimer / Mies van der Rohe: Lafayette Park, Detroit*, edited by Charles Waldheim, 95–111. Case. Munich: Prestel, in association with the Harvard University Graduate School of Design, Cambridge, MA.

Corssen, Meta. 1924. "Hausarbeit." In *Sozialistische Monatshefte* 30, no. 1 (January): 51–53.

Coyner, Sandra Jean. 1975. "Class Patterns of Family Income and Expenditure during the Weimar Republic: German White-Collar Workers as Harbingers of Modern Society." PhD diss. Rutgers University.

Currell, Sue. 2017. "You Haven't Seen Their Faces: Eugenic National Housekeeping and Documentary Photography in 1930s in America." In *Journal of American Studies* 51, no. 2: 481–511.

Curtis, William J. R. 1996. *Modern Architecture since 1900*. London: Phaidon.

Dallmayr, Fred R., and Thomas A. McCarthy. 1977. *Understanding and Social Inquiry*. Notre Dame: University of Notre Dame Press.

Danforth, George. 1988. "Hilberseimer Remembered." In Pommer, Spaeth, and Harrington 1988, 8–15.

Davidovici, Irina. 2017. "Ludwig Hilberseimer: The New City, 1944." In *Manuale zum Städtebau: die Systematisierung des Wissens von der Stadt 1870–1950*, edited by Vittorio Magnago Lampugnani, Katrin Albrecht, Helene Bihlmaier, Lukas Zurfluh, Melchior Fischli, Andri Gerber, Vittorio Lampugnani, Christopher Metz, Christiane Post, and Harald R. Stühlinger, 265–85. Berlin: DOM.

Davis, Ujjiji. 2018. "The Bottom: The Emergence and Erasure of Black American Urban Landscapes." In *The Avery Review*, no. 34 (October). https://www.averyreview.com/issues/34/the-bottom. Accessed July 14, 2020.

Delbaere, Denis. 2004. "Table rase et paysage: Projet d'urbanisme et contextualité spatiale dans le Plan Voisin de Le Corbusier (1925) et la cité Concorde de Le Maresquier (1954)." PhD diss. Paris, EHESS.

Delbaere, Denis. 2005. "La description 'infralocale' du centre de Paris dans le plan Voisin de Le Corbusier." In *Figures de la ville et construction des savoirs*, edited by Frédéric Pousin, 73–85. Paris, CNRS Editions.

Deleuze, Gilles. 1982. "Sur le cinéma : classifications des signes et du temps." https://www.webdeleuze.com/textes/76.

Denny, Philip, and Charles Waldheim. 2020. "Reconsidering Hilberseimer's Chicago." In *Urban Planning* 5, no. 2: 243–48.

Der Aufbau. 1959. "Profile: Ludwig Hilberseimer." In *Der Aufbau* 14 (March): 107–10.

"Der neue Direktor—der neue Kurs." 1930. In *Bauhaus. organ der kostufra. sprachrohr der studierenden*, no. 3 (September): n.p. [4–6].

Der Städtebau. 1928. "Die Hilberseimerische 'Nekropolis.'" In *Der Städtebau*, no. 10: 256.

Divendal, Simone. 2019. "The Functional City: The Contribution of Bauhaus Students Jan and Kees van der Linden to the 1933 CIAM Congress." In Simon Thomas and Brentjens 2019, 126–34.

Droste, Magdalena. 1998. *Das Bauhaus webt: Die Textilwerkstatt am Bauhaus*. Berlin: GH Verlag.

Dyja, Thomas L. 2014. *The Third Coast: When Chicago Built the American Dream*. New York: Penguin.

Easterling, Keller. 2021. *Medium Design: Knowing How to Work on the World*. London: Verso.

Edificación. 1940. No. 34 (July–September).

Eggeling, Viking. 1921. "Elvi Fejtegetesek a Mozgomüveszetröl [Theoretical Presentation of Dynamic Art]." *MA*, no. 8: 105–6.

Eisenschmidt, Alexander. 2019. *The Good Metropolis: From Urban Formlessness to Metropolitan Architecture*. Berlin: Birkhäuser.

Elder, R. Bruce. 2007. "Hans Richter and Viking Eggeling: The Dream of Universal Language and the Birth of the Absolute Film." In *Avant-Garde Film*, edited by Alexander Graf and Dietrich Scheunemann, 3–53. Amsterdam: Rodopi.

El Lissitzky. 1929. "Old City—New Buildings." In El Lissitzky 1970, 50–56.

El Lissitzky. 1970. *Russia: An Architecture for World-Revolution*. Translated by Eric Dluhosch. Cambridge, MA: MIT Press.

Elste, Judith. n.d. "Die Werkstatt für Weberei am Bauhaus in Weimar." Manuscript. Archiv der Moderne, Weimar, Estate Schädlich, Bu-02-20.50-53.

Fabricius, Daniela. 2013. "Who's Afraid of Ludwig Hilbers-eimer? Spectrality and Space in the Groszstadt." In *Journal of Architectural Education* 67, no. 1: 39–51.

Fehl, Gerhard, and Juan Rodríguez-Lores, eds. 1997. *"Die Stadt wird in der Landschaft sein und die Landschaft in der Stadt": Bandstadt und Bandstruktur als Leit-bilder des modernen Städtebaus.* Basel: Birkhäuser.

Fernandez, Lilia. 2012. *Brown in the Windy City: Mexi-cans and Puerto Ricans in Postwar Chicago.* Chi-cago: University of Chicago Press.

Fezer, Jesko, Christian Hiller, Alexandra Nehmer, and Philipp Oswalt, eds. 2015. *Kollektiv für sozialis-tisches Bauen: Proletarische Bauausstellung / Col-lective for Socialist Architecture: Proletarian Building Exhibition.* Leipzig: Spector.

Ford, Henry, and Samuel Crowther. 1922. *My Life and Work.* New York: Doubleday.

Fort Dearborn Project. 1956. *A New Frontier for Down-town Chicago: The Fort Dearborn Project.* Chicago: The Project.

Exner, Lisbeth. *Fasching als Logik: Über Salomo Fried-laender / Mynona.* Munich: Belleville, 1996.

Fortey, Stuart, Horst Kopleck, Helen Galloway, and Ve-ronika Schnorr, eds. 2006. *Collins German Dictio-nary.* 5th ed. Glasgow: Harper Collins Publishers.

Forty, Adrian. 2000. *Words and Buildings: A Vocabulary of Modern Architecture.* London: Thames & Hudson.

Foucault, Michel. 1983. "Afterword: The Subject and Power," in *Beyond Structuralism and Hermeneutics*, ed. Hubert L. Dreyfus and Paul Rabinow, 208–26. 2nd ed. Chicago: University of Chicago Press.

Foucault, Michel. 1997. "The Technologies of Self." In *Eth-ics: Subjectivity and Truth*, vol. 1 of *The Essential Works of Foucault*, edited by Paul Rabinow, trans-lated by Robert Hurley and others, 223–51. New York: New Press.

Frank, Rike. 2015. "Materials at an Exhibition." In Rike and Watson 2015, 22–35.

Frank, Rike, and Grant Watson, eds. 2015. *Textiles: Open Letter.* Vienna: Sternberg Press.

Frazier, E. Franklin. 1932. *The Negro Family in Chicago.* Chicago: University of Chicago Press.

Freundlich, Otto. 1982. "Der Raum [1919]." In *Schriften: Ein Wegbereiter der gegenstandslosen Kunst*, ed-ited by Uli Bohnen. Cologne: DuMont.

Friedlaender, Salamo. 1907. "Goethe." In *Berliner Tage-blatt und Hanelszeitung* 37 (March 18). Reprinted in *Salamo Friedlaender / Mynona, Philosophische Abhandlungen und Kritiken 1896–1946*, edited by

Detlef Thiel, 2 volumes (Herrsching: Waitawhile, 2006): 239–44.

Friedlaender, Salamo. 1911. *Friedrich Nietzsche: Eine Intellektuelle Biographie.* Leipzig: G. J. Göschen.

Friedlaender, Salamo. 1913. "Das Individuum und die so-ziale Frage." In *Die Aktion* 3, no. 51 (December 29): cols. 1182–86.

Friedlaender, Salamo. 1918. *Schöpferische Indifferenz.* Munich: Georg Müller Verlag.

Friedlaender, Salomo. 1919. "Kant und die Freiheit nach Ernst Marcus." In *Der Sturm*, no. 9: 144–46.

Fulmer, Jeffrey. 2009. "What in the World Is Infrastruc-ture?" In *PEI Infrastructure Investor* (July/August): 30–32.

Geddes, Patrick. 1915. *Cities in Evolution.* London: Wil-liams & Norgate.

Geerken, Hartmut, ed. *Der Einzige.* 2 vols. Munich: Kraus Reprint, 1980.

Geist, Johann Friedrich, Klaus Kürvers, and Dieter Rausch. 1993. *Hans Scharoun: Chronik zu Leben und Werk.* Berlin: Akademie der Künste.

Giaccaria, Paolo, and Claudio Minca. 2016. "For a Tenta-tive Spatial Theory of the Third Reich." In *Hitler's Geographies: The Spatialities of the Third Reich*, ed-ited by Paolo Giaccaria and Claudio Minca, 19–44. Chicago: University of Chicago Press.

Giedion, Sigfried. 1995. *Building in France, Building in Iron, Building in Ferroconcrete.* Los Angeles: Getty Center for the History of Art and the Humanities.

Ginzburg, Moisei. 1927. "Constructivism as Method of Laboratory and Teaching Work." In *SA* 6: 160–66

Ginzburg, Moisei. 2017 (1934). *Dwelling: Five Year's Work on the Problem of Habitation.* London: Fon-tanka Publications.

González Martínez, Plácido. 2013. "Ludwig Hilberseimer at the Illinois Institute of Technology: Architectural Education, Organic Democracy and Colonization." In *Docomomo International Journal* 49: 34–39.

González Martínez, Plácido. 2015. *In Light of Hilbers-eimer: The Genesis and the Legacy of The New City.* Seville: Vibok Works.

Gottmann, Jean. 1961. *Megalopolis: The Urbanized Northeastern Seaboard of the United States.* New York: Twentieth Century Fund.

Graeff, Werner. 1962. "Über die sogenannte 'G-Gruppe.'" In *werk und zeit*, no. 11: 5.

Graham Foundation. 1987. *Ludwig Hilberseimer. The Man and the Work. A Concordia.* Chicago: Graham Foun-dation, 47.

Graham, Steve, and Simon Marvin, eds. 1996. *Telecom-munications and the City: Electronic Spaces, Urban Places*. London: Routledge.

Graham, Steve, and Simon Marvin. 2001. *Splintering Urbanism: Networked Infrastructures, Technological Mobilities and the Urban Condition*. London: Routledge.

Günther, Sonja. 1993. *Wils Ebert: Ein Bauhausschüler, 1909–1979: Die Arbeit eines Architekten und Städtebauers*, with contributions by Annemarie Lancelle, Günther Kühne, and Christian Wolsdorff. Berlin: Kupfergraben.

Haar, Sharon. 2010. *City as Campus: Urbanism and Higher Education in Chicago*. Minneapolis: University of Minnesota Press.

Haffner, Jeanne. 2013. *The View from Above: The Science of Social Space*. Cambridge, MA: MIT Press.

Hahn, Peter, ed. 1981. *Bauhaus Archiv, Museum. Architektur, Design, Malerei, Graphik, Kunstpädagogik. Sammlungskatalog*. Berlin: Gebr. Mann Verlag.

Hahn, Peter, ed. 1985. *Bauhaus Berlin: Auflösung Dessau 1932, Schließung Berlin 1933, Bauhäusler und Drittes Reich: Eine Dokumentation zusammengestellt vom Bauhaus Archiv Berlin*. Weingarten: Kunstverlag Weingarten.

Hake, Sabine. 2008. *Topographies of Class: Modern Architecture and Mass Society in Weimar Berlin*. Ann Arbor: University of Michigan Press.

Harbusch, Gregor, Daniel Weiss, Konstanze Sylva Domhardt, and Muriel Pérez. 2014. "Germany: Established Modernists Go into Exile, Younger Members Go to Athens." In Van Es et al. 2014, 162–95.

Häring, Hugo. 1926. "Zwei Städte." In *Die Form*, no. 8: 172–75.

Harrasser, Karin. 2016. "Synthesis as Mediation: Inner Touch and Eccentric Sensation." In *Cultural Studies* 30, no. 4: 704–16.

Harrington, Kevin. 1988. "Ideas in Action: Hilberseimer and the Redevelopment of the South Side of Chicago." In Pommer, Spaeth, and Harrington, 69–88.

Hausmann, Raoul. 1919. "Schnitt durch die Zeit." In *Die Erde* (October 1).

Hausmann, Raoul. 1921. "PRÉsentismus: gegen den Puffkeismus der teutschen Seele." In *De Stijl* 4, no. 9: 136–43.

Hays, K. Michael. 1992. *Modernism and the Posthumanist Subject: The Architecture of Hannes Meyer and Ludwig Hilberseimer*. Cambridge, MA: MIT Press.

Herscher, Andrew. 2020. "Black and Blight." In *Race and Modern Architecture: A Critical History from the Enlightenment to the Present*, edited by Irene Cheng, Charles L. Davis II, and Mable O. Wilson, 291–307. Pittsburgh: Pittsburgh Press.

Herzogenrath, Wulf, ed. 1968. *50 Jahre Bauhaus*. Exh. cat. Würtembergischer Kunstverein Stuttgart; Royal Academy, London; Stedelijk Museum, Amsterdam. Stuttgart: Württembergischer Kunstverein.

Higgins, Hannah. 2009. *The Grid Book*. Cambridge, MA: MIT Press.

Hilberseimer, Ludwig. n.d. "The City as Idea: Contemporary Planning Proposals: Their Roots and Trends," typed manuscript, n.d., Ludwig Karl Hilberseimer Papers, Ryerson and Burnham Archives, The Art Institute of Chicago. Series 8/2, Box 2.5.

Hilberseimer, Ludwig. 1914. "Die Architektur der Großstadt," handwritten outline on 15 folios, Ludwig Karl Hilberseimer Papers, Ryerson and Burnham Archives, The Art Institute of Chicago. Series 8/3, Box 1.1.

Hilberseimer, Ludwig. 1919a. "Der Naturalismus und das Primitive in der Kunst." In *Der Einzige* 1, no. 8 (March 9): 88–89.

Hilberseimer, Ludwig. 1919b. "Form und Individuum." In *Der Einzige* 1, no. 3 (February 2): 6–7.

Hilberseimer, Ludwig. 1919c. "Kunst und Wissen." In *Der Einzige* 1, no. 11 (March 30): 127–128.

Hilberseimer, Ludwig. 1919d. "Schöpfung und Entwicklung." In *Der Einzige* 1, no. 1 (January 19): 5–6.

Hilberseimer, Ludwig. 1919e. "Umwertung in der Kunst." In *Der Einzige* 1, no. 2 (January 26): 4–5.

Hilberseimer, Ludwig. 1921a. "Archipenko." In *Sozialistische Monatshefte* 27, no. 9 (May): 465–66.

Hilberseimer, Ludwig. 1921b. "Bewegungskunst." In *Sozialistische Monatshefte* 27, no. 9 (May): 467–68.

Hilberseimer, Ludwig. 1921c. "Freundlich." In *Sozialistische Monatshefte* 27, no. 9 (May): 466–67.

Hilberseimer, Ludwig. 1922a. "Das Hochhaus." In *Das Kunstblatt* 6, no. 12: 525–31.

Hilberseimer, Ludwig. 1922b. "Filmmöglichkeiten." In *Sozialistische Monatshefte* 28, no. 12 (August): 741–43.

Hilberseimer, Ludwig. 1922c. "Konstruktivismus." In *Sozialistische Monatshefte* 28, no. 13 (September): 831–34.

Hilberseimer, Ludwig. 1923a. "Der Wille zur Architektur." In *Das Kunstblatt* 7, no. 5: 133–40.

Hilberseimer, Ludwig. 1923b. "Vom städtebaulichen Problem der Großstadt." In *Sozialistische Monatshefte* 24: 352–57.

Hilberseimer, Ludwig. 1925a. "Bauwirtschaft und Wohnungsbau." In *Sozialistische Monatshefte* 31, no. 5 (May): 285–91.

Hilberseimer, Ludwig. 1925b. *Großstadtbauten: Neue Architektur*. Hannover: Apossverlag.

Hilberseimer, Ludwig. 1925c. "Stadt- und Wohnungsbau." In *Soziale Bauwirtschaft* 5, no. 14 (July 15): 187–88.

Hilberseimer, Ludwig. 1926a. *Großstadtbauten, Merz 18/19*. Hannover: Merz Verlag.

Hilberseimer, Ludwig. 1926b. "Kunstgewerbe." In *Sozialistische Monatshefte* 32, no. 1 (January): 63–65.

Hilberseimer, Ludwig. 1926c. "Nicht Lesen, Verbotener Film!" In *G: Zeitschrift Für Elementare Gestaltung*, no. 5/6: 136.

Hilberseimer, Ludwig. 1926d. "On Standardizing the Tenement Block." In *Metropolis Berlin: 1880–1940*, edited by Iain Boyd Whyte and David Frisby, 480–81. Berkeley: University of California Press, 2012. Originally published as "Über die Typisierung des Mietshauses." In *Die Form* 1 (1926): 338–39.

Hilberseimer, Ludwig. 1927a. "Die Wohnung als Gebrauchsgegenstand." In *Bau und Wohnung: Die Bauten der Weißenhofsiedlung in Stuttgart errichtet 1927 nach Vorschlägen des Deutschen Werkbundes im Auftrag der Stadt Stuttgart und im Rahmen der Werkbundausstellung "Die Wohnung,"* edited by Peter Behrens and Deutscher Werkbund, 68–75. Stuttgart: Akademischer Verlag Dr. Fritz Wedekind & Co.

Hilberseimer, Ludwig. 1927b. *Großstadtarchitektur*. Stuttgart: Julius Hoffmann.

Hilberseimer, Ludwig. 1928. *Internationale neue Baukunst*. Stuttgart: Julius Hoffmann.

Hilberseimer, Ludwig. 1929a. "Arbeitssitz und Arbeitstisch." In *Die Form* 4, no. 13 (July): 362.

Hilberseimer, Ludwig. 1929b. "Arbeitssitz und Arbeitstisch." In *Sozialistische Monatshefte* 35, no. 9 (September): 870.

Hilberseimer, Ludwig. 1929c. "Großstädtische Kleinwohnungen." In *Zentralblatt der Bauverwaltung* 49, no. 32 (August 7, 1929): 509–14.

Hilberseimer, Ludwig. 1929d. "Kleinstwohnungen: Größe, Grundriß und städtebauliche Anordnung." In *Bauhaus: Vierteljahr-Zeitschrift für Gestaltung* 3, no. 2: 1–4.

Hilberseimer, Ludwig. 1929e. Reply to Martin Wagner, "Das Formproblem eines Welstadtplatzes." In *Das neue Berlin* 2: 39–41.

Hilberseimer, Ludwig. 1929f. "Vorschlag zur City-Bebauung." In *Das Kunstblatt* 13, no. 3 (March): 93–95.

Hilberseimer, Ludwig. 1929g. "Würdigung des Projektes Mies van der Rohe." In *Das Neue Berlin*, no. 2: 39–40.

Hilberseimer, Ludwig. 1930a. "Glas und Festigkeit." In *Technisches Blatt der Frankfurter Zeitung* (March 20): 3. Ludwig Karl Hilberseimer Papers, Ryerson and Burnham Archives, The Art Institute of Chicago. Series 9/5, Box 1.4.

Hilberseimer, Ludwig. 1930b. "Vorschlag zur City-Bebauung." In *Die Form* 5, no. 23/24 (December 15): 608–11.

Hilberseimer, Ludwig. 1931a. "Die Kleinstwohnung im treppenlosen Hause." In *Bauhaus: Zeitschrift für Gestaltung* 4, no. 1: 1–3.

Hilberseimer, Ludwig. 1931b. "Die Wohnung unserer Zeit." In *Die Form* 6, no. 7: 249–70.

Hilberseimer, Ludwig. 1931c. "Entwurf für die Stadthalle Nürnberg." In *Die Form* 6, no. 10 (October): 390–92.

Hilberseimer, Ludwig. 1931d. "Flachbau und Stadtraum." *Zentralblatt für Bauverwaltung* 51, no. 53/54 (December 23): 773–78.

Hilberseimer, Ludwig. 1931e. *Hallenbauten*. Leipzig: J. M. Gerhardt.

Hilberseimer, Ludwig. 1931f. "Vorschlag zur City-Bebauung." In *Moderne Bauformen* 30, no. 3 (March): 55–59.

Hilberseimer, Ludwig. 1932. "Entwurf: Architekt Ludwig Hilberseimer, Berlin; Bauausführung: A. Christ, Berlin." In Wagner 1932, 72–75.

Hilberseimer, Ludwig. 1935. "Raumdurchsonnung." In *Moderne Bauformen* 34: 29–36.

Hilberseimer, Ludwig. 1936. "Raumdurchsonnung und Siedlungsdichtigkeit." In *Moderne Bauformen* 35: 69–76.

Hilberseimer, Ludwig. 1940a. "The Elements of City Planning." In *Armour Engineer and Alumnus* 6, no. 2 (1940/1941): 4–13.

Hilberseimer, Ludwig. 1940b. "The Settlung Americas." Unpublished manuscript, January 1940. Ludwig Karl Hilberseimer Papers, Ryerson and Burnham Archives, The Art Institute of Chicago. Series 8/3, Box 8.22.

Hilberseimer, Ludwig. 1944. *The New City: Principles of Planning*. Chicago: Theobald.

Hilberseimer, Ludwig. 1945a. "Cities and Defense." In Pommer, Spaeth, and Harrington 1988, 89–93.

Hilberseimer, Ludwig. 1945b. "Le Corbusier and City Planning." Ludwig Karl Hilberseimer Papers, Ryerson and Burnham Archives, The Art Institute of Chicago. Series 8/3, Box 2.28.

Hilberseimer, Ludwig. 1947. "Elemente der Stadtplanung." In *Der Bauhelfer* 2, no. 19: 3–8.

Hilberseimer, Ludwig. 1949. *The New Regional Pattern: Industries and Gardens, Workshops and Farms.* Chicago: Theobald.

Hilberseimer, Ludwig. 1952. "Hugo Häring und das Neue Bauen." In *Die neue Stadt* 6: 188–91.

Hilberseimer, Ludwig. 1955. *The Nature of Cities: Origin, Growth, and Decline, Pattern and Form, Planning Problems.* Chicago: Theobald.

Hilberseimer, Ludwig. 1956–59. "Project Notes on Hyde Park Redevelopment Plan, 1956–1959." Ludwig Karl Hilberseimer Papers, Ryerson and Burnham Archives, The Art Institute of Chicago. Series 6, OP 3.

Hilberseimer, Ludwig. 1957a. "Die Umformung einer Großstadt." In *Medizin und Städtebau: Ein Handbuch für gesundheitlichen Städtebau,* edited by Paul Vogler and Erich Kühn, 2:533–50. 2 vols. Munich: Urban & Schwarzenberg.

Hilberseimer, Ludwig. 1957b. "Großstädtische Planungsaufgaben." In *Baukunst und Werkform* 10: 13–17.

Hilberseimer, Ludwig. ca. 1960. "City Architecture: The Trend Toward Openness." In Pommer, Spaeth, and Harrington 1988, 102–13.

Hilberseimer, Ludwig. 1963a. "Dankesworte." In *Technische Universität Berlin, Akademische Reden* 22: 15–18. Ludwig Karl Hilberseimer Papers, Ryerson and Burnham Archives, The Art Institute of Chicago. Series 2, Box 3.6.

Hilberseimer, Ludwig. 1963b. *Entfaltung einer Planungsidee.* Bauwelt Fundamente 6. Berlin/Frankfurt a.M./Vienna: Ullstein.

Hilberseimer, Ludwig. ca. 1963. "The Human Environment: The Development of a Planning Idea," typed manuscript. Ludwig Karl Hilberseimer Papers, Ryerson and Burnham Archives, The Art Institute of Chicago. Series 8/1, Box 5.5.

Hilberseimer, Ludwig. 1964a. *Contemporary Architecture: Its Roots and Trends.* Chicago: Paul Theobald and Company.

Hilbersheimer [sic], Ludwig. 1964b. "Stadtarchitektur und Gesellschaft." In *Bauen + Wohnen* 19, no. 3: 103–6.

Hilberseimer, Ludwig. 1967a. "A Tall, Bold Slugger: Chicago, Density and Traffic." In *Arena/Interbuild* 83, no. 14 (October): 41–43.

Hilberseimer, Ludwig. 1967b. *Berliner Architektur der 20er Jahre.* Mainz: Kupferberg (Neue Bauhausbücher).

Hilberseimer, Ludwig. 2012. *Metropolisarchitecture and Selected Essays.* Edited by Richard Anderson, translated by Richard Anderson and Julie Dawson. New York: GSAPP Books. Translation of Hilberseimer 1927b.

Hilberseimer, Ludwig, and Julius Vischer. 1928. *Beton als Gestalter.* Stuttgart: Julius Hoffmann.

Hirsch, Arnold R. 1983. *Making the Second Ghetto: Race & Housing in Chicago, 1940–1960.* Cambridge: Cambridge University Press.

Hoffacker, Heinz Wilhelm. 1989. *Entstehung der Raumplanung, konservative Gesellschaftsreform und das Ruhrgebiet, 1918–1933.* Essen: Hobbing.

Hoffmann, Hubert. 1930. "Kleinhaus oder Hochhaus." In *Wohnungswirtschaft* 7, no. 13 (April 1): 136–37.

Hoffmann, Hubert. 1966. "Persönliches: Ludwig Hilberseimer 80 Jahre." In *Werk-Chronik* 9 (September): 215–16.

Howard, Ebenezer. 1902. *Garden Cities of To-Morrow.* London: Swan Sonnenschein & Co.

Hunt, D. Bradford. 2005. "Photography and the History of the Chicago Housing Authority." In *The Promise of Public Housing, 1936–1983: Photographs from the Archives of the Chicago Housing Authority and the Chicago Historical Society,* edited by Michael Ensdorf and Kathy Pilat. Chicago: Roosevelt University.

Hvattum, Mari. 2006. "'Unfolding from Within': Modern Architecture and the Dream of Organic Totality." In *Journal of Architecture* 11, no. 4 (2006): 497–509.

Jacobs, Jane. 1963. *Tod und Leben großer amerikanischer Städte.* Bauwelt Fundamente 4. Berlin/Frankfurt a.M./Vienna: Ullstein.

James-Chakraborty, Kathleen. 2012. "From Chicago to Berlin and Back Again." In *Chicago Makes Modern: How Creative Minds Changed Society,* edited by Mary Jane Jacob and Jacquelynn Baas, 91–109. Chicago: University of Chicago Press.

Kamleithner, Christa. 2020. *Ströme und Zonen: Eine Genealogie der "funktionalen Stadt."* Basel: Birkhäuser.

Kamleithner, Christa. 2021a. "Dangerous Congestions: Cholera, Mapping and the Beginnings of Modern Urbanism." In *gta papers* 5: 38–49.

Kamleithner, Christa. 2021b. "Dessau, das Bauhaus und die Ästhetik der Rationalisierung." In *Neue Perspektiven auf die Bauhaus-Rezeption*, edited by Bauhaus-Institut für Geschichte und Theorie der Architektur und Planung, 114–27. Berlin: Jovis.

Kegler, Harald. 2015. *Landesplanung Mitteldeutschland: Spiel-Räume: Die Entstehung der wissenschaftlichen Raumordnung in Deutschland*. Arbeitsberichte der ARL 15. Hannover: Akademie für Raumforschung und Landesplanung.

Kegler, Karl R. 2015. *Deutsche Raumplanung: Das Modell der "Zentralen Orte" zwischen NS-Staat und Bundesrepublik*. Paderborn: Schöningh.

Kegler, Karl R. 2016. "Towards the Functional Society: Paradigm Shifts in the Regional Planning of West and East Germany." In *Re-Scaling the Environment: New Landscapes of Design, 1960–1980*, edited by Ákos Moravánszky and Karl. R. Kegler, 153–72. Basel: Birkhäuser.

Kepes, György. 1956. *The New Landscape in Art and Science*. Chicago: Theobald.

Kestner-Gesellschaft. 1951. *Gropius. Mies van der Rohe*. Hannover: Kestner-Gesellschaft.

Kilian, Markus. 2002. "Großstadtarchitektur und New City: Eine planungsmethodische Untersuchung der Stadtplanungsmodelle Ludwig Hilberseimers." Diss. Universität Karlsruhe.

Killian, Johann. 1937. *Der Kristal*. Berlin: P. Zsolnay.

King, F. H. 1911. *Farmers of Forty Centuries, or Permanent Agriculture in China, Korea and Japan*. Madison, WI: Mrs. F. H. King.

Kirkland, Wallace. 1951. "The Mecca: Chicago's Showiest Apartment Has Given Up All but the Ghost." Photo essay in *Life* (November 19, 1951): 133–34, 136, 139.

Klodt, Henning. n.d. "Infrastruktur." In *Gabler Wirtschaftslexikon*. https://wirtschaftslexikon.gabler.de/definition/infrastruktur-39955. Accessed March 7, 2022.

Klose, Walther. 1911. "Die räumliche Verteilung und Dichtigkeit der Bevölkerung." In *Die Statistik in Deutschland nach ihrem heutigen Stand*, edited by F. Zahn, 236–56. Munich: J. Schweitzer Verlag.

Klove, Robert C. 1948. "City Planning in Chicago: A Review." In *Geographical Review* 38, no. 1: 127–31.

Köhler, Daniel. 2016. *The Mereological City: A Reading of the Works of Ludwig Hilberseimer*. Bielefeld: Transcript.

Kollektiv für Sozialistisches Bauen. 2015. *Proletarische Bauausstellung / Proletarian Building Exhibition*.

Berlin: Haus der Kulturen der Welt Berlin; Leipzig: Spector.

Kracauer, Siegfried. 1930. *Die Angestellten: Aus dem neuesten Deutschland*. Frankfurt am Main: Societäts-Verlag.

Krauss, Rosalind E. 1999. "Grids." In *The Originality of the Avant-Garde and Other Modernist Myths*, edited by Rosalind Krauss, 8–22. Cambridge, MA: MIT Press.

Kropotkin, Piotr. 1907. *Fields, Factories and Workshops; or, Industry Combined with Agriculture and Brain Work with Manual Work*. New York: Putnam.

Kunsthochschule Berlin, ed. *Selman Selmanagić: Festgabe zum 80. Geburtstag am 25. April 1985*. Beiträge 10. Berlin: Kunsthochschule Berlin.

Landesplanung für den Engeren Mitteldeutschen Industriebezirk. 1932. *Landesplanung im engeren mitteldeutschen Industriebezirk Merseburg: Ihre Grundlagen, Aufgaben und Ergebnisse*. Merseburg: Landesplanung.

Larkin, Brian. 2013. "The Politics and Poetics of Infrastructure." In *Annual Review of Anthropology* 42: 327–43.

Latour, Bruno. 1990. "Drawing Things Together." In *Representation in Scientific Practice*, edited by Michael Lynch and Steve Woolgar, 19–68. Cambridge, MA: MIT Press.

Lauterbach, Burkhart, ed. 1995. *Großstadtmenschen: Die Welt der Angestellten*. Exh. cat. Münchner Stadtmuseum. Frankfurt am Main: Büchergilde Gutenberg.

Law Whyte, Lancelot. 1951. *Aspects of Form: A Symposium on Form in Nature and Art*. London/Bradford: Lund Humphries.

Le Corbusier. 1925. *Urbanisme*. Paris: G. Crès & Cie.

Le Corbusier. 1929. *Städtebau*. Translated by Hans Hildebrandt. Stuttgart: Deutsche-Verlags-Anstalt.

Le Corbusier. 1931. "Invite à l'action." In *Plans* 1, no. 1: 49.

Leendertz, Ariane. 2008. *Ordnung schaffen: Deutsche Raumplanung im 20. Jahrhundert*. Göttingen: Wallstein.

Lefebvre, Henri. 1991. *The Production of Space*. Oxford, UK: Blackwell.

Liebmann, Hans. 1920. "Film und Bewegung." In *Das Werk: Mitteilungen des Deutschen Werkbundes*, no. 5: 3–7.

Liston, James M. 1963. "Marina City." In *Popular Science* 222, no. 4 (April): 82–85, 194.

Littell, Robert. 1961. "Spain's Villages of Hope." In *Reader's Digest* (August): 177–80.

Llobet i Ribeiro, Xavier. 2007. *Hilberseimer y Mies: La metrópolis como ciudad jardín*. Barcelona: Fundación Caja de Arquitectos.

Mächler, Martin. 1921. "Das Siedelungsproblem." In *Sozialistische Monatshefte* 27, no. 4 (February): 182–87.

Mackay, John Henry. 1898. *Max Stirner: Sein Leben und sein Werk*. Berlin: Schuster & Loeffler.

Manly, Chesly. 1954. "How Chicago Is Winning the War Against Slums." In *Chicago Daily Tribune* (December 19), 20.

Manzke, Dirk. ed. [1994]. *Festschrift Hubert Hoffmann zum 90 Geburtstag*. Dessau: Bauhaus Dessau.

Marciniak, Ed. 1986. *Reclaiming the Inner City: Chicago's Near North Revitalization Confronts Cabrini-Green*. Washington, DC: National Center for Urban Ethnic Affairs.

Martin, Reinhold. 2003. *The Organizational Complex: Architecture, Media, and Corporate Space*. Cambridge MA: MIT Press.

Martin, Reinhold. 2014. *Mediators: Aesthetics, Politics, and the City*. Minneapolis: University of Minnesota Press.

May, Ernst. 1931. "Moscow: City Building in the USSR." In El Lissitzky 1970, 188–203.

Mayne, Alan. 2017. *Slums: The History of a Global Injustice*. London: Reaktion Books.

Mazower, Mark. 2008. *Hitler's Empire: How the Nazis Ruled Europe*. New York: Penguin Press.

Mengin, Christine. 2007. *Guerre du toit et modernité architecturale: Loger l'employé sous la république de Weimar*. Paris: Publications de la Sorbonne.

Mengin, Christine. 2011. "1929: Welcher Standardgrundriss? Und für welche soziale Klasse?" In *Neues Wohnen 1929/2009: Frankfurt und der 2. Congrès International d'Architecture Moderne*, edited by Helen Barr, 68–79. Berlin: Jovis Verlag.

Mertins, Detlef. 2009. "Hannes Meyer, German Trade Unions School, Bernau, 1928–30." In *Bauhaus 1919–1933: Workshops for Modernity*, edited by Barry Bergdoll and Leah Dickerman, 256–61. New York: Museum of Modern Art.

Mertins, Detlef. 2013. *Mies*. New York: Phaidon.

Meyer, Hannes. 1926. "Die Neue Welt." In *Das Werk* 13, no. 7: 205–24.

Meyer, Hannes. 1927. "Curriculum Vitae, Basel, 15.2.1927." In Meyer 1980, 10–14.

Meyer, Hannes. 1928. "bauen," *bauhaus* 2, no. 2: 12–13.

Meyer, Hannes. 1930. "Mein Hinauswurf aus dem Bauhaus." In Meyer 1980, 69.

Meyer, Hannes. 1980. *Bauen und Gesellschaft: Schriften, Briefe, Projekte*, edited by Lena Meyer-Bergner and Klaus-Jurgen Winkler. Dresden: Verlag der Kunst.

Meyer, Kurt. 1931. "Zu den Grundfragen des Städtebaus Moskaus." In *Von Adenauer zu Stalin: Der Einfluss des traditionellen Städtebaus in der Sowjetunion um 1935*, edited by Harald Bodenschatz and Thomas Flierl, 106–12. Berlin: Theater der Zeit, 2016.

Miljutin, N. A. [Nikolaj Aleksandrovič]. 1930. *Sozgorod: Die Planung der neuen Stadt*. Translated by Kyra Stromberg. Basel: Birkhäuser, 1992.

Mittag-Fodor, Etel. 2014. *Not an Unusual Life for the Time and the Place / Ein Leben, nicht einmal ungewöhnlich für diese Zeit und diesen Ort*. Translated by Kerstin Stutterheim and Michael Wetzel. Bauhäusler 3. Berlin: Bauhaus-Archiv.

Moholy-Nagy, László. 1976. *Malerei, Fotografie, Film*. Berlin.

Monroe, Harriet. 1896. *John Wellborn Root: A Study of His Life and Work*. Cambridge: The Riverside Press.

Montgomery, Roger. 1965. "Improving the Design Process in Urban Renewal." In *Journal of the American Institute of Planners* 31, no. 1 (February): 7–20.

Moreno, Carlos, Zaheer Allam, Didier Chabaud, Catherine Gall, and Florent Pratlong. 2021. "Introducing the '15-Minute City': Sustainability, Resilience and Place Identity in Future Post-Pandemic Cities." In *Smart Cities* 4, no. 1: 93–111. https://doi.org/10.3390/smartcities4010006.

Mullin, John R. 1982. "Henry Ford and Field and Factory: An Analysis of the Ford Sponsored Village Industries-Experiment in Michigan, 1918–1941." In *Journal of the American Planning Association* 41: 419–31.

Mumford, Eric. 2000. *The CIAM Discourse on Urbanism, 1928–1960*. Cambridge, MA: MIT Press.

Nerdinger, Winfried. 2019. *Walter Gropius: Architekt der Moderne, 1883–1969*. Munich: C. H. Beck.

Neumann, Eckhard, ed. 1964. *Bauhaus: Idee—Form—Zweck—Zeit, Zeit: Dokumente und Äußerungen*. Frankfurt am Main: Göppinger Galerie.

Neumann, Eckhard, ed. 1971. *Bauhaus und Bauhäusler: Bekenntnisse und Erinnerungen*. Bern: Hallwag.

Neumeyer, Fritz. 1986. *Mies van der Rohe: Das kunstlose Wort*. Berlin: Siedler.

Oechslin, Werner, and Gregor Harbusch, eds. 2010. *Siegfried Giedion und die Fotografie: Bildinszenierungen der Moderne*. Zurich: gta Verlag.

Neumeyer, Fritz. 1993. "Manhattan Transfer: The New York Myth and Berlin Architecture in Context of Ludwig Hilberseimer's High-Rise City." In *Berlin/New York: Like and Unlike: Essays on Architecture and Art from 1870 to the Present*, edited by Josef Paul Kleihues and Christina Rathgeber, 315–29. New York: Rizzoli.

Oeckl, Albert. 1935. *Die deutsche Angestelltenschaft: Eine sozialpolitische Studie unter besonderer Berücksichtigung der Gagfah*. Munich: Gerber.

Oscar Katov and Company, Public Relations. 1956. Press release, February 1. 5 pages. Ludwig Karl Hilberseimer Papers, Ryerson and Burnham Archives, The Art Institute of Chicago. Series 6, Box 3.6.

Oswalt, Philipp, ed. 2019a. *Hannes Meyers neue Bauhauslehre: Von Dessau bis Mexiko*. Bauwelt Fundamente 164. Basel: Birkhäuser.

Oswalt, Philipp. 2019b. "Ludwig Hilberseimer und die Städtebaulehre." In Oswalt 2019a, 153–74, here 169–72.

Ozenfant, Amédée, and Charles-Edouard Jeanneret. 1923. "Umschau: Imitative Kunst." In *Das Kunstblatt*, no. 9 (September): 280–83.

Panarchos [Raoul Hausmann]. 1919. "Zu Kommunismus und Anarchie." In *Der Einzige* 1, no. 2 (January 26): 5–7.

Panzini, Franco. 1985. "Risolvere i problemi della casa." In *La tessitura del Bauhaus 1919–1933. Nelle collezioni della Repubblica Democratica Tedesca*, edited by Georg Oppitz and Franco Panzini, 33–41. Venezia: Marsilio.

Pârvulescu, Constantin. 2006. "After the Revolution: The Individualist Anarchist Journal Der Einzige and the Making of the Radical Left in the Early Post-War I Germany." PhD diss. University of Minnesota.

Pârvulescu, Constantin. 2018. *The Individualist Anarchist Discourse of Early Interwar Germany*. Cluj-Napoca: Presa Universitară Cluejeană.

Passanti, Francesco. 1993. "Le Corbusier et le gratte-ciel: aux origines du Plan Voisin." In *Américanisme et modernité*, edited by Jean-Louis Cohen and Hubert Damisch, 171–89. Paris: Flammarion.

Perren, Claudia, Torsten Blume, Alexia Pooth, and Stiftung Bauhaus Dessau, eds. 2016. *Moderne Typen, Fantasten und Erfinder: Große Pläne! Zur Angewandten Moderne in Sachsen-Anhalt 1919–1933*. Bielefeld: Kerber.

Peters, John Durham. 2015. *The Marvelous Clouds: Toward a Philosophy of Elemental Media*. Chicago: University of Chicago Press.

Poerschke, Ute. 2018. "Data-Driven Design in High Modernism: Hilberseimer's Solar Orientation Studies." In *ARCC Conference Repository*, September. https://www.arcc-journal.org/index.php/repository/article/view/557.

Pommer, Richard. 1988. "'More a Necropolis than a Metropolis': Ludwig Hilberseimer's Highrise City and Modern City Planning." In Pommer, Spaeth, and Harrington 1988, 16–53.

Pommer, Richard, David Spaeth, and Kevin Harrington. 1988. *In the Shadow of Mies: Ludwig Hilberseimer, Architect, Educator, and Urban Planner*. Chicago: Art Institute of Chicago and Rizzoli International Publications.

Preston, Richard E. 2009. "Walter Christaller's Research on Regional and Rural Development Planning During World War II." In *METAR – Papers in Metropolitan Studies* 52: 3–38.

Rancière, Jacques. 2003. *Le destin des images*. Paris: La Fabrique Éd.

Rathenau, Walther. 1899. "Die schönste Stadt der Welt." In *Die Zukunft* 26, no. 1.

Ratzel, Friedrich. 1882. *Anthropogeographie, oder Grundzüge der Anwendung der Erdkunde auf die Geschichte*. Vol. 1. Stuttgart: Engelhorn.

Ratzel, Friedrich. 1903. "Die geographische Lage der großen Städte." In *Die Großstadt: Vorträge und Aufsätze zur Städteausstellung*, edited by Theodor Petermann, 33–72. Dresden: Zahn & Jaensch.

Ratzel, Friedrich. 2018 [1901] "Lebensraum: A Biogeographical Study," translated by Tul'si (Tuesday) Bhambry. In *Journal of Historical Geography* 61 (July): 59–80.

Reichsforschungsgesellschaft für Wirtschaftlichkeit im Bau- und Wohnungswesen e. V. [Reichsforschungsgesellschaft], ed. 1930. *Die billige, gute Wohnung: Grundrisse zum zusätzlichen Wohnungsbauprogramm des Reichs*. Berlin: Verlag Die Baugilde.

Reckwitz, Andreas. 2019. *Das Ende der Illusionen. Politik, Ökonomie und Kultur in der Spätmoderne*. Berlin: Suhrkamp.

Richter, Hans. 1921. "Prinzipielles zur Bewegungskunst." In *De Stijl* 4, no. 7: 109–12.

Richter, Hans. 1923. "Demonstration des Materials." In *G: Material zur elementaren Gestaltung*, no. 1: 2–3.

Richter, Hans. 1924. "G." In *G: Zeitschrift für elementare Gestaltung*, no. 3: 3–5.

Richter, Hans. 1967. *Köpfe und Hinterköpfe*. Zurich: Arche.

Richter, Hans. 2010. "Demonstration of the Materials." In *G. An Avant-Garde Journal of Art, Architecture, Design, and Film*, edited by Detlef Mertins and Michael W. Jennings, translated by Steven Lindberg and Margareta Ingrid Christian, 102. Los Angeles: Getty Research Institute.

Robbers, Lutz. 2012. "Modern Architecture in the Age of Cinema: Mies van der Rohe and the Moving Image." PhD diss. Princeton University.

Robbers, Lutz. 2017. "'This Type Lives': Montages of Architectonic Imagery." In *Mies van Der Rohe: Montage Collage*, edited by Andreas Beitin, 86–103. London: Koenig Books.

Rosellini, Anna. 2020. "La cité des illusions: Stratégies narratives et formes de représentation des visions urbanistiques de Le Corbusier." In *Scienza & Politica* 31, no. 62: 63–94.

Rössler, Mechtild. 1989. "Applied Geography and Area Research in Nazi Society: Central Place Theory and Planning, 1933 to 1945," *Environment and Planning D: Society and Space* 7, no. 4 (December): 419–31.

Ruest, Anselm. 1906. *Max Stirner: Leben, Weltanschauung, Vermächtnis*. Berlin: Verlag von Hermann Seemann Nachfolger.

Ruest, Anselm. 1919a. "Die Einzige bewährt sich als Egoisten. Zwei offene Briefe." In *Der Einzige* 1, no. 3 (February 2): 29–30.

Ruest, Anselm. 1919b. "Die letzte Revolution." In *Der Einzige* 1, no. 1 (January 19): 1–4.

Ruest, Anselm. 1919c. "Getrennt marschieren – vereint schlagen!" In *Der Einzige* 1, no. 8 (March 9): 85–88.

Rukser, Udo. 1919a. "Arthur Willners Fugen." In *Der Einzige* 1, no. 5 (February 16): 7–8.

Rukser, Udo. 1919b. "Janthur, der Maler." In *Der Einzige* 1, no. 7 (March 2): 79–80.

Rukser, Udo. 1919c. "Von der Form des Menschen." In *Der Einzige* 1, no. 9 (March 16): 104.

Rykwert, Joseph. 1984. "Die Stadt unter dem Strich: Eine Bilanz." In *Modelle für eine Stadt*, edited by Vittorio Magnago Lampugnani, translated by Thomas Bachmann, Gerhard Poppenberg, Agnes Kohlmeyer, Bernd Samland and Renate Schein, 118–128. Berlin: Siedler (Schriftenreihe zur Internationalen Bauausstellung Berlin, vol. 1).

Schätzke, Andreas. 2000. "Die Remigration deutscher Architekten nach 1945." In *Exil: Forschung, Erkenntnisse, Ergebnisse* 20, no. 1: 5–27.

Scheffler, Karl. 1903. "Ein Weg zum Stil." In *Berliner Architekturwelt*: 291–95.

Scheffler, Karl. 1907. *Moderne Baukunst*. Berlin: Julius Bard.

Scheffler, Karl. 1910. *Berlin: Ein Stadtschicksal*. Berlin: E. Reiss.

Scheffler, Karl. 1913. *Die Architektur der Großstadt*. Berlin: Bruno Cassirer Verlag.

Scheiffele, Walter. 2003. *Bauhaus, Junkers, Sozialdemokratie: Ein Kraftfeld der Moderne*. Berlin: form+zweck.

Schelling, F. W. J. 1834. *Philosophische Untersuchungen über das Wesen der menschlichen Freiheit und die damit zusammenhängenden Gegenstände*. Reutlingen: Enßlin.

Schelling, F. W. J. 2006 (1834). *Philosophical Investigations into the Essence of Human Freedom*. Translated by Jeff Love and Johannes Schmidt. Albany: State University of New York Press.

Schlögel, Karl. 2016. "The German Case: Space as Obsession." In *In Space We Read Time: On the History of Civilization and Geopolitics*, translated by Gerrit Jackson, 32–38. New York: Bard Graduate Center.

Schubert, Dirk. 2000. "The Neighbourhood Paradigm: From Garden Cities to Gated Communities." In *Urban Planning in a Changing World: The Twentieth Century Experience*, edited by Robert Freestone, 118–38. London: E & FN Spon.

Schulz, Günther. 2000. *Die Angestellten seit dem 19. Jahrhundert*. Munich: R. Oldenbourg Verlag.

Schumacher, Fritz. 1931. *Darstellungen des soziologischen Zustandes im Hamburgisch-Preussischen Landesplanungsgebiet*. Hamburg: Kommissionsverlag von Lütcke & Wulff.

Schumacher, Fritz. 1951. *Vom Städtebau zur Landesplanung und Fragen städtebaulicher Gestaltung*. Tübingen: Ernst Wasmuth.

Schwartz, Frederic J. 1997. *The Werkbund: Design Theory and Mass Culture before the First World War*. New Haven: Yale University Press.

Seidlein, Peter C. von. 1957. "Weg zu einer künftigen Umwelt: Zum Werk von Ludwig Hilberseimer, Chicago." In *Baukunst und Werkform* 10: 11–12.

Selmanagić, Selman. 1976. "Entwurf einer Arbeitersiedlung." In *Form und Zweck* 8, no. 6: 31–32.

Sieverts, Thomas. 2000. "Eine Begegnung mit Ludwig Hilberseimer." In *Architektur im 20. Jahrhundert: Deutschland*, edited by Romana Schneider, Winfried Nerdinger, and Wilfried Wang, 12–19. Munich: Prestel.

Simmel, Alice. 1929. "Die neue Küche." In *Die Form* 4, no. 11 (June): 289–91.

Simmel, Alice. 1931. "Die Wohnung unserer Zeit." In *Frauenwelt* 8, no. 20: 470–71. Ludwig Karl Hilberseimer Papers, Ryerson and Burnham Archives, The Art Institute of Chicago. Series 9/2, Box 3.28.

Simmel, Georg. 2002. "The Metropolis and Mental Life." In *The Blackwell City Reader*, edited by Gary Bridge and Sophia Watson, 11–19. Malden, MA: Blackwell Publishing.

Simon Thomas, Mienke, and Yvonne Brentjens, eds. 2019. *Netherlands Bauhaus: Pioneers of a New World*. Exh. cat. Museum Boijmans van Bouningen, Rotterdam. Bruges: Drukkerij Die Keure.

Smith, T'ai. 2014. *Bauhaus Weaving Theory: Craft to Mode of Design*. Minneapolis: University of Minnesota Press.

Smith, T'ai. 2015. "The Event of a Thread." In Frank and Watson 2015, 76–87.

Somer, Kees. 2007a. *The Functional City: The CIAM and Cornelis van Eesteren 1928–1960*. Rotterdam: NAi.

Somer, Kees. 2007b. "Congress Preparations in Moscow." In Somer 2007a, 112–17.

Soria y Mata, Arturo. 1882. "Madrid remendado y Madrid nuevo," *El Progresso* (March 6).

South Side Planning Board. 1952. *Community Appraisal Study: Report on Housing and Social Survey*. Chicago: South Side Planning Board.

South Side Planning Board 1956. *An Opportunity for Urban Renewal on Chicago's Near South Side*. Chicago: South Side Planning Board.

"Sozialistischer Städtebau in der UdSSR. Vortrag von Ernst May." 1931. In *Bauhaus. organ der kostufra. sprachrohr der studierenden*, no. 6 (July): n.p. [5–6].

Spaeth, David. 1981. *L. K. Hilberseimer: An Annotated Bibliography and Chronology*. New York: Garland Publishing.

Spaeth, David. 1988. "Ludwig Hilberseimer's Settlement Unit: Origins and Applications." In Pommer, Spaeth, and Harrington 1988, 54–68.

Stalder, Laurent. 2009. "'Cluster Buildings.'" In *Bauten der Boomjahre: Paradoxien der Erhaltung / Architecture de la croissance: Les paradoxes de la sauvegarde*, edited by Ute Hassler and Catherine Dumont d'Ayot, 44–55. Gollion: Infolio éditions.

Star, Susan Leigh, and Karen Ruhleben. 1996. "Steps Toward an Ecology of Infrastructure: design and Access for Large Scale Information Spaces." In *Information Systems Research* 7, no. 1 (March): 111–34.

Stengel, Anne. 2019. "Baupraxis als Lehre." 2019. In Oswalt 2019a, 130–42.

Stevenson, Angus, and Maurice Waite, eds. 2011. *Concise Oxford English Dictionary*. 12th ed. Oxford: Oxford University Press.

Stierli, Martino. 2018. *Montage and the Metropolis: Architecture, Modernity and the Representation of Space*. New Haven: Yale University Press.

Stirner, Max. 1845. *Der Einzige und sein Eigentum*. Leipzig: O. Wigand.

Stirner, Max. 1907. *The Ego and His Own*. Translated by Steven T. Byington. New York: Benjamin R. Tucker.

Stölzl, Gunta. 1931. "Die Entwicklung der Bauhaus-Weberei," *bauhaus* 5, no. 2: 2–5.

Stölzl, Gunta. 1987. *Weberei am Bauhaus und aus eigener Werkstatt*. Berlin: Kupfergraben.

Sugrue, Thomas. 1996. *The Origins of the Urban Crisis*. Princeton: Princeton University Press.

Tafuri, Manfredo. 1998. "Toward a Critique of Architectural Ideology." In *Architecture Theory since 1968*, edited by Michael K. Hays, 2–35. Cambridge, MA: MIT Press.

Tavares, Andre. 2016. *The Anatomy of the Architectural Book*. Zurich: Lars Müller and Canadian Centre for Architecture.

Taylor, Seth. 1990. *Left-Wing Nietzscheans: The Politics of German Expressionism 1910–1920*. Berlin: Walter de Gruyter.

Technische Universität Berlin. 1963. "Verleihung der akademischen Würde Doktor-Ingenieur Ehren halber an Herrn Professor Dr. of Laws Ludwig Hilberseimer durch die Technische Universität Berlin. 21. Juni 1963." *Akademische Reden* 22. Berlin (West): Technische Universität.

Tessenow, Heinrich. 1996. *Ich verfolgte bestimmte Gedanken: Dorf, Stadt, Großstadt – was nun?* Schwerin: Helms.

Thöner, Wolfgang. 2005. "From an 'Alien, Hostile Phenomenon' to the 'Poetry of the Future': On the Bauhaus Reception in East Germany, 1945–70." In *From Manhattan to Mainhattan: Architecture and Style as Transatlantic Dialogue, 1920–1970*, edited by Cordula Grewe, 115–37. Washington, DC: German Historical Institute.

Thrall, Grant. 2010. "Christaller, Walter." In *Encyclopedia of Geography*, edited by Barney Warf, vol. 1, 410. Los Angeles: Sage.

Thrasher, Frederick. 1927. *The Gang: A Study of 1,313 Gangs in Chicago*. Chicago: University of Chicago Press.

"Über den Vortrag von Stadtbaurat Meyer, Leiter des sozialistischen Städtebaues Moskau, gehalten anlässlich der proletarischen Bauausstellung." 1931. In *Bauhaus. organ der kostufra. sprachrohr der studierenden*, no. 6 (July): n.p. [10–11].

Urban, Florian. 2004. "Recovering Essence through Demolition: The 'Organic' City in Postwar West Berlin." In *Journal of the Society of Architectural Historians* 63, no. 3 (September): 354–69.

Vallye, Anna. 2020. "'Balance-Sheet' City: Martin Wagner and the Visualization of Statistical Data." In *Journal of Urban History* 46 (January): 334–63.

Van Doesburg, Theo. 1921. "Abstracte Filmbeelding." In *De Stijl* 4, no. 5: 71–75.

Van Doesburg, Theo. 1925. "Contemporary City for 3 million people. Le Corbusier's ville contemporaine"." In *Het Bouwbedrijf,* no. 1 (January): 32–38. On European architecture: complete essays from Het Bouwbedrijf 1924–1931, Birkhäuser 1990.

Van Doesburg, Theo. 1926. "Toward a new cityscape. Ludwig Hilberseimer's Hochhausstadt"." In *Het Bouwbed- rijf,* no. 2 (February): 74–78. On European architecture: complete essays from Het Bouwbedrijf 1924–1931, Birkhäuser 1990. Van Es, Evelien, Gregor Harbusch, Bruno Maurer, Muriel Pérez, Kees Somer, and Daniel Weiss, eds. 2014. *Atlas of the Functional City: CIAM 4 and Comparative Urban Analyses*. Rotterdam: THOTH Publishers; Zürich: gta Verlag.

Vasold, Georg. 2015. "Woven Thinking: Textile Art and the Advent of Modern Art Scholarship." In Frank and Watson 2015, 166–79.

Vidler, Anthony. 1992. *The Architectural Uncanny*. Cambridge, MA: MIT Press.

Wagner, Martin. 1932. *Das wachsende Haus: Ein Beitrag zur Lösung des Städtischen Wohnungsfrage*. Leipzig: Deutsches Verlagshaus Bong & Co.

Waldheim, Charles. 2016. *Landscape as Urbanism: A General Theory*. Princeton: Princeton University Press.

Wagenführ, Max. 1919. "Architektonische Entwürfe von L. Hilberseimer." In *Deutsche Kunst und Dekoration* 22, nos. 7–8 (April/May): 208–16.

Wallenstein, Sven-Olov. 2009. *Biopolitics and the Emergence of Modern Architecture*. New York: Princeton Architectural Press.

Weber, Alfred. 1922. *Über den Standort der Industrien*. Tübingen: J.C.B. Mohr.

Weber, Max. 1922. *Grundriss der Sozialökonomik, III. Abteilung: Wirtschaft und Gesellschaft*. Tübingen: J.C.B.Mohr.

Weber, Max. 2019. *Economy and Society*, edited and translated by Keith Tribe. Cambridge, MA: Harvard University Press.

Wedepohl, E[dgar]. 1928. "Bücherschau: Hilberseimer, Ludwig. Großstadtarchitektur." In *Der Städtebau*, 23, no 7: 161.

Weipert, Matthias. 2006. *"Mehrung der Volkskraft": Die Debatte über Bevölkerung, Modernisierung und Nation, 1890–1933*. Paderborn: Schöningh.

Weiss, Daniel. 2010. "Eine Reise in die Sowjetunion, Dezember 1932." In Oechslin and Harbusch 2010, 222–23.

Westheim, Paul. 1928. "Die Minute der Lebenden, Ludwig Hilberseimer." In *8 Uhr-Abendblatt* (May 21). Ludwig Karl Hilberseimer Papers, Ryerson and Burnham Archives, The Art Institute of Chicago. Series 9/6, Box 1.32.

Whiting, Sarah. 2001. "Bas-Relief Urbanism: Chicago's Figured Field." In *Mies in America*, edited by Phyllis Lambert, 642–91. New York: Harry N. Abrams, Centre Canadien d'Architecture, Whitney Museum of American Art, and Museum of Modern Art New York.

Whiting, Sarah. 2009. "Super!" In *Log*, no. 16 (Spring/ Summer): 19–26.

Wigley, Mark. 2001. "Network Fever." In *Grey Room* 2, no. 4: 82–122.

Wingler, Hans M., 1962. *Das Bauhaus, 1919–1933: Weimar Dessau Berlin*. Bramsche: Rasch.

Wingler, Hans. M. 1967. "Nachwort des Herausgebers." In Hilberseimer 1967b, 101–3.

Wingler, Hans. M. 1979a. *Bauhaus-Archiv Berlin: Museum für Gestaltung*. Braunschweig: Westermann.

Wingler, Hans M. 1979b. "Junkers baut für seine Arbeiter." In Wingler 1979a, 115–16.

Winkler, Klaus-Jürgen. 1989. *Der Architekt Hannes Meyer: Anschauungen und Werk*. Berlin: Verlag für Bauwesen.

Winkler, Klaus-Jürgen. 2003. *Baulehre und Entwerfen am Bauhaus 1919–1933*. Weimar: Universitätsverlag.

Wirth, Louis. 1928. *The Ghetto*. Chicago: University of Chicago Press.

Wölfflin, Heinrich. 1915. *Kunstgeschichtliche Grundbegriffe: Das Problem der Stilentwicklung in der neueren Kunst*. Munich: Bruckmann.

Wölfflin, Heinrich. 1950. *Principles of Art History: The Problem of the Development of Style in Later Art*. Translated by M. D. Hottinger. New York: Dover Publications. Translation of Wölfflin 1915.

Wollen, Peter. 1997. "Lund Celebrates Dada Child." In *PIX*, no. 2: 146–56.

Wood, Elizabeth. 1945. "Realities of Urban Redevelopment." In *The Journal of Housing* 3, no. 1 (December): 12–14.

Worringer, Wilhelm. 1908. *Abstraktion und Einfühlung*. Munich: Piper Verlag.

Wortmann Weltge, Sigrid. 1993. *Bauhaus Textiles: Women Artists and the Weaving Workshop*. London: Thames & Hudson.

Zipp, Samuel. 2010. *Manhattan Projects: The Rise and Fall of Urban Renewal in Cold War New York*. Oxford: Oxford University Press.

Zorbaugh, Harvey Warren. 1976 (1929). *The Gold Coast and the Slum: A Sociological Study of Chicago's Near North Side*. Chicago : University of Chicago Press.

Authors' Biographies

Andreas Buss is an architect and research associate in the Department of Architectural Theory and Design at the University of Kassel. He works there on the research project Laubenganghäuser (Houses with Balcony Access) by Hannes Meyer. In 2019, together with Philipp Oswalt, he led the temporary reconstruction of a wooden house by Hilberseimer at the Bauhaus World Heritage Site in Dessau.

Benedict Clouette is a doctoral candidate in architectural history and theory at Columbia University, where his research focuses on the visual cultures of urban design and planning in postwar America. With Marlisa Wise, he is the author of *Forms of Aid: Architectures of Humanitarian Space* (Birkhäuser, 2017), and the principal of Interval Projects, an architecture and urbanism practice based in New York City.

Scott Colman teaches architectural and urban history, theory, and design at the Rice University School of Architecture in Houston. His monograph on Ludwig Hilberseimer will be published in the Bloomsbury Studies in Modern Architecture series, edited by Tom Avermaete and Janina Gosseye, in 2022.

Magdalena Droste has been professor of art history at the Brandenburg Technical University in Cottbus for many years. Previously she was curator at the Bauhaus Archive Berlin. She is editor and author of numerous books, essays and curator of all aspects of the Bauhaus and the history of design. Her two monographs on the history of the Bauhaus (new edition 2019) have been translated into eleven languages. The most recent book is Oskar Schlemmer and Otto Meyer-Amden, *Das Seelenpostbuch. Briefwechsel 1909–1933* (ed. with Elisa Tamaschke, 2020).

Alexander Eisenschmidt is a designer, theorist, and Associate Professor at the University of Illinois at Chicago's School of Architecture. He directs the Visionary Cities Project and speculations on new forms of architectural urbanism, and he leads the architecture and urban design practice Studio Offshore. Eisenschmidt has edited numerous volumes, is author of *The Good Metropolis* (2019), and has exhibited internationally in venues such as the Venice Biennale.

Alison Fisher is the Harold and Margot Schiff Curator of Architecture and Design at the Art Institute of Chicago. She specializes in alternative histories of modern architecture, urbanism, and design and has curated many exhibitions. Her work has been recognized with grants and awards from the Graham Foundation for Advanced Studies in the Fine Arts and the Society of Architectural Historians, and she also teaches architectural history at Chicago-area universities.

Plácido González Martínez is professor at the College of Architecture and Urban Planning at Tongji University in Shanghai, Executive Editor of the journal *Built Heritage*, and Vice President of the Association of Critical Heritage Studies. His research focuses on architectural and urban heritage conservation and on modern architecture as heritage. His book *A la luz de Hilberseimer* (2015; English version published as *In Light of Hilberseimer*) was awarded the Research Prize of the 2018 Spanish Architecture Biennale.

Christa Kamleithner is an architectural theorist and cultural historian whose research focuses on the epistemological and cultural history of built spaces. After holding several academic positions in Austria and Germany, she is currently a research associate at the Centre for Cultural Inquiry (Zentrum für Kulturwissenschaftliche Forschung, ZKF) at the University of Konstanz. Her PhD thesis *Ströme und Zonen*, published in Birkhäuser's Bauwelt Fundamente series in 2020, reconstructs the genealogy of the "functional city" as a process of abstraction in which statistics, thematic maps, and economic models played an important role.

Christine Mengin has been associate professor in the history of architecture and heritage at the University of Paris 1 Panthéon-Sorbonne since 1995. The various institutional responsibilities she held led her to take an interest in a variety of subjects (the built heritage of Porto-Novo, Benin, the architectural evolution of the French National Library, the restoration of Le Corbusier's work and now the architectural and urban history of the city of Tianjin, China). In the 1980s, she devoted three masters theses to Hilberseimer's German period (gathering biographical elements, establishing his bibliography, analyzing his writings on the big city, art critics, housing plans) before devoting her PhD to the housing of the white-collar workers during the Weimar Republic.

Sandra Neugärtner is a research associate at Leuphana University Lüneburg. She is leading a DFG project in which she is investigating Lena Meyer-Bergner's concept of modernity in a transcultural perspective (starting in 2021). She studied design, economics, cultural studies and art history in Dessau, Berlin and Zurich. From 2017 to 2018, she was a visiting fellow at the Department History of Art and Architecture at Harvard University.

Philipp Oswalt is professor of Architectural Theory and Design at the University of Kassel. He was previously, among other things, editor of the architecture magazine *Arch+*, collaborator in the office OMA/Rem Koolhaas, co-leader of the European research project Urban Catalyst, head of the project Shrinking Cities of the Federal Cultural Foundation and Director of the Bauhaus Dessau Foundation (2009–2014). He is part of the Future Stages Frankfurt initiative (2020 onwards) and the critical learning site Garnisonkirche Potsdam (2020 onwards).

Lutz Robbers currently teaches architectural theory at the Jade University in Oldenburg. His research and publications explore the media conditions of architectural knowledge. He served as editor of the journal *Candide – Journal for Architectural Knowledge.*

Andreas Schätzke is a research associate at the Bauhaus Dessau Foundation. Previously, he worked at the Berlin State Museums and taught at the Technical University of Kaiserslautern and the University of Applied Sciences in Wismar. Among his research areas are architecture and urban development in the 20th century, as well as migration and cultural transfer in the field of architecture and the visual arts. He has been curator of several architecture exhibitions.

Robin Schuldenfrei is the Tangen Reader in 20th Century Modernism at The Courtauld Institute of Art, University of London. She has written widely on modernism and especially on the Bauhaus. Her publications include *Luxury and Modernism: Architecture and the Object in Germany 1900–1933* (2018). She is currently writing a book on objects in exile and the displacement of design which includes a study of Hilberseimer.

Florian Strob is the research associate to the director of the Bauhaus Dessau Foundation, head of the research project *Bauhaus im Text / Bauhaus Written Heritage* (2020–2022), and curator for the Bauhaus Residency Program as well as for several architecture exhibitions. He has published numerous books and articles on the architecture and literature of modernity; his critical edition of Ludwig Hilberseimer's *The New City* is forthcoming.

Anna Vallye is an assistant professor of Art History and Architectural Studies at Connecticut College. Her research focuses on modern architecture and urban planning in the United States and Western Europe, with particular interest in the intersections of design, the social sciences, and state governance. She is currently at work on a book titled *Model Territories: German Architects and the Shaping of America's Welfare State*, about the American careers of emigrant architects such as Hilberseimer, Gropius, and Martin Wagner in the interwar and immediate postwar period.

Charles Waldheim is a North American architect and urbanist. He is John E. Irving Professor of Landscape Architecture at Harvard University's Graduate School of Design where he directs the School's Office for Urbanization. He also serves as the Ruettgers Curator of Landscape at the Isabella Stewart Gardner Museum in Boston. He has been a visiting scholar at the Architectural Association School of Architecture in London and the Bauhaus in Dessau. Waldheim's research and practice examine the relations between landscape, ecology, and contemporary urbanism. He coined the term "landscape urbanism" to describe the emergent discourse and practices of landscape in relation to design culture and contemporary urbanisation. On these topics, Waldheim is author of *Landscape as Urbanism: A General Theory* (2016) and editor of *The Landscape Urbanism Reader* (2006).

Index of Names

Image Credits

Front cover: Detroit area, planning diagram, c. 1945, published in: Hilberseimer, Ludwig. 1949. *The New Regional Pattern: Industries and Gardens, Workshops and Farms*. Chicago: Theobald, p. 173

Back cover and p. 7: Weißenhof Settlement Single-family residence, Weißenhofsiedlung © RBA

p. 9: SBD (I 6527 F) / © (Pahl, E. Pius) Pahl, Peter Jan

p. 10: The House Alice Built. 2018 © Mona Mahalls and Asli Serbests

p. 11: © Adrian Phiffer

p. 19: Ludwig Hilberseimer with Alfred Caldwell, The City in the Landscape, 1942, published in: Hilberseimer, Ludwig. 1944. *The New City: Principles of Planning*. Chicago: Theobald, 146

p. 30: © BHA

p. 31: © BHA

p. 35: Illustration from: Miljutin, Nikolai A. 1992 [1930]. Sozgorod: Die Planung der neuen Stadt. Basel, Berlin: Birkhäuser

p. 39: Ernst Mittag, Südliche Siedlung Mosigkauer Heide (Southern housing estate Mosigkauer Heide), before 1932 © HNI

p. 47: Cover of: Deutscher Werkbund, ed.. 1927. Bau und Wohnung: Die Bauten der Weißenhofsiedlung in Stuttgart. Stuttgart: Akad. Verlag Dr. Fritz Wedekind & Co, 1927

p. 51: Ludwig Hilberseimer with students in the classroom, c. 1949. © RBA

p. 52: Mineral Creek Valdez, Source: The Great Alaska Earthquake of 1964. 1968. vol. 1, pt 1. Washington DC: National Research Council. © Valdez Museum & Historical Archive

p. 61: City slum, published in: Hilberseimer, Ludwig. 1955. *The Nature of Cities: Origin, Growth, and Decline, Pattern and Form, Planning Problems*. Chicago: Theobald, 109

p. 65: Mildred Mead, "Down Some Alley," Fort Dearborn Project, Chicago Land Clearance Commission, Near North Side Survey Area, 1953. © Chicago Department of Urban Renewal Records, Chicago Public Library Special Collections

p. 67: Skidmore, Owings & Merrill, Architectural model for a civic center, 1954, photo: William C. Hedrich for Hedrich-Blessing. © Chicago Department of Urban Renewal Records, Chicago Public Library Special Collections

p. 83: Ludwig Hilberseimer, Desk in a living room designed by Ludwig Hilberseimer for the exhibition *Die Wohnung unserer Zeit*, 1931, published in: Alice Simmel. 1931. "Die Wohnung unserer Zeit." In: *Frauenwelt* 8, p. 20

p. 86: Bauhaus Dessau, building department, Dessau-Törten Housing Estate, construction phase, 1930; the contextualization of the mixed-use development is shown on the left, and its smallest unit on the right: two construction fields with pergolas and three types of low-rise buildings. © ADM, Bauhaus-Universität Weimar, PSD 5 001 363

p. 88: Bauhaus Dessau, building department, isometric view of the four model houses on the Bauhaus test site in Kleine Kienheide, 1930. © Konnte nicht ermittelt werden

p. 89: Dessau city map (detail), c. 1930. Hofbuchdruckerei von C. Dünnhaupt, G.m.b.H. Dessau

p. 90: Ludwig Hilberseimer (design), Andreas Buss (drawing), the isometry of L-types in a row was reconstructed on the basis of the plan documents of the time of their creation, 1930 (design), 2021 (drawing)

p. 96: Ludwig Hilberseimer (design), Andreas Buss (drawing), reconstructed perspective along the housing street with low-rise buildings and House with Balcony Access from south, 1930 (design), 2021 (drawing)

p. 101, fig. 1: Bare building frame in Schöneberg, Martin-Luther-Straße, in: Karl Scheffler, *Die Architektur der Großstadt*, 1913, p. 34

p. 101, fig. 2: Heinrich Tessenow, worker's row house for a family in Hellerau, in: Karl Scheffler, *Die Architektur der Großstadt*, 1913, p. 168

p. 102: Alfred Messel, department store A. Wertheim in Berlin, Leipziger Straße and Leipziger Platz, photograph c. 1906

p. 104: Ludwig Hilberseimer, "Die Architektur der Großstadt", handwritten folio, 1914, p. 10. © RBA

p. 106: Ludwig Mies van der Rohe, Concrete Office Building, Berlin, perspective project, 1923. © ARS, New York / VG BK

p. 107: Burnham & Root, Monadnock building at Jackson Boulevard, Chicago, 1891, in: Ludiwg Hilberseimer, *Großstadtarchitektur*, 1927, p. 65

p. 110: Hannes Meyer, Co-op Zimmer, 1926. © gta Archiv /
ETH Zürich, Hannes Meyer

p. 115: Ludwig Hilberseimer, page of the travel diary for
Holland and Paris, with a sketch of the villa Ozenfant,
October 1924. © RBA

p. 116: Paul Westheim's buisness card, front and back.
© FLC / VG BK

p. 120: Le Corbusier, model of the Plan Voisin, 1930,
photo: Marius Gravot. © FLC / VG BK

p. 124: The employee's desk, published in: Heinrich
Helfenstein / Martin Steinmann. 1985. "Eine Deut-
sche Versicherungsgesellschaft um 1930." In: O.R.
Salvisberg: Die andere Moderne, Dokumente zur
modernen Schweizer Architektur, ed. by Claude
Lichtenstein, 130–141. Zurich: Gta-Verlag. © gta
Archiv / ETH Zürich, Otto Rudolf Salvisberg

p. 127: Ludwig Hilberseimer, Desk in a living room de-
signed by Ludwig Hilberseimer for the exhibition
Die Wohnung unserer Zeit, 1931, published in: Alice
Simmel. 1931. "Die Wohnung unserer Zeit." In:
Frauenwelt 8, p. 20

p. 128: Ludwig Hilberseimer in his Berlin office. © RBA

p. 138: Alexander Klein, Floor plan studies, c. 1927
© konnte nicht ermittelt werden

p. 139: Jean Nicolas Louis Durand, Précis des leçons
d'architectures données à l'École Polytechnique,
1802–1805

p. 141, fig. 4: Lotte Stam-Beese, Rotterdam Pendrecht,
1949–1953, Aerophoto Nederlands, n.d. , Aerophoto
Neterlands, Rotterdam City Archives III-492.
© Roel Dijkstra

p. 141, fig. 5: Akademie der Künste: Hans-Scharoun-
Archiv Nr. 3788 F. 170/69; photographer: Hans
L.(eopold) Minzloff, © Thomas Minzloff

p. 143: Population distribution in the Chicago region,
1950, published in: Hilberseimer, Ludwig. 1963.
Entfaltung einer Planungsidee. Berlin/Frank-
furt a.M./ Wien: Ullstein, p. 108

p. 145: Ludwig Hilberseimer, Schematic application of
Christaller's Theory of the Distribution of towns as
service centers. Southern German, published in:
Ludwig Hilberseimer, 1949, *The New Regional Pat-
tern: Industries and Gardens, Workshops and Farms*.
Chicago: Theobald, p. 100. © LIL

p. 146: Walter Christaller, diagram, published in: Ludwig
Hilberseimer, 1949. *The New Regional Pattern:
Industries and Gardens, Workshops and Farms*.
Chicago: Theobald, p. 101. © LIL

p. 157: Ludwig Hilberseimer, Warsaw, a diagram for its
proposed replanning, published in: Ludwig Hilberseimer, 1949, *The New Regional Pattern: Industries
and Gardens, Workshops and Farms*. Chicago:
Theobald, p. 179

p. 165: Entwicklungstendenzen, Dessau analysis,
1932/33. © HNI / EEST 4.361-15

p. 166: Wilhelm Hess, Dessau analysis: settlement plan,
1932/33. © HNI / EEST 4.361/362

p. 168: Der Personenzugverkehr auf den mitteldeutschen
Reichsbahnen (passenger traffic on Central German
railroads), planning atlas, 1931, published in:
*Landesplanung im engeren mitteldeutschen Indus-
triebezirk Merseburg: ihre Grundlagen, Aufgaben
und Ergebnisse* (Merseburg: Landesplanung, 1932),
plate 15

p. 173: Recommended system of interregional highways in
relation to the population distribution of the United
States, 1944, published in: *Interregional Highways:
Message from The President of the United States
Transmitting a Report of the National Interregional
Highway Committee* (Washington: US Government
Printing Office, 1944), p. 16

p. 175: Land reclaimed by man, US Soil Conservation
Service, from: Hilberseimer, Ludwig. 1949. *The New
Regional Pattern: Industries and Gardens, Work-
shops and Farms*. Chicago: Theobald, p. 119

p. 176: Strip cropping and contour cultivation, US Soil
Conservation Service, 1956

p. 180: Walter Christaller, diagram, published in: Hilbers-
eimer, Ludwig. 1949. *The New Regional Pattern:
Industries and Gardens, Workshops and Farms*.
Chicago: Theobald, p. 99. © LIL

p. 181: Alfred Weber, Calculation of site location according
to transport distance, published in: Weber, Alfred.
1922. *Über der Standort der Industrien*. Tübingen:
J.C.B. Mohr.

p. 183: Ludwig Hilberseimer, Theoretical population
distribution on an island: past, present, and possible
future, published in: Hilberseimer, Ludwig. 1949.
*The New Regional Pattern: Industries and Gardens,
Workshops and Farms*. Chicago: Theobald,
p. 84–86

p. 184: Ludwig Hilberseimer, Centric System, published
in: Hilberseimer, Ludwig. 1949. *The New Regional
Pattern: Industries and Gardens, Workshops and
Farms*. Chicago: Theobald, p. 164

p. 185: Walter Christaller, Population distribution in Southern Germany analyzed through the central place system, published in: Christaller, Walter. 1933. *Die zentralen Orte in Süddeutschland: Eine ökonomisch-geographische Untersuchung über die Gesetzmäßigkeit der Verbreitung und Entwicklung der Siedlungen mit städtischen Funktionen.* Jena: Fischer. © LIL

p. 193: Hilberseimer, Ludwig. 1930. "Vorschlag zur City-Bebauung." In: *Die Form: Zeitschrift für gestaltende Arbeit* 5: 608–611, p. 609

p. 195: Cover of: *Der Einzige.* 1919, 1, 1 (January 19), 1919

p. 201: Cover of: Salamo Friedlaender. 1918. *Schöpferische Indifferenz*, Munich: Georg Müller

p. 202: Hannah Höch, *Schnitt mit dem Küchen- messer durch die letzte Weimarer Bierbauchkulturepoche Deutschlands* © bpk / Nationalgalerie, SMB / Jörg P. Anders, © (Höch, Hannah) / VG BK

p. 213: Ludwig Mies van der Rohe, Urban Design Proposal for Alexanderplatz, Berlin-Mitte, aerial perspective, 1929. © Artists Rights Society (ARS), New York / VG BK

p. 216: Viking Eggeling. Drei Momente des Horizontal-Vertikalorchesters. c 1921, published in: *De Stijl*, vol. 4, nr, 7 (July 1921): facing p. 112

p. 226: Margaretha Reichardt, *Sie brauchen das Bauhaus* (You Need the Bauhaus), 1928. Stiftung Bauhaus Dessau (I 248 G) / © (Reichardt, Margaretha (Grete)) Kaiser, Gisela

p. 229: Konrad Püschel, traffic study for the general development plan Dessau, from the architecture theory lessons (basics of urban planning) of Ludwig Hilberseimer at Bauhaus Dessau, 1928. Stiftung Bauhaus Dessau (I 6950 G) / © (Püschel, Konrad) Erbengemeinschaft nach Konrad Püschel

p. 230: Unidentified city and land-use studies, noted on the back: "Den Haag/Berlage/See Stübben p. 569". © RBA

p. 231: Margaretha Reichardt, fabric for upholstery, 1928–30. © ADM

p. 232: Pius Pahl, floor plan studies, left: floor plan in axonometric view, right: perspective view, from the architecture theory lessons of Ludwig Hilberseimer, 1931–32. SBD (I 6509 F) / © (Pahl, E. Pius) Pahl, Peter Jan

p. 240: Ludwig Hilberseimer, first page of the manuscript "Gesellschaft und Städtebau", n.d. © RBA

p. 242: Ludwig Hilberseimer, First page of translation for The New City with manuscript changes, n.d. © RBA

p. 247: Siegfried Risch, List of broad leaved trees on the back of a typescript of the translation for *The New City*, n.d. © RBA

p. 248: Hilberseimer, Ludwig. 1944. *The New City: Principles of Planning.* Chicago: Theobald, p. 99

p. 250: Hilberseimer, Ludwig. 1940. Letter to Dearstyne, 20th Nov 1940. © RBA

p. 251: Hilberseimer, Ludwig. 1944. *The New City: Principles of Planning.* Chicago: Theobald, p. 181

p. 262: Hilberseimer, Ludwig. 1947. „Elemente der Stadtplanung." In: *Der Bauhelfer* 2, 19: p. 3

p. 268: Cover of: Hilberseimer, Ludwig. 1967. *Berliner Architektur der 20er Jahre.* (Mainz: Kupferberg, design by Herbert Bayer) © VG BK

p. 273: Ludwig Hilberseimer in 1927, standing in front a tower made of six of his fifteen-story buildings from the "Welfare City" model. © RBA

p. 274, fig. – p. 286, fig. 24: Ludwig Hilberseimer, first publications as mentioned © AIC

p. 287, fig. 25: © SBD

p. 288, fig. 26 – 309, fig. 60: Ludwig Hilberseimer, first publications as mentioned or © AIC

p. 310, fig. 61: © VG BK

p. 311, fig. 62: Ludwig Hilberseimer, Ludwig Mies van der Rohe and Alfred Caldwell, Lafayette Park, preliminary site plan, 1956. © AIC

p. 311, fig. 63: © VG BK / AIC

p. 312, fig. 64 – 314, fig. 67: Ludwig Hilberseimer, first publications as mentioned or © AIC

Abbreviations

ADM   Archiv der Moderne

AIC   The Art Institute of Chicago / Art Resource, NY

ARS   Artists Rights Society

BHA   Bauhaus-Archiv / Museum für Gestaltung, Berlin

FLC   Fondation Le Corbusier

HNI   Collection Het Nieuwe Instituut

LIL   Leibniz-Institut für Länderkunde

RBA   Ludwig Karl Hilberseimer Papers, Ryerson and Burnham Art and Architecture Archives, Art Institute of Chicago

SBD   Stiftung Bauhaus Dessau – Bauhaus Dessau Foundation

VG BK   VG Bild-Kunst, Bonn 2022